The Beatest State in the Union:
An Anthology of Beat Texas Writings

The Beatest State in the Union:
An Anthology of Beat Texas Writings

Edited by

Christopher Carmona
Rob Johnson
Chuck Taylor

LAMAR UNIVERSITY
LITERARY PRESS

ISBN: 978-1-942956-08-2
Library of Congress Control Number: 2015958957

Book Design: Theresa L. Ener

Lamar University Literary Press
Beaumont, Texas

Acknowledgments

"Tripping Down to the Big Mango" is reprinted with permission from the publisher of "The Quixote Cult" by Genaro González (©1998 Arte Público Press-University of Houston).

Excerpts from "Strangelove Outtake" from Now Dig This, copyright © 2001 by The Terry Southern Literary Trust. Used by permission of Grove/Atlantic, Inc. Any third party use of this material, outside of this publication, is prohibited.

Excerpts from *Last Words*, copyright © 2000 by William S. Burroughs. Used by permission of Grove/Atlantic, Inc. Any third party use of this material, outside of this publication, is prohibited.

White Collar by C. Wright Mills (1951) 1000w from pp. 220-224.

"Amarillo Highway" © Terry Allen, 1975, Green Shoes Pub.

"One Fuse of A Summer" From *Bonfire of Roadmaps* by Joe Ely, Copyright© 2007. By permission of the University of Texas Press.

"Wild Night in Brownsville," "San Antonio," " El Paso" reprinted by permission of SLL/Sterling Lord Literistic, Inc. Copyright by the Estate of Jack Kerouac.

Selection from *Troia: Mexican Memoirs* used by permission from Dalkey Archive Press, Copyright© 2007.

White Collar by C. Wright Mills (1951) used by permission from Oxford University Press.

"Letter to Jack Kerouac" and "Dear Neal" reprinted by permission of the estate of Allen Ginsberg.

"On The Road to Texas" by Tomás Rivera (reprinted by permission of ©1998 Arte Público Press-University of Houston).

"Thoughts on a Breath" by Allen Ginsberg reprinted by permission of HarperCollins ©2007.

Excerpt from "Strange Peaches" reprinted by permission of the estate of Edwin "Bud" Shrake.

"To Jack Kerouac" by Neal Cassady reprinted by permission of the estate of Neal Cassady.

"Beauty Contest: Ms. More Usual Person" and "Things" are reprinted by permission from My Own Alphabet (Coffee House Press, 1989). Copyright © 1989 by Bobbie Louise Hawkins.

Excerpt from "City of Night" by John Rechy used by permission of Grove/Atlantic, Inc. Any third party use of this material, outside of this publication, is prohibited.

Books from Lamar University Literary Press

Jean Andrews, *High Tides, Low Tides: the Story of Leroy Colombo*
Charles Behlen, *Failing Heaven*
Alan Berecka, *With Our Baggage*
David Bowles, *Flower, Song, Dance: Aztec and Mayan Poetry*
David Bowles, *Border Lore, Folktales and Legends of South Texas*
Jerry Bradley, *Crownfeathers and Effigies*
Kevin Casey, *Four-Peace*
Julie Chappell and Marilyn Robitaille, editors, *Writing Texas, 2013-14*
Terry Dalrymple, *Love Stories, Sort Of*
Chip Dameron, *Waiting for an Etcher*
Robert Murray Davis, *Levels of Incompetence: An Academic Life*
William Virgil Davis, *The Bones Poems*
Jeffrey Delotto, *Voices Writ in Sand*
Gerald Duff, *Memphis Mojo*
Ted L. Estess, *Fishing Spirit Lake*
Mimi Ferebee, *Wildfires and Atmospheric Memories*
Ken Hada, *Margaritas and Redfish*
Michelle Hartman, *Disenchanted and Disgruntled*
Michelle Hartman, *Irony and Irreverence*
Katherine Hoerth, *Goddess Wears Cowboy Boots*
Lynn Hoggard, *Motherland, Stories and Poems from Louisiana*
Dominique Inge, *A Garden on the Brazos*
Gretchen Johnson, *The Joy of Deception*
Gretchen Johnson, *A Trip Through Downer, Minnesota*
Laozi, *The daodejing*, tr. David Breeden, Steven Schroeder, Wally Swist
Christopher Linforth, *When You Find Us We Will Be Gone*
Tom Mack and Andrew Geyer, editors, *A Shared Voice*
Jim McJunkin, *Deep Sleep*
Jeanetta Calhoun Mish. *Oklahomeland*
Laurence Musgrove, *Local Bird*
Dave Oliphant, *The Pilgrimage, Selected Poems: 1962-2012*
Janet McCann, *The Crone at the Casino*
Erin Murphy, *Ancilla*
Kornelijus Platelis, *Solitary Architectures*
Harold Raley, *Louisiana Rogue*
Carol Coffee Reposa, *Underground Musicians*
Jim Sanderson, *Trashy Behavior*
Jim Sanderson, *Sanderson's Fiction Writing Manual*
Jan Seale, *Appearances*
Jan Seale, *The Parkinson Poems*
Carol Smallwood, *Water, Earth, Air, Fire, and Picket Fences*
Glen Sorestad, *Hazards of Eden, Poems from the Southwest*
Melvin Sterne, *The Number You Have Reached*
W.K. Stratton, *Ranchero Ford/Dying in Red Dirt Country*
John Wegner, *Love is Not a Dirty Word and Other Stories*
Robert Wexelblatt, *The Artist Wears Rough Clothing*
Jonas Zdanys, *Pushing the Envelope*

For more information about these and other books, go to
www.LamarUniversityPress.Org

Special Thanks to Those That Made This Anthology Happen:

Jo Ann Carmona
PW Covington
Amy Cummins
Dash
Steve Davis
Suzanne Denson
Lauren Dixon
Billie Duncan
Amber Foster
Ben Fountain
Hedwig Gorski
Kathleen Hudson
David Juarez
Jeremiah Kelly
Griff Mangan
Janet McCann
Lupe Mendez
Michelle Miller
Karen Minzer
Alan Oak
Oscar Peña
Octavio Quintanilla
Harold Rodinsky
Luis Rodriguez-Abad
David Searcy
Matt Stefon
Melissa Studdard
Susan Summers
Jim Welton
Lowell Mick White
Steve Wilson
Witliff Collection

CONTENTS

Note: Authors' works are placed under their home region unless the work is primarily set in another part of Texas.

Beat Austin

Beat Dallas

Beat East Texas

Beat Houston

Beat West Texas

Beat El Paso

Letter from Joan Vollmer to Allen Ginsberg trying to entice him to come and stay with her and William S. Burroughs on a ranch outside of New Waverly, Texas.

March 23, 1947

Dear Allen,

Here, finally, are those shirts you said you thought you could use, selected by [Herbert] Huncke, who says he'll write shortly, and sends his regards.

We're coming along quite well down here, although already we're being attacked by hordes of all sorts of dreadful bugs, including scorpions, to which William [Burroughs] has taken quite a fancy.

Give my regards to John [Kingsland] and Kerouac, if you should see them.

How's your last year at Columbia winding up? If you feel like seeing the beatest state in the union for a while during the summer, we'd all be awfully glad to see you. By that time, I guarantee, the plumbing will be systematized satisfactorily. Bring your own insecticides, however.

Yours,
Joan

Introduction: a Taped Discussion Among Editors
Christopher Carmona
Chuck Taylor
Rob Johnson

CC: What initially attracted the original Beats like Burroughs, Kerouac, and Ginsberg to Texas?

CT: Well, I think everyone knows about this one. Burroughs had a lot of fantasies of Texas being in the Wild West and in a place where everyone could own guns. Texas seemed to have more freedom than other places, but maybe he bought too heavily into the myth. Eventually he got disillusioned living in East Texas and even in South Texas things were a little better.

RJ: They used to call him Billy down here because he had a Billy the Kid Wild West syndrome. He liked to shoot on the fly from his hip, throw a grapefruit in the air and shoot it down. So down here in South Texas, it did have the Wild West frontier flavor to it that California didn't have and almost nowhere did.

CC: I think the Beats were looking for a new West. If you look at someone like Neal Cassady, he's the new rebel, the new cowboy; I mean, he stole cars and that made him an outlaw figure.

CC: If you look at the East Texas experiment, Jack Kerouac would always talk about having a ranch where all of their writer friends would go work the land and they would write and live together on this kind of farming commune. That was his dream and Ginsberg tried to do that in Cherry Valley, but I think in Texas when Burroughs had his ranch here they all tried to get there but they were never there all at the same time. Kerouac never got to come there.

RJ: Kerouac never came down to the Valley but he went through Laredo into Mexico and came back through Brownsville in 1952 and writes about it in his journal. Ginsberg and Cassady and Huncke were up at Burroughs' East Texas farm. Cassady supposedly visited down in South Texas but I never found any record of it. Kerouac called Texas "inevitable." In fact, they were all over Texas, and another thing about Texas and the Beats is Texas is the gateway to Mexico. They went back and forth east to west and then finally they got sensible and thought why don't we head south and they ended up down in Mexico and to do that they had to go through Texas—it has 1200 miles of Mexican border.

CC: Even people like Bonnie and Ray Bremser came through Matamoros to get to Brownsville.

RJ: When Kerouac went to Mexico in 1949, right after Burroughs had moved down there, they had opened the Pan American highway just ten years earlier, all 770 miles of it, and that was the highway from Laredo all the way down to Mexico City and Burroughs writes about it in *Naked Lunch*. He's driving and getting into this mountain town called Tamazunchale and because he had driven through it so many times, he had a nickname for it, they called it "Thomas and Charlie." That was an adventurous road for Americans because it was the first major highway in Mexico and it came in through Laredo, which is why they would go through San Antonio because San Antonio to Laredo is the route and it still is the biggest port of entry on the Texas border. Kerouac went all over Texas and I think Texas is the only state that he drives all the way through east, west, north, and south in *On The Road.*

CC: Well, we've discussed what the original Beats interest was in Texas, but now I want to talk about the effect that they had on the writers here in Texas.

CT: This is moving up into the 60s and 70s and 80s with Texas being a place that beats people down. Our support of the arts is 50th out of the 50 states in the union. It's very interesting because I can remember when you could drive around in Texas with an open beer can and I suppose the Beats appreciated that. But there is a strong confederate authoritarian tradition here also. Part of Texas is the West and its influence is the cowboy mythology and freedom and being an individual, but then you have the confederate and religious influence pushing in from the East and so it is a place that doesn't like artists very much that don't tow the line and is suspicious of people who are in writing or other arts and so it pushes writers into the margins where the Beats live making them angry and rebellious. So in a way this will always be the beatest state in the union because it is one of the hardest places to be an artist.

RJ: Well, you have artists like Robert Rauschenberg and Janis Joplin coming out of Port Arthur, and Rauschenberg is gay and a pop artist even before Warhol and Janis Joplin is voted the "Ugliest Man on Campus" at UT and she was ridiculed for her bohemian look. So, yeah, it was a lot easier to be an artist in the East Village or San Francisco than in Port Arthur, Texas. Here in Texas it was a different story, they really were beat here.

CC: That's true in many areas especially like the Dallas scene with Bud Shrake and the Mad Dog scene, and the Austin Beat Punk scene in the 1970s and 80s, your era Chuck.

RJ: I don't think there was anything resembling a Beat scene in Texas until the Beats started publishing their work except that there really were "beat" Texans. But then when it came out, the Texas writers picked up on it real fast. You had one of the original Crickets who played with Buddy Holly opening up a Beatnik coffee shop in the late 50s. You had Terry Allen reading *On The Road* and writing Beatnik poetry and actually getting encouraged by his high school teacher to write.

CC: Joe Ely was influenced by the Beats.

RJ: Yeah, they read them and it did take root here with them. Even with the Mexican American writers like Genaro Gonzalez in McAllen, who was reading the Beats in the 60s and Dagoberto Gilb …

CC: I believe the Beat writings gave a lot of writers license to write about their own lives because mostly what they were reading were people like Hemingway and Fitzgerald and 19th-century privileged writers that they could not connect with. Here came Kerouac, Burroughs, Ginsberg, and others coming along showcasing an America that most underprivileged people could relate to as opposed to Americans abroad in Europe or the upper classes of New York City. Kerouac featured a lot of the poorer areas of America in his work and they highlighted Mexico and the border regions of America and these writers like Dagoberto Gilb and Raul Salinas picked up on the fact that they were writing about poor people and Mexican peoples.

CT: John Rechy is out there in El Paso and this guy named Dru Lagndon had a magazine that was publishing Ed Dorn in El Paso, but I think it was the Chicanos that have kept the spirit of the Beats going with the moviemento poets, with Ricardo Sanchez who was interested in the Beats, Raul Salinas goes up to Lowell to look at the monument to Kerouac there, Rechy is definitely writing in Beat style. It is the Mexican-American writers who have the strongest identification with the Beat writers and they have continued the literary tradition. These were people who were living the Beat life, reading the Beats, and definitely were influenced by them. These are the young ones who are starting out in the sixties.

RJ: I think Dagoberto is a good case study. He's from El Paso and what he told me, like you said earlier Chris, was that he was a teenager trying to read great literature and all he could get was Hemingway and what are Hemingway characters doing? Oh, they are vacationing in Europe and the only reason they remember the cities they went to was that they tried some new drink there and they are going to bull fights and dancing drunk in fountains. F. Scott Fitzgerald lived the same sort of rich expatriate lifestyle and Dagoberto said that as a young Mexican-American writer that he couldn't relate to those people at all because they had more money than he would ever have in his life, but then he read the Beats. And you read Jack Kerouac and at one point, he is eating grass, he's so hungry. And he does at least try to pick some crops in the fields and so he said that those were the only writers that he could relate to. Henry Miller was unavailable in the United States. There was just the Beats unless you were reading *Tobacco Road* or maybe some Steinbeck and a few other things. You had to wait for the Beats to get any sort of working class literature that would appeal to Mexican Americans in Texas and the Southwest. Then Chicano literature comes around in the 60s, but the Beats were getting popular in 1956, '57, '58.

CC: The Beats gave them license to write about their own lives in their own language and that's what really opened the door for a lot of these writers, people like Raul Salinas and Ricardo Sanchez. The Beats opened them up to the idea that they don't have to write like Ivy League writers, they can write in their own voice and that is really what the Beats were doing. Especially someone like Kerouac, who seems to be the most influential on people nowadays. I think that's because he wrote about people in their own language, in their own way, he recorded what he heard like an audio recorder and spit it back out in poetic prose. He turned the attention away from the rich and put his focus on the salt of the earth and the outlaw and made it okay for a writer to make their own life into a novel or a poem and show that it was just as interesting as the New York elite. It opened up a different writer.

RJ: Surely, but now let me ask a question. Are there really Texas Beat writers?

CC: Yes, there are. Look at Bud Shrake. He's a Beat Texas writer.

RJ: Steven Davis calls him one in his book *Texas Literary Outlaws*.

CC: Terry Southern wrote *Dr. Strangelove*. You have people like Larry McMurtry ...

RJ: McMurtry wrote his undergraduate honors thesis on the Beats in 1958.

CC: And he was hanging out with Ken Kesey at Stanford.

CC: It hits about the 60s, 70s, and by the 80s it was big in Austin. There were a lot of poets in Austin around the 70s and 80s. You had people like Chuck—that was your era.

RJ: Well, you're a small press publisher, Chuck, and you've being doing that since 1973. Slough Press is, from what I've read, the longest running small press in Texas.

CT: Bryce Milligan, the guy that runs Wings Press in San Antonio, we have a friendly argument about who started theirs first. Jim Cody had a press called Place of Heron's Press and he was a student of Gary Snyder. He was an Eco-poet. There was Dave Oliphant who did Prickly Pear Press, but nobody was really publishing marginalized and radical writers. When I was living in El Paso you really saw how little bookstores had a lot of Beat literature and Henry Miller and there were intellectuals out there who weren't associated with the university and they were going over to Mexico and they were hard drinkers and it was a very inexpensive place to live. There's a place called Chase Mansion where Ginsberg and Snyder came through and read. When these writers were heading west they would come through there.

CC: The one thing we have learned since putting this book together is how many Beat writers there are in Texas. When we first began we had no idea there were so many Beats here and what this book is doing is connecting everyone like Ginsberg connected everyone when he read "Howl." It is showing the world that we are not alone, we are here, and we are Beat. When we started to talk to the various writers in El Paso, Dallas, Houston, Austin, they all realized that they were all kind of Beat and they all had this Beat influence and Beat attitude, but they just never had a space where they could be represented together as Beat. We have people like Gene Keller and Donna Snyder in El Paso, Karen Minzer, who was Allen Ginsberg's student, and Opalina Salas in Dallas, Ken Jones in Houston, from the L.A./Austin punk rock scene.

CT: And we also have this surprising woman up in Lamesa, Connie Williams. She went up to Naropa.

RJ: She was in love with Ferlinghetti, which she says quite openly. And she's even in Chuck Workman's documentary film of the Beat Generation, *The Source*.

CC: She says that it was Ferlinghetti that turned her on to writing. She sketched out Ferlinghetti and that is in this book. So, Texas ends up being a place you wouldn't think would be Beat influenced but it is.

CT: One of the false perceptions about the Beats is that it was New York, Denver, San Francisco.

RJ: You're right. If you just tell the story of the Beats from an East Coast/West Coast perspective you have San Francisco and New York and they spent some time in Chicago where Herbert Huncke was from and then you throw in Colorado in the middle and you are leaving out the fact that Texas was a big center of it. The grandfather of the Beats, William S. Burroughs, spent a lot of time here and got them all to come down here and introduced them to Mexico and that was a huge part of their development as writers. Instead of becoming European-American writers they became Mexican-American writers because their Europe was Mexico. They were the first ones to say that you don't have to go to North Africa to see pyramids—if you are in Texas you get in your car and drive for about ten hours south and there they are.

CC: No other state can make the claim that Texas can, I mean you look at New York and it's actually New York City and you look at California, but it's actually San Francisco, but Texas has pockets of activity all over from El Paso to South Texas to Dallas to Houston and Austin.

Part II

RJ: What were you and Chuck looking for when you put together your list of contemporary Beat writers?

CC: The way we went about it was through Chuck. Chuck knows all of these Beat writers like Karen Minzer and Donna Snyder and Ken Jones and others who all had direct links to the Beats.

RJ: Like the punk rock movement and otherwise, right?

CC: Yeah, Karen was a disciple of Allen Ginsberg. Donna Snyder has had a lot Beat writers go through her Tumblewords series over the years. That is how we started. We went to people who had connections to the Beats and also Raul's bookstore, Resistencia. Rene Valdez, Raul's executor and now manager of Resistencia, told us of all the Beat writers that Raul knew. That was where our search began seeking out these certain writers. Well, Chuck you know Jose Olivera out there in El Paso, who is a Mexican-American Beat writer.

RJ: And then you connected through him to other writers and so on and so on?

CT: I had a friend write me a letter for a promotion I am bucking for and he described me as a scrappy Beat writer and in Texas anyone who is not an academic they either call them street poets or Beat writers. They are considered very strange and black sheep, certainly many of the writers in this book, who for most of their lives were not academics.

CC: You have people like Opalina Salas, a Dallas Beat Chicana poet who was a Slam champion back in the 90s and she is not an academic, but she ran a little Beat bookstore in Dallas for awhile. She's directly influenced by the Beats and labels herself a Beat, which she certainly is. Even though they write about the original Beats they write their own stuff that is not imitative of the original Beat work, but is something new and different but still Beat. They are picking up on the style but they are creating something different.

RJ: Like Chuck was saying these are the outsiders who might be associated with academia off and on but a lot of them are writers in their own right. Ken Jones for example. Ken is a lawyer and he does teach but he teaches at the Art Institute of Houston and he's a former punk rocker and he's a poet and he's got that DIY attitude. So, these are the writers you carry the Beat tradition through and are doing their own thing.

CT: Like Joe Hoppe who comes from a working class background—he's a Michener Fellow—and writes working class poetry. A lot of these writers write about people who are not rich. Hedwig Gorski spent some time at Naropa and she was an Austin poet, doing performance poetry.

CC: I think the current Beat writers keep the spirit of the Beats in their own voices and there is for most a connection to the original movement which has created this lineage. Karen goes and sets up Wordspace in Dallas and brings lots of writers through, Beat and otherwise. Same thing in El Paso and in South Texas with PW Covington and Edward Vidaurre and Erika Garza; in Austin you have people like Thom the Worldpoet and others.

CT: The Sun poet there in San Antonio is another, Rod Stryker, he's very Beat.

CC: Raul set up a different type of Beat writer scene, which is very Chicano. He taps into the Pinta poetry scene since he was a prisoner and he understands the transformative power of poetry and how the Beats spoke to him. I think the Beats have been successful at creating spaces for poets to create more poets and it is certainly so here in Texas.

RJ: Let a thousand flowers bloom is a Ginsberg idea.

CT: Hedwig Gorski when she was living in Austin was trying to be a Beat playwright and so she found this abandoned house and it became the set for her play. She did have a couple of professional actors but mostly the cast was made up of street people and I published the book about the play with photographs and such. There was a lot of weird stuff going on in Texas.

RJ: Erika Garza and Veronica Sandoval and Daniel Garcia Ordaz in the Valley have been doing renegade readings for over a decade, all outside of and even in spite of academia. They, and others, are our outlaw poets. Most recently, Edward Vidaurre, originally from El Salvador and now in south Texas via East Los, he sets up a lot of the readings down here and he's a restaurant manager who didn't start writing poetry until fairly recently but has a good ear for poetry, a rich tragic life experience, and he's very open-minded. People like that who have no academic training are doing poetry. That's Beat.

Beat South Texas

begins with San Antonio and extends to the Rio Grande on the Mexican border, then to the Gulf of Mexico. The place consists of forty-one counties, and many businesses in Houston have the words "South Texas" in their titles. With its vast and sparsely populated lands and mesquite trees it resembles West Texas. One editor calls the area MexAmerica because Mexican-American culture is dominant. Beat literature flourishes here, especially in the border cities along the Rio Grande, because Mexican Americans maintain a special attachment to Beat writers and can relate to the marginality in the Beat sensibility. Beat South Texas possesses a bustling economy and culture, yet one can enjoy walking the citrus fields irrigated by the Rio Grande, or strolling at night the golf course behind Edinburg's Echo Hotel where William Burroughs once killed a rattlesnake with a golf club. Poetry readings in South Texas along the Rio attract large audiences of artists, poets, and regular citizens looking for exploration of important issues, like immigration. A popular venue that has been operating for years, run by the Beat influences poet Edward Vidaurre, is called Poetry and Pasta and provides food for body and soul. A number of vibrant small presses are active.

Jack Kerouac

[Jack Kerouac traveled extensively in Mexico in the early 1950s and often stayed with his friend William S. Burroughs in Mexico City. He wrote several of his novels there, including *Tristessa* and *Dr. Sax*. In this excerpt from Kerouac's selected journal entries, *Windblown World*, he crosses back into the U.S. via Matamoros/Brownsville.]

Wild Night in Brownsville

BROWNSVILLE TEXAS TO ROCKY MOUNT, JULY 1952

Hitchhiking all the way, with a 5-dollar bill and a big packbag: time to stop cause I wanta be home for 4th July - Start off walking from Mexican bus across Matamoros, out dusty streets, to border, American guards, & into Brownsville - out to connecting highway, where I'm picked up by Hotrod Johnny Bowen of Brownsville which wants me to have a beer with him - A few beers in roadhouse - Now he wants me to drink with him all night - wants me to get a job in Brownsville - He is a crazy lonely kid - wants me to go see his pregnant wife - we drink and do, she throws him out (they're separated) - Wants me to meet his Drive-In sister, she says "I don't wanta be told who to go out with" - he's crazy -

He plays pinball machine all up & down the highway, we get drunk, drive 100 mph thru intersections, play pool with a buncha Mexicans downtown Brownsville one of whom "borrows" $1 from me & I so drunk I give it, out of my 5

At dawn I'm broke - we sleep in his house, Texas cottage - Next day I'm sick & also dysentery fever

- Have soda, he gives me back my $5 - I go out on road & am sick in gas station toilet - sit a long while resting - Then I hitch - Got 3000 miles to go - Immediate ride to Harlingen along endless fence of King Ranch, with old hillbilly who hearing of Mexican whores thinks it wd. be a good idea to bring a truckload to Chicago - Long wait in hot sun at Harlingen, I drink cokes, - Get ride to Rosenberg Texas from young Mexican medical student - Then spot ride into Houston where drunken construction worker invites me into his motel room for shower & when I come out he on his belly naked begging me to screw him - I leave, wont do it - he's crying - I get ride from little faggot who owns Dandy Courts, says "Hitch out here in front of my court (motel), if

ALL THOSE BLACKEYED PEAS

you don't get a ride come in & sleep" but I do get ride from oil truck driven by wild talking rhythmic Cherokee Indian mentioned on p. 74 of DHARMA BUMS, to Liberty Texas at dawn, where I sleep on railroad loading platform - There ride with flat truck carrying pile of black-eyed peas in bags, we stop to fix load under "tarpolian" he called it, thru Beaumont to Baton Rouge - Hot sunny highway I suck on flavored ice in a cup, get a ride up to Mississippi from some pleasant Mississippian -

Ted Marak

[Ted Marak was a friend of William S. Burroughs and Kells Elvins, Burroughs' longtime friend from St. Louis whose father had bought Valley citrus in the land rush of the 1930s. Exiled for various reasons and somewhat disoriented by the border, they all lived in south Texas in the late 1940s and partied at Kells' farmhouse on S. Jackson Road in Pharr, Texas. Their exploits are chronicled in *The Lost Years of William S. Burroughs: Beats in South Texas*, by Rob Johnson. In 2003, Johnson recorded Marak (who died in 2009) reading the following excerpt from a "little short story" he was writing about the "south Texas Beats," including Marak, Tiger Terry, and Kells' "live-in" girlfriend Obie Dobbs. The "orgone accumulator" in the story was a walk-in box designed by Wilhelm Reich to harvest vital energies from the atmosphere. Burroughs built his first orgone accumulator in an orange grove on Kells' property. Local Mexicans thought the crazy gringos were practicing *brujería*, or black magic. In the story, a spotted rooster isn't producing spotted chicks so they put him in the accumulator. The result is spotted chicks. Burroughs used a portable version of the accumulator, made from a gas can, for sexual stimulation.]

South Texas Beats

Six o'clock was drinking time. Hard and fast rule ... As the minute hand slowly approached its zenith on the Ingersoll clock, you could have heard a gnat fart except for the dripping of the condensation on the glasses.

"That damn thing stop?" asked Elvins.

"Oh, shut up," said Obie, as she moved the glass closer to her mouth. "You never heard of an Ingersoll that just stopped. They just slowed down and died, according to my Mother."

"Oh can't you talk about anything but your family?"

Terry let out an acceptable burp saying that the five-gallon bottle of Ozark gin water was getting low. Kells said he'd send Eusabio across the river tomorrow for his usual five-gallon purchase. That to Terry seemed a major decision. He smiled and felt a little more secure, since gin and quinine water along with a little pot were the sustaining factor of this particular group.

Suddenly Terry's brain clicked and went into high gear, and he asked Kells what he thought about raising cockroaches. Now cockroaches was about as bad a word as clap in a whorehouse. Three of the "brains" went into shock at the sound of the word. Bopper's [the dog's] ears even went up; before they went down, Terry was explaining how he was trying to find out from an off-duty border patrolman how to get a line on some mushrooms. Well one thing led to another. Dickie Dean had mentioned that cockroaches were on-hoof chicken feed. Then, after guzzling most of his drink, how easy it was to grow them and dry them and make them into pellets.

"You're out of your mind, Terry," hollered Obie. "You been on the mushroom again?"

"Naw, I'm off that shit," replied Terry indignantly. "Kells, can't you get that gal off of me? She's always downing me like I'm some kind of embryo."

"Embryo? You mean imbecile, Terry," Obie chirped.

"I mean you treat me like I'm so dumb I wasn't even born yet," [said Terry].

"Naw," said Kells, "You know Obie's all bark. Besides," he said, addressing Obie, "it was Terry who came up with the orgone accumulator."

"Yeah, yeah," said Obie. "Spotted chickens and a bunch of hardons. Can't you guys come up with some logic, or at least make some money?"

"It would have made money if it hadn't been for those members of the White Legged Breeders Association accusing us of having mutilated the breed," [said Terry].

"Not mutilated," said Obie, shaking her head. "Mutation was the reason why, Terry."

"Well, whatever I had in mind didn't mean killing the sonsofbitches. Besides, you had to admit that these longhorns were a damn site prettier with spots on them. On top of that, it would be commercially enviable if you had meat that winked."

"Oh Terry."

Juan Ochoa

[Eugene "Tiger" Terry was a ne'er-do-well from Corsicana, Texas, who was sent to the Rio Grande Valley by his parents so "he wouldn't get in trouble." Had it not been for Terry's unusual death by mauling, his life might have very well gone unnoticed. Someone who did take note of Terry's life and death was renowned Beat Generation writer William S. Burroughs, who had a crush on Terry and would often include the young man in his "routines." It was during one of these routines, in which Eugene played a punch-drunk boxer, that he acquired the "Tiger" moniker. Terry's death in Jose Ortega's infamous Reynosa border bar/ restaurant, Joe's Place, helped cement the popular belief among locals that it was bad luck to hang out with Anglos. Most people south of the Rio Grande who still remember that fateful night in November when Terry was killed agree it was Terry who caused the lion's death and not the other way around.]

El Corrido de Tiger Terry

This tragedy happened on a warm night in 1950 and I wish I couldn't remember
How Tiger Terry was killed by a lion in a Reynosa bar in the month of November

Oh Tiger Terry what have you done,
That lion doesn't care that you're a rich man's son
Your parents would've never sent you to Pharr
Had they known you'd be killed in a Reynosa bar

He was at the HUB café in Pharr laughing with Nevada, George, and his friend Willey too
Terry decided he would cross into Mexico to Joe's and pet the cats before the night was through

His friends thought him crazy but why not grab a few drinks at a place called Joe's
The friends thought they would go with Terry into Mexico and catch the Princess's show

Princess La Homa dances sweet and never rough,
She was enough for them to call Terry's bluff

But Terry stood by his promise to pet the cats and drove straight to Joe's
Gunning his truck he named the black death as fast as it would go

"This won't be the first time, I've done it before," said Terry when they stood at the cage door
Luis Allejos heard Terry's boast as he tuned his guitar, "Terry won't learn until he gets another scar."

Oh Tiger Terry what have you done,
That lion doesn't care that you're a rich man's son.
Your parents would've never sent you to Pharr
Had they known you'd be killed in a Reynosa bar

Terry walked into the cage and slapped a she lion across the face
The friends were impressed for Terry acted like he owned the place

But then she rose with a blood-thirsty roar and pounced on Terry tooth and hide
While his friends ran out and shut the door leaving poor Tiger Terry trapped inside

Luis saw George and Willy run from the cage
And knew Terry must still be facing the lion's rage

Jaime Torres and Luis ran to help Terry, Roberto Perez went too
Hitting the lion with the whiskey glasses and chairs they threw

Terry tried to escape by climbing the wall but was brought down with a claw
The lion soon had Terry firmly in her jaw thrashing him around like an old rag doll

Luis and Jaime rush the lion with bottles and chairs
Forcing the lion off of Terry leaving him just lying there

Roberto Perez keeps the beast at bay with only his valor, a chair and a gun
He gets off a shot and fierce eyes go grey while Luis checks on the American

Oh Tiger Terry what have you done,
That lion doesn't care that you're a rich man's son
Your parents would've sent never you to Pharr
Had they known you'd be killed in a Reynosa bar

They wrap Terry in tablecloths and sheets
The bloody scene brings cries from the crowd on the street

Into the back of Joe's Cadillac a bloody Terry is laid
Jaime heads for McAllen but at the bridge is delayed

To the Mexican Red Cross Terry is driven
And it is there that last rites are given

Tiger Terry I have sung your corrido
But to Mexicans you are no hero

You woke a sleeping lion and this shouldn't come as a surprise
Those men risked their lives because some kid thought he couldn't die

A disco now stands at the place that was called Joe's
And no one remembers Princess La Homa's show

But Blondie and the old timers are around and still remember
The night Tiger Terry was killed by a lion in the month of November

Oh Tiger Terry what have you done,
That lion doesn't care that you're a rich man's son
Your parents would've never sent you to Pharr
Had they known you'd be killed in a Reynosa bar

William S. Burroughs

[Burroughs wrote at least two versions of the Tiger Terry story (this one was apparently written in the 1980s) and mentions it repeatedly in his works. "KE" in the story is Kells Elvins. Burroughs was living in Mexico City at the time of Terry's death and heard the story from Elvins and through newspaper accounts. An earlier version of the story, now lost, was described by Jack Kerouac as "exquisite and macabre." Burroughs wrote the earlier version in 1954 as a veiled attempt to write about the death of Joan Vollmer, yet another example of a fatal accident—as he rather defensively saw it—that could have been prevented had sensible bystanders intervened.]

Tiger Terry

It was one of those drunken Texas Interludes. We'd driven down from Pharr to the island off Corpus Christi, to a motel on the beach. There was KE and his lady of the period was it Golden or I forget they all ended up weeping on my shoulder about Kells who after three drinks would start declaiming.

"Show me a good woman ANYTHING."

Couldn't stand them couldn't live without them.

And there was young Terry, like all of us a farmer didn't know shit about farming, we had farmers for that.

"What's that growing on my land?" I ask KE.

"Tomatoes."

"Why?"

"Get 'em off early we get ten cents a pound."

"I understand." We take a bright positive view of things.

And there was someone named Mike, looked like a cop, seemed to know a lot of cops (in fact he reeked of cop, 200 pounds of hard fat and muscle) had a girl with him named Pat who every few seconds would scream out,

"BEER BEER BEER, said the private."

And I'm drinking whiskey out of a chamber pot with a filthy yachting cap on and they call me the Old Engineer and I tell one of my dirty jokes only got two.

Strip tease in London music hall ...

Nice one skips out.

"Oh blimey, look at 'er!"

And this blasé bloke next to him says, "I've 'ad 'er!"

One after another, "I've 'ad 'er!"

So finally the most luscious bird of them all skips out.

"So what about 'er, mate?"

"Shuuuuush, I'm 'aving 'er now."

At one point Terry has a hard-on in the corridor, necking with one of the tomatoes.

Papa didn't grow no peas last year.

Papa didn't grow no taters.

But Oh Christ tomatoes.

Late getting them off you can sell 'em to the canneries for one cent a pound or you can plough them under. We ploughed them under wouldn't you?

"BEER BEER BEER said the private."

''I'm 'aving 'er now.''

So she grabs Terry's cock and turns to Coppy Mike and says, "My gawd! Feel it!"

And Mike says, "What I wanta feel his old peter for?"

Later Dick Tracy gets really smashed, strips off all his clothes and walks into the water like a great big laughing baby.

"Be careful he don't drown hisself!" Pat screeched and I went out and beached him like a whale.

Next day he says, "And I'm usually the son of a bitch goes around telling everyone else what they did last night."

On the beach next day we run into this retired army sergeant weather-beat face close-cropped gray hair and cold hostile crazy gray eyes very pale in the face and we tell him this is Tiger Terry the coming champ and Terry hams it up shadow boxing and spitting and the 20 year man doesn't like it one bit but he doesn't want trouble with Mike and KE. So he went away muttering curses. The rest I hear second hand.

There was a restaurant bar called Joe's in Reynosa, Mexico ... we used to drive across to eat and drink.

"Let's go to REYNOSA!" someone sings out and off we go, me and these good sports. Joe had game dinners like quail and dove and venison and sometimes it was good and sometimes it would just kill you. Usually we ate out on the patio.

Joe had picked up this mangy old lioness from a stranded carnival and kept her in a cage as an attraction. So Terry gets drunk and goes in the cage and pets the lioness ... "Petting the cat," he called it. When Joe heard about this he told the bartender to keep the key behind the bar and see to it the gringo loco didn't get his hands on it. But Terry sneaked in behind the bar and got the key.

"Time to pet the cat," he said.

And those were his last words. The lioness is sleeping, he goes in with a flashlight, shines it in her eyes and the cat comes up on him, knocks him down biting and clawing at him. The two kids from Texas who were with him said, "We don't want to get in any trouble in Mexico!" and got in their car and drove away.

The Mexican waiter went in with a chair and tried to get the lion off Terry but the lion dragged him off into a corner perhaps with culinary intentions, but the bartender gracefully vaults over the bar with his .45 goes in the cage like a matador and blasts the lion from a distance of six inches.

Tiger Terry was DOA Red Cross Reynosa with a broken neck, a fractured skull, a crushed chest like the cat has broken every bone in his body. He was 22 years old.

Now I had a shotgun I'd left with Kells at some point and Kells loaned the gun to Terry. It was a good double-barrel .12 gauge belonged to my father and I wanted it back. When Kells talks to Mr. Bickford, Terry's father, who has come down from Tyler Texas or someplace to settle things, Bickford comes on dead nasty.

"I don't know anything about any shotgun."

Seems Terry owed a lot of money around town and many of the debts were not in writing.

So Kells says, "Look Mr. Bickford, if you think I'm lying, we'll just forget it."

Next day he runs into Bickford again and Bickford says, "Are you in a settling mood?"

And Kells says, "Mr. Bickford, I couldn't care less one way or the other."

And Bickford slips him a hundred dollar bill.

So Kells passes the C note on to me, and I can see he feels a bit guilty for lending the gun to Terry. But who could have imagined that Terry would be dead a week later killed by an African lion in a border town bar. So we call it square and that is the last I ever hear of Tiger Terry.

Fights between lions and tigers have been staged. The tiger always wins.

Brian Allen Carr

[Editor's Note: Carr's story is a loose re-telling and re-imagining of aspects of William S. Burroughs' life in south Texas in the late 1940s. In the citrus groves on Kells Elvins' land Burroughs would shoot grapefruit perched on his common-law wife Joan Vollmer's head. In September of 1951 at an apartment in Mexico City, he tried the same trick with a drink glass and put a bullet in Joan's forehead, killing her.]

The Paint from Her Hands

When the baby came dead they held her for a few hours on the kitchen floor with their legs tangled in the purged amniotic fluid, and Tabitha cried with her head thrown back against the refrigerator door, and Barrow didn't say a thing. He even breathed quiet, drawing the burnt-almond scented air through his nose, his thoughts as puzzled as dust floating in light. They had been to the flea market the week before and had seen a woman with a stand where she made dolls in the likeness of real babies for mementos, and they had smiled and laughed with her and had said they'd see her in a few weeks, and the doll maker held her hand against Tabitha's belly and said, I'll wait for the day. Wait for the day? Barrow and Tabitha had walked away smiling, holding hands. An hour passed since the birth. Barrow, Tabitha said, Barrow. Her shoulders shook and so did her voice, her tears muddling her throat, so Barrow's name lowed from her achingly. What we gonna, she said. Barrow, what we gonna do? Gonna do? Gonna do? Barrow stumbled the phrase through his mind as he thumbed the small thing's lips. Smooth beneath his weathered finger. Gonna do? He thumbed the lips. Gonna do? It's face like a pebble. He'd heard they'd come that way. Like statues unmoving that drew breaths and became themselves. But this one hadn't breathed. It was still when its face hit the light, it stayed still as he dragged the umbilical cord across his blade. He put a thumb against one of its cold, tiny palms, and Tabitha watched for something to come from Barrow's lips. Then Barrow stood, baby in hand. Barrow, Tabitha said. Nothing. Barrow? He shook his head. Barrow? He couldn't look at her. Barrow? Fluid spat from the soles of his shoes as he exited the kitchen.

The trees in the orchard beyond the yard of their home were heavy with green grapefruit. They'd ripen in the weeks to come and grow pale orange out from the stem. Summer was coming on. The heat brought sweat to Barrow's chest within a dozen steps, and his shirt stuck to him. He lowered a strap from his coveralls. He set the baby in the yard. He ran his hands down his shirt undoing the buttons. He flung the shirt into the grass. He reshouldered his coverall strap. He picked up the baby. The plum-colored cord dangled loose from its belly. Barrow walked toward a row of the orchard. Ten months back he and Tabitha had stood in the grass with ripe fruit in piles about them, the perfume of the citrus cutting the damp air. It was an earlier growing season, and they'd hired a half-dozen Mexicans to pick. The Mexicans had run out of boxes and had made mounds of grapefruit in the grass, and Tabitha had taken a grapefruit and set it on her head, and told Barrow, I bet you can't hit it, and Barrow pulled his revolver from his pocket and shot the fruit clean off her skull from ten yards away. One of the Mexicans crossed himself when he saw the juice spray in the air, shaking his head when the rind came down a moment or so later, and then the air was hot with gunpowder, and Tabitha laughed and laughed and rubbed her burgeoned belly. Barrow's feet sank in the soft earth with each step down the row. He kept an orgone accumulator at the center of his orchard. He had built it using a schematic a poet friend had sent him in the mail. It'll unshrink you, the poet friend had written, and Barrow had spent an hour in the box every day since its construction. He opened the pine door and stepped into the sheet-iron lined box. He sat down on the stool inside. He cradled the baby in his arms. He closed the accumulator door.

Barrow couldn't make out her words. He heard her palm strike the accumulator door. The accumulator thumped like a drum and Tabitha's dampened voice swam through the dark. He touched the baby's cheek to his own. It was soft and chill. He wished it warm. He put his palm against the door. Was the box rebuilding him? Could it rebuild the baby? He pressed the door open. It swung soft. Outside Tabitha held tight to a grapefruit-tree branch with one hand. With the other hand she held her dirtied-white gown bunched beside her. Her legs trembled. Her face was damp and pale. Her toes clenched the dirt. What we gonna do? she asked. Barrow dragged Tabitha back toward the house. He slung her arm over his shoulder and held the baby in his free arm. Tabitha's feet caught against the dirt. Barrow looked at her face. Her eyes closed. He dragged her back to the yard and laid her in the grass. He found his flung shirt. He spread it open. He laid the still baby on the shirt and it looked like a shadow, and one of its eyes glazed open, and Barrow flipped the lid closed with a finger, crossed its arms and wrapped it up in a bundle. He lifted Tabitha from the grass and hoisted her to his shoulder. He lifted the bundled baby in his palm. He carried them both into the house. He took Tabitha to the back room. He lit a candle that smelled of lavender. He went to the kitchen and ran cold water over a wash cloth. He rang the cloth. Beads of water drummed the sink. He went back to the bedroom. He folded the cloth over twice and spread it across Tabitha's brow. She took angry, unconscious breaths. Barrow looked into the bundle. Still the child was still and colored dimly.

The woman at the market cracked an egg open and emptied it into her hand. She dropped the shell into the soil of a potted hibiscus on the ground beside her and she spread her fingers and tilted her palm and let the egg white slip into a metal mixing bowl. She then slid the yolk into a granite molcajete and took up a pestle and swirled it through the yolk before raising and mashing the bright yellow sack with the dull instrument. She had already formed the face from polymer clay. She had looked down upon the still baby as her thumbs worked the soft mound. She pulled a body from the shelf. It was intact, a small cloth abdomen with plastic arms and legs. The arms and legs were near-ivory white. She took a canister of powdered lapis lazuli from a cabinet behind her. She scooped a measure of the blue powder and sprinkled it into the yolk and she added other powders and mashed the paste, and Barrow watched the woman and then looked at the baby's face. He watched the woman and then looked at the baby's face. A chime rang and the woman reached for the small oven door and pulled it open. She grabbed a pair of tongs from the table beside her, took the baby's head from the oven and laid it on a cooling rack on a separate work station. The woman then looked at Barrow. She looked at the gun which he'd pulled from his pocket the moment he'd reached her stand. She reached for the rich blue paint in the molcajete. Barrow cocked his gun. Want it to look right don't ya? the woman said. Barrow shook his head. The face, the woman said as she picked up the molcajete, the same blue. Then Barrow shot the paint from her hands.

Barrow laid both babies in the passenger seat of the pickup and drove out to a bluff overlooking the river. He parked the car near an olive tree and got down and grabbed a narrow-bladed shovel from the bed of the truck and dug a hole where a mass of fallen white blossoms had landed and turned the color of tobacco. The ground was soft and the shovel blade passed with the softest press from his boot, and it only took a few scoops to go a foot down, and it needed to be so narrow that the grave was dug in just a few minutes, and he was able to lay the still baby down in the soft black dirt, and then Barrow felt rotten because it looked like a giant grub worm that he had once used to fish with. Then he thought about fishing with the baby as bait. He didn't mean to. The image came to his mind. So he kissed the thing's face, as if to apologize, stood up and took off his hat. He'd been to a funeral or two in the past. He always liked to listen to the ministers. He liked to hear them talk about the people in the coffins. He liked to hear about them flying off to heaven. Barrow didn't know whether or not babies went to heaven, but he wished a minister was there to tell him they did. He wished there was somebody there to say something, anything, but it was quiet except for the sound of the slow river in the distance. He watched the water for a moment moving. Then Barrow covered the thing with the soft mound of unearthed soil beside him.

Barrow had to shake Tabitha awake, and when she came to she'd forgotten a moment, Barrow could tell by the peace in her face, and then the reality came awake in her, and her eyes tightened in the corners. Again she asked Barrow what they should do, and again Barrow was quiet. He looked down at his lap. Tabitha looked down too. Barrow had bundled the fake baby in a small cotton blanket. He picked it up in his hands. He shrugged his shoulders and looked at Tabitha, and Tabitha pulled at the edge of the blanket, and it fell open just enough for her to see the ivory face. She lifted her head back surprised. She touched the thing's head with the tip of a fingernail. Her nail clicked against the skin of it, and she nodded and looked at Barrow who had wet in his eyes. Tabitha leaned back against her pillow. She opened her arms. Barrow laid the baby in them, and Tabitha pulled it to her chest. She looked down at it. She asked it questions that Barrow didn't understand, but Barrow could see from Tabitha's expression that the baby had a silent way of answering her. The thing's actions could solve riddles. And then he knew the thing was kin.

Genaro González

[Genaro González is a professor of psychology at the University of Texas Rio Grande Valley and is the author of four critically-acclaimed works of fiction about the south Texas border. In this excerpt from *The Quixote Cult*, De La O (González's alter-ego in the novel) and his Beat-inspired friend Lucio travel from McAllen, Texas, to Mexico City in 1968 looking for remnants of the Beat Mexico written about by Jack Kerouac and William S. Burroughs. They arrive there only a few months after the conclusion of the 1968 Olympics, an event remembered to this day in Mexico City less for the athletic competition than for the Mexican government's murder of hundreds of students who organized peaceful protest marches during the Olympics.]

Tripping Down to the Big Mango

Lucio comes home for the holidays with plans for a Thanksgiving trip to Mexico City. He wants me and Pablo, the part-time checker at his father's store, to come along. He's never expressed an interest in Mexico except as a source of drugs. Now he's talking about adventures like the kind Kerouac had down there, so I'm sure his college friends have sold him on the idea.

Pablo's lukewarm until Lucio personalizes the sales pitch: "I heard some Olympic athletes stayed over for follow-up games."

Pablo, who talks about last month's games in Mexico City as though they were still going on, says he hasn't seen anything of the sort in the sports pages.

"Well, that's what I heard at UT." Lucio shrugs to show that's all he knows. Even though Pablo is older and already a junior in college, in some ways he still looks up to Lucio.

That evening Pablo has us talk to his compadre, who's been to Mexico City several times. Pablo immediately asks him about any events carried over from the Olympics.

"Not that I've read about," he says. "Then again, people want to forget about October. Who knows, maybe now's the time to keep the public distracted."

Pablo wonders aloud who would want to forget the Olympics.

I ask, "Didn't their National Guard open fire on some demonstrators?"

Compadre simply shakes his head, implying it was no big thing. "They just popped a few people, that's all. College kids. Troublemakers."

He glances at me out of the corner of his eyes. "Leave those Chicano buttons on the side. And keep that hair tucked under your collar."

Something tells me he knows a lot more than he's letting on, but by now our main concern is finding bus seats during Thanksgiving. Then I remember a bus trip I once took during the holidays with the old man to his hometown in Mexico. That was when I found out that Mexicans didn't celebrate Thanksgiving.

Once that matter is settled, I start getting excited about the trip. I know full well that Lucio's invitation is partly because of his father's insistence that Pablo and I go along to keep Lucio half way straight. But since he's footing the bill, that's all that matters. And since I intend to stay straight the whole trip, setting the example should be no great sacrifice. The one thing that bothers me, up to the afternoon we're ready to leave, is Lucio's lying to Pablo about the Olympics.

"So what's going to happen," I ask Lucio, "when we get there and Pablo finds out there's nothing going on?"

"I never said I was sure. Anyway, we'll take in a fight at the Coliseo."

"Why not tell him that from the start?"

"Because the Olympics are what's pushing him, even if it's just left-overs. He talked all summer about going but never did. Now he wants to believe that athletes are still there. They're his ghosts, just like yours are the places where Villa and Zapata walked, and mine where Burroughs and the Beats hung out."

Then he adds, "I saw some Bunuel films at UT. The Mexican Bus Ride, and"—he pauses to make sure his Spanish comes out straight—"La illusion viaja en tranvia. Just think, we'll be doing both in one trip! Bus rides and illusions."

I argue that for Pablo the return trip will be more disappointment than illusion, but Lucio insists, "What difference does it make? What's important is that he's coming along. He can help out if there's trouble."

"What do you mean?"

"Well, you never know."

In fact I don't really know until we board the bus across the border. No sooner do we take our seats in back than Lucio shows a small bag of pills held by the elastic of one sock. Above the other I see the tips of several joints.

"Camus must be rolling in his grave at the absurdity," he says. "Some guys risks his ass crossing the shit over the river, just so that we can cross it right back."

I point out a more immediate absurdity. "You've heard those horror stories about Mexican prisons?"

"That's why I bought the stuff in the States." He pretends to peer into the dim light of the bus. "You think I'd trust any of these maniacs?"

What I mean, of course, is that all that trouble could be avoided—provided we traveled clean. But that provision is either too tall an order for Lucio or else too trifling. He'd sooner go insane trying to unravel Wittgenstein than swallow an ounce of common sense. I try hard to keep the little I have left, even as a part of me enjoys the excitement too.

At our first rest stop, Lucio swallows a couple of uppers. Pablo drops one too, saying he doesn't want to miss out on anything during the trip even though it's already turning dark. I simply mention that the last time I took pills I ended up going to a curandera. The anecdote amuses them to no end. I hold out until we reach Monterrey, where I become the man who takes a potion and sacrifices his sanity in order to fit in with the madmen around him. Besides, I tell myself, the quicker we use up the stuff the sooner we'll be home free.

Once the uppers kick in I sit next to a mexicano who's also headed for Mexico City and who ends up as my sounding board for the night. He's about my age, but with a calm maturity that makes him pause every so often for the right word, which only makes me more self-conscious about my own non-stop speech on speed. I make an effort to do more listening and less talking, but not before confessing that I'm a Chicano activist.

It truly is a confession. Before we left, the compadre warned me against discussing politics. "Their revolution's been over for fifty years," I told the compadre back home. "The bad guys won."

"Maybe, but the government doesn't like being reminded," he said, "especially by outsiders."

"I'm no outsider."

"You will be, in Mexico. Anyway, the place is still a powderkeg." He left me with a look that hinted I asked too many questions.

If I do, it's a habit I can't break. I start asking the young mexicano about last month's protests. He speaks reluctantly, with the same nervousness the compadre gave the matter. Finally he starts talking about his involvement in the student movement in the capital. He explains how, some weeks back, students and workers in Mexico City tried using the international spotlight on the Olympic Games to highlight their grievances. "We didn't think the government should spend that kind of money with so much poverty around. I was amazed at the public support we got, considering how fanatical our people get about sports. At first the government ignored us, then they started calling us unpatriotic."

"Sounds familiar."

"In the beginning it was hard work but also fun, the same way you talk about your own movement. We organized, talked to students and workers. We'd demonstrate, then the government would demonstrate back."

"You mean the government threw its own protests?"

"It's nothing new. Every time elections roll around they round up villagers and truck them over to their candidates' rallies. They did the same thing in the city, except now you had bureaucrats herded to demonstrations on buses. The districto federal is one huge, bureaucratic beehive, so they were everywhere. They weren't crazy about going, but they also weren't crazy enough to lose their jobs. So they'd board, bleating like sarcastic sheep all the way. 'Ba-aa! Please don't make us go! Baa-aaaaaa!' That's how it went for a while. We'd take to the streets one day, then the next day it was the government's turn. But with the Olympics around the corner, they were afraid we'd embarrass them before the world, so they called a meeting at Las Plaza De las Tres Culturas. 'For a meaningful dialogue,' they said. We brought housewives and children, workers and the elderly. The government brought its gunmen and grenadiers. Then they closed the gates, corralled everyone inside and opened fire. Pistols, rifles, machine guns, you name it. Even a helicopter hovered overhead, illuminating the crowd, and later I heard it too opened fire. I couldn't tell, though, I was running like everyone else, terrified I'd die. There was screaming all around, and I tried to yell, 'Stop the screaming!' as though that might somehow stop the shooting. But the moment I opened my mouth I started screaming too. Or at least I felt something in my chest. I couldn't even hear myself scream. I kept stumbling towards the gates when suddenly a barrage of bullets hurled a woman against some railings, like a scrap of iron yanked to a magnet. It happened so fast I couldn't tell whether she was a young girl or an old woman, I only knew she seemed so frail. An instant later she was too disfigured to tell. I started sobbing, when I noticed a man on the other side of the gates, waving his arms like a madman for someone to let him in. For a moment I imagined he was my father. He seemed desperate to get in. Here people were forming human pyramids trying to get out of that hell and there he was, dying to get in."

He turns quiet for a moment, and I ask, "So then it wasn't like the papers said, about a few protesters being shot?"

He shakes his head in anger. "Hundreds died. Even people in the high-rises surrounding the park were hit. Afterwards they were pulling out bodies from the elevators and halls."

"You were lucky, then." My mouth, already dry from the amphetamines, now feels parched.

"They say the lucky ones were those who ended up in the morgue or in mass graves. The rest of my friends were either in Lecumberri Prison or will be there soon."

"So why are you going back? Sounds like it's still dangerous."

"They took in my younger sister for questioning. That was three days ago. I'm the one they want. Not that I think it'll save her, but I have no choice."

We say very little after that. No wonder Pablo and his compadre told me to keep quiet about politics.

We arrive the following morning and end up on the fourth floor of a hotel without a working elevator. For once I'm glad Lucio brought uppers, but after staying up for the second straight day and night, we collapse on the beds.

The next day we stroll around Chapultepec Park, where Lucio decides that the weekend crowd is ideal cover for smoking some joints. We're supposed to take turns smoking cigarettes to camouflage the smell, but I balk, arguing with a perverse prudishness that I'll smoke a straight cigarette. Later Pablo lights up our last joint while on a chalupa we rent out in Lake Xochimilco. Luckily our guide not only looks the other way but has the decency to lower the side awnings.

Lucio finds the episode entertaining, like something out of a Beat novel. "Imagine when the guy gets home. 'Honey, you'll never guess what happened while I was pushing the chalupa this afternoon.'"

"I don't think the guys here call their wives honey," says Pablo.

Though I'm enjoying the trip in a nervous way, I know full well that if we're busted it's Lucio, with his well-off dad, who's most likely to return home.

A couple of blocks from a main avenue, I come face to face with silent reminders of the massacre. Posters of Zapata, with his piercing, accusative stare, are plastered so tightly on the walls that nothing short of razors could scrape away their message: "Yesterday they assassinated Zapata. Today they assassinate students. Why?"

I try not to think much about the chavo I met on the bus, or the fate of his sister, until it's time for us to leave. We're taking a cab to the bus station when I ask the driver, "There's a prison around here. Le ... Lechu ..."

The cab driver, somewhat startled, answers, "Lecumberri?"

"That's the one. Where is it?"

He doesn't give a direct answer but simply says, "That's where they locked up rebels in the days of Porfirio Díaz."

"Is it close by?"

"Close by? It's closed! Anyway, you don't want to go there."

"But if it's closed, what's the harm?"

"People insist the place is haunted, that you can still hear ghosts from the old days. And you know what they say about the dead."

I don't know what they say, nor do I bother to ask. I suppose it's the same thing they say here about the missing—nothing.

Bonnie Bremser

[Bonnie Bremser's *Troia*, published in 1969, is the first authentic memoir by a woman of the Beat Generation. Written in a style inspired by Kerouac's *On the Road* and *Dr. Sax*, the book follows Bremser and her husband Ray's flight to Mexico in 1960 after Ray is accused of committing armed robbery (he says he is innocent). In Mexico, Bremser prostitutes herself to support her daughter Rachel and her husband's ambitions as a poet. In this excerpt, Ray has been arrested in Mexico, deported, and incarcerated in a jail in Laredo, Texas.]

Troia: Mexican Memoirs

Rachel and I checked into a concrete structure called a hotel, far back from the border in Nuevo Laredo. I should always differentiate Nuevo Laredo from Laredo; I insisted on living on the Mexican side. I was afraid of the Texas police, and I wanted a better position from which to operate. After all, I have found it not too greatly illegal to hustle in Mexico, and even the head of immigration (though he has threatened that if I am caught causing any trouble in Nuevo Laredo that he would have to make me leave) has looked at me sympathetically. I know that the police on the American side would like to get me on anything. In fact, they are constantly threatening to put me in jail for just standing beneath Ray's window and talking to him, and they tell Ray that they are going to put me in jail and Rachel in an orphanage if I don't stop that, but I am stubborn, wildly defiant of any discipline so I do it even more often to bug them, I guess, and also just to be alone close to Ray. It was a long walk from our new concrete stucco hotel, and the windows out on some secondary plaza of Nuevo Laredo let in too much morning sun. Rachel lays in a basket, our baggage consists mostly of baskets. On the way back, final trip from Mexcity, the bus stopped in a dawn plaza of Indian basketry and I bought a covered basket to serve as a suitcase.

Once or twice I exceeded the friendship of B the cop, who considered himself my steady. Though he only gave me dribbles of money and help, I considered him my mainstay, mostly because of the insecurity of the police situation there, and I knew he was sympathetic. Nonetheless one late afternoon when I needed money badly, had nothing, funny to get down to not even Coca-Cola bottles to cash in a strange place. I get dressed in the freshest I got (and funny also how it is not up to me, but an attraction which occurs like Ray says, Monk eyeing the keys while someone else, probably Milt Jackson or John Lewis, is also up to something, and then it happens, like flies making it in midair), and a young man digs me on the street. I somehow find change to have lemonade in a patio parlor alone, so he can dig me better and approach. I am not often so cool, he is shy to the point of sweetness, and I think at first that he is too young, but a good possibility in this town of no visual hustle, everyone on the streets is busy hustling the Americans and I am not interested or able to try them yet (my prejudices). The young man asks to sit down and I allow him to join me. His youth is a motivation for me to set the price as soon as I can. I am nervous, he tells me how impressed he was by my entire profile in silhouette, like a queen, a young queen I think he specified, and I quickly find out his business, salesman, and his inclinations to pay me. He is short of money and reluctant at first to pay the 300 pesos I ask for, but when we get to his room, and we retire there immediately in the setting evening, I lay the whole story on him of the baby sleeping back in the hotel and Ray across the river, and he came across with what I needed. His room was in a triangular, jutting-out building, which I will come to know again later, slatted doors, sign of the tropics, tile hallways, double-centered windows. In fact his room is so full of windows we had to shut out evening with blinds to avoid the eyes of the adjoining market. I let myself go a little, he wants love (doesn't everyone), but he is young and better able to talk me into it. We somehow achieve a good enough fuck and unity through conversation that when it is done it is a clearing away of the day's cares, good healthy boy and girl fuck. He wants me to sleep there and give him more, but in my impatience to get away, my suntan naked persuasion, my means are twisted and he is more desirous of another good clean fuck. The second was an aftermath and reluctant for me, for I never want to do twice what I am getting paid for once, with no money in hand, though I have insisted that it be in sight on the table, because from there on I am capable of self-protection, so it was just a cool evening laying aside one another, no interesting perversions, just kiss and give a feel. Let him admire me, he gets hot again, there are some struggles of tension, and then it is in, up and down and over and I quickly dress and make arrangements to see him again sometime, and out, money in pocket. I have succeeded in taking care of business.

Oh, it is good to eat after several days of nothing but worry, and good to know that in the morning I will go to the jail across the bridge, no problem with the nickel toll; I will probably even ignore the tollkeeper as I pass and hitch the baby higher on my hip, and buy peaches for Ray, enormous ones that make a whole meal for our shrunken stomachs, and sit square down on the sidewalk between the courthouse and Ray's jail window, almost hidden by trees as it is by bars mesh of superfluous shading, sit there and eat the peach I have saved from Ray's and know that he is watching and know that his watching makes me hotter than any Laredo sun, the baby cooing among the grass roots of courthouse sprinkler lawn. Don't no one care, not till the sheriff comes along and I hear about it on our next visit. That's how it will be tomorrow, window Ray, the shadow god that leaves little more than a footprint on mirrors.

But now it is night and the creepy blueness comes to haunt me, the dull starless night. I know that Ray will be glad that I pulled this trick O.K., no burn, no fear, but the light of indescribable conscience shines at me from beyond the darkness I know lies over the river—maybe it was better to have no money and not wonder about this specter that I fear will be our downfall. Sure I have to take care of the baby, and I am proud that I can do it independently of American law, but the light and the dark still haunts me, I am so close to the brink of being ashamed, maybe because I liked it—this is an esoteric problem especially to bug me while Ray is in jail. The emptiness makes more sense to me than all of this nighttime flourish of tourist shop jade earrings and gaucho pants and beautiful puckered shirts, the emptiness below which stands for the roast goat I see in all the restaurant advertisements, the lost dog howl I never hear in town, no mongrel dog Mexico this, this is tourist-ville, and loneliness knowing even the Mexicans here are almost Americans. I eat, check Rachel, play music on the jukebox, and watch the other late-nighters.

The music is really too much for me to ignore; gaucho's gaiety accelerated to an amazing polka tempo getting faster and even more aboriginal in Texas even, poor Texas, as if it were occupied, cannot always maintain its square crew-cut, is swung out beyond its intention, way far out of its intention swings, but it is an underground sense that I have become used to picking up like the Indian continuation of life and music in Mexico—there is a doughnut place in Laredo, across from the post office but hidden by trees and a street that from the middle of the square (Laredo despite its intentions has a plaza also, which it mars by putting KEEP OFF signs up) dwindles off into intentional nothing, where truck drivers and Texan rummies scoff doughnuts and hear wild polkas sung by cowboys who have never seen a singing movie. So I linger there mornings on my dwindling American dimes, speak Spanish at every opportunity, implying the truth I am too paranoid to proclaim, knowing the weird fallout of Texas. Texas is the most vicious atmosphere I have ever suffered. We are into September already, two weeks in this place have lacerated and nearly killed us, we wait news about bail, wait news about a bail bondsman, and meanwhile try to do feeble damage to the enormous government of clerks and memos from Washington by pressuring the sheriff and his deputies who feature themselves total Texans and incorporate Mexican heritage they are anxious to deny and which I see as a mutual betrayal in them and love to bring to their attention.

I call them wetbacks and turncoats, which they don't understand too well, and they reply, "we are more American than you are," and I silently say, "yeah man, and you can have it, too, you are fully welcome to your keep-off-the-grass parks and courthouse lawns which furnish me with the corrupted surface to spit on, having become the face of your earth, return me to the other side which, though also corrupted, is mine."

One afternoon, B the cop informs me that he has someone in town for me to meet and that he will pick me up that evening to take me there and that I should be nice to this guy as he is a friend of B's from businesses long back. It hits me that B is very experienced like Humberto, the Mexican revolutionary, who has friends all over. So I fix myself up, anxious for something lucrative to come of this, and B and I drive in his truck way out of town beyond bus routes, not talking much, knowing that this is not the night for our own personal pitch, neither of us coming on, except he with his friend, dual reasons for wanting me to make it here. He raises the pitch mightily as we get to the motel with the swimming pool, calls in by house phone, opens the door to the individual suite, which we are immediately introduced to as the bridal apartment, that phony. This cat was wearing a horrible ugly Hawaiian shirt which contrasts with his Batista Florida come-on of riches. He invites us in for drinks which B accepts, but I am so disgusted I poke B in the ribs, which he ignores. I am twisted into sitting on a bed and drink the Scotch he has given me, which I do not like either, and invited to converse; dinner is offered to both of us, but B professes business and intimates to leave me behind till he returns, I do not talk, only briefly and bugged answering questions directly put to me. We sit there for an hour or so, B leaning on a bed pillow keeps the conversation going in phony family business talk, they make some kind of deal business-wise friendly, making a big thing of trusting each other.

Through all this, which seems to have no real meaning, comes some kind of indefinite pitch from the disgusting dark cat who no doubt is driving a Cadillac (which later proved to be true. I sometimes sense a whole scene, my instincts are good); it turns out he is out of money and wants B to get him a check cashed, which makes the whole scene fall apart anyway, so that I am visibly justified in not wanting any more to do with even the person's proximity and start acting jively insistent with B to the point of insulting his friend and we all split together. He wants us to go in his Cadillac, which I nix, and we drive back to town with him following, B and I not talking at all, except that I am completely out of money, and smiling he lets me off at my hotel and gives me a couple of dollars loan, left alone with his own problem of the cat who is no doubt trustworthy, though it is funny in this instance he has to prove it.

... Another mysterious pickup late that night of need—back to the hotel with shuttered doors, a sneak entrance with me reserving the room and the cat who has something to fear from the public follows me in and fucks. I remember he was a creepy, short, fifty-year-old man, fag-looking type who fucked like a satyr—furious and wanted badly for me to suck him off, paid well for me to do it in the shower and likewise mysteriously disappeared from the room before my exit from it. I saw him later in town, he wanted me to be his mistress, which offer I absorbed with enthusiasm, for his wallet bulges were more healthy than I have ever seen on a walking person, especially a mark which he obviously was, and after he left I smoked a cigarette on the bed at his instructions not to leave immediately. The light is out, I am half-clothed, a timid knock at the door, it is the little brown, grown-up chiclet seller of the street I saw out front near the desk as I entered. I start to put him down to protect myself thinking he wants a free peek, but he offers me fifty pesos to do it—"do it"—I figure, oh well, to save trouble, and his brown cock in me, his head reaches the breast level of my prone front and he loves my nipples as if I were his mother. I keep my eyes peeled for attempts at him stealing my stash of pesos, but he is sincere, and pays …

Sometimes with all the excitement I lose track of what I am doing—like the second night in one of the hotels I stayed in. I asked the desk clerk to wake me the next morning and he asks me to leave the key in case I don't hear him knock, and I, in fact, never heard him knock but woke to sensations of a husbanded bed and though I wake slowly I see the boy there already undressed ready to jump in sitting on my bed playing. Arg, I up and scream at him and he is out the door half clothed before I am fully awake, my first fear for the baby. Alone in the world and disgusted, berated by Ray, for this, I have to move out super fast that day to protect my confidence. I had only moved in a day before after a bad scene at the last hotel where I awoke at dawn with a great hole burning by my head on the bed. So someone had given me a lead on a Casa De Huespedes, a boarding house where I got bed and two meals a day for fifty pesos a week, but it was well away from the border again. I had become used to roving in the center of town near the immigration gates, but I hire a horse drawn cart and get straight and move immediately.

So I have learned to lower my eyes and hide what I know—learned to pick up on what people thought I said instead of persisting in my own vulnerable blunder, have learned to turn on the vacuum so that people can express whatever outgoing tendencies they have toward me, and it is a strain, for I learned soon enough where it leads—to an endless involvement which I am forced to believe as valid as any other contact with people.

Letter to Ray:

> *… 11:30—Just got in, been walking for three hours, made the rounds looking for a familiar face to touch for money, but nothing, have to wait for Monday. I walked by the jail quietly because I felt you were uneasy, and up pops an old codger with a flashlight shining in my eyes. I shield them with my writing book and say, "What do you want?" He pipes in a crotchety voice, "I'm the guard of the courthouse and I have charge of all the grounds around it!!!" I say, "Well, what's the matter?" "What's your name?" he asks. I answer lowly, leaving him in silence (he doesn't want to betray his bad hearing, already lacking the virility of a fat rump, which is the badge and dignity of a real cop, and also the foundation of law enforcement, foundation on which rests the pistol proud and hard making up for what lacks in that other limp and useless tool) and he says, "Well, you come on with me. I want them to identify you around front, see if you're the same one they're looking for," so I say O.K. and he walks off while I light a cigarette. He gets ten feet away and discovers I'm gone and does a double take and then tries to take the double take back and squeaks gruffly, "Come on you and don't give me any trouble or I'm gonna arrest you," so I say, "O.K., O.K., don't get excited," and catch almost up to him and then slow down again. He's trying to hurry me, keeps turning anxiously to see if I'm still there and I say, "On what charges you gonna arrest me?"—he says "Well, we're going to walk around here and see if this guy recognizes you. You got any children?" I say, "What's that to you, old man?" and he is offended and, not knowing the dialectics of the beat 'em first, book 'em later philosophy, he says, "Well, of course you don't have to answer my question, but I just asked that one straight from me and it's a good honest … " I interrupt him: "But you're not in a good honest business, old man, and I don't plan to*

answer any questions." He does a double take again, not hearing right, and says indignantly, "Well, I don't know what questions you'd want to ask me. I'm a sheriff's deputy, I got my card right here, and you'd better be careful or I'm gonna arrest you right here and you won't even have a chance." So I am silent and we walk, slowly gaining the front corner of the jail yard and his sense of accomplishment grows as he starts to turn the corner. I stop and say, "I think you'd better go down to the police station and get a cop and arrest me then." He squeaks furiously, "But I am a cop! I been a sheriff's deputy for twenty-seven years." I say, "Well, let me see your papers then." He whips out a thin plastic ID case with one other card in it and I take it as he says, "See my pistol here?" He pats it and it flops like a toy, being very small, above his drooping buttocks. "I got a badge, too, look, with my name on it and everything." I bend close to look at it. It is one-half inch in diameter. I inspect his card; there is a space for a picture. I say there's no picture here, and look at it closer. He shouts, "But you don't have to have a picture! You better come with me to be identified or they're gonna pick you up tomorrow with a warrant!" I hand him his card and cross the street, saying, "Well, I'll wait till tomorrow then." "They're gonna git you," he says, and I walk back across the river ...

I reach the second corner in North Laredo and take in an English conversation behind me, viewing the participants from the corner of my eye: a middle age, clean cut, suntanned Texas businessman, and a tall twenty-eight-year-old fellow who is probably his son, obviously a repressed homosexual, bulging waistline, amply rounded hips, crew-cut, who watches me walk while his father is talking and says, "Que bonito!" for my ears alone. I keep walking and the other guy keeps talking unheard and this cat (the one who is such great cop material) moves up behind and beside me thinking he's gonna score and speaking in English, thinking I have mistaken him for a Mexican, asking me something about the C.O.D. postal rate, thinking I am a Mexican. I turn slightly toward him and spit juicily on his feet and he jumps back and angrily says, "I'd like to see you do that again—I'll kick you into the street!" and his father shuts up in confusion, sensing a dangerous international situation. All the Mexicans are watching, and I turn casually still walking and spit again and he calls me a goddamn whore and falls back, at which point I turn again and say loud and clear: "I'm not a whore! You're a pimp and a stupid American, and if you want to pick up a silly bitch on the street you'd better go back to the other side where you belong!"

... And that was the last letter I wrote as our plans for suicide reached consummation. The next morning I go to the lawyer's sidestreet office; he has always permitted my most far out put-downs of personal property and even consented to most of them. He lives a leather-covered sofa life of shambled house and has a companion "friend," a young fellow with a Volkswagen and very motherly pipesmoking face. But I don't care any more about them, my interest is exhausted, I have summoned myself to his burning afternoon-sun step with the baby too many times to be able to make it any more, and have been more impressed by the Mexican family across the street who rescued us into their house from one rainstorm. But I go, slowly, to see him, my routine, my walk of thoughts in the air, besides we already have a solution, we are going to die and my heart's eye is thusly fixed. Beyond other considerations, I do not even worry about the next meal anymore.

And he is waiting to tell me that the bondsman has arrived and is going to get Ray out today; I should go see him at such and such a place.

Damp wind across the river and ominousness in the air. Baby Rachel is at M's. M runs a beauty parlor in the neighborhood near the red-light section of the town. It is too bad I do not remember the real

Mexican border name for this three square blocks of Orphic song, but I connect it with the name Lolo which rings in my head like a guitar string. B the cop took me there one night looking for him so we could hear him sing, a street singer, Lolo, of this three block square area of bright lights, advertising a happy night of visiting in this or that house, no discretion necessary in this open scene of welcome if you are an American with money or a Mexican hustler of some sort, but don't be anything in between, except as I was, with an official escort. Anyway, M's beauty parlor used to house the baby and also I took my wardrobe there for it to be washed and ironed, all for very little money, though I never got complete devotion like in Veracruz. No, Nuevo Laredo was a mixed scene and, as sensed all along, a precarious one for me and Rachel, but at least more sure than that in Laredo. That would have been beyond comprehension, we would have had to beg at the doors of the Salvation Army or Catholic Charities, which I considered a couple of times anyway, and tried the blood bank which never works, should be the other way around, I should have gone for a transfusion.

I am wearing the blue French hustler's beret given to me by Marge C in Hoboken, one of those tokens of friendship in my life, like the amethyst ring I gave Malcolm S soon after I received the hat, getting the giving feeling. I wore the hat all around Mexico, and didn't lose it until two years afterwards, consider that in relation to people, consider all that I have lost for less tangible reasons than that that hat had to exist on my head. Anyway, that day I wore it and some far-out Indian skirt; not a hustling costume at all, but just an expression of I don't give a fuck for we both are soon going to be dead anyway. So that is how I appeared to Tom, the bondsman from Forth Worth. I didn't have much to say to him, already filled with disgust with reports of him from the F's. He was Texas on the hoof appraised me immediately and told me to get my things together—that we were leaving for Ft. Worth in two hours. So I told him I didn't have any money, and he told me to meet him at his hotel in a couple of hours, just like that, shit, and I told him I need money to pick up my things in Nuevo Laredo so he gives me ten, and I make it to M for the baby double time, buying her a new pair of pink Mexican baby shoes on the way—a goodbye to Mexcity, Veracruz, and New Laredo. We dress in the casa de huespedes and go through customs which we had never even considered the whole time we were there, not ever having officially crossed. It is somehow illegal to live on the other side, especially if you are hustling. So I stop in with the baby to say goodbye to my friends at immigration, and I don't think they even checked us. No, for I had a bag of groceries or something, and certainly they knew us by then, only on the American side we checked in and I gave a special Mexican flourish—fuck you, Laredo border patrol of the streets and awful turnstile nickels and liquor tax, which I finally end up paying on an impulsive bottle of tequila.

At the hotel where I was supposed to make some scene with the bondsman I find Ray already out. I am numb, the height of the miracle does not extinguish the tragedy. Maybe this is the way Ray felt when he came out to Hoboken with me waiting for him pregnant and fucked in every direction; feeling that someone has made an enormous fool of you. This isn't the way it should be; I wonder what caused it: extreme exhaustion, despair, I have never ever felt such despair as in Laredo. Even as leveled as it may seem in writing, I cannot help but come back to the human trying to tell what it is like to come back to life again without wanting to …

And then there is the baby Rachel, and Ray's physical presence. The first thing he wants on the street is a piece of chocolate cake. I am extremely self-conscious with him and we talk of the business. We are in the presence of the bondsman, this is meant to be just an interlude of legal delay until Ray is sent back to New Jersey. There is also a sheriff sitting in the front seat, the baby and Ray and me in the back. I am ashamed; it had something to do with that ten dollars, it had something to do with the dinner we were invited to along the road and had to say, well, of course we didn't have any money and he, big-hearted hospitality, bought us all steaks and bragged about the quality of the restaurant we were going to and joked with Ray and me and I didn't answer him and Ray protected me, but I think it made him sick, too. Ray is in control I discover later, and I am just a useless wife who was so tired out that I did not dare to enjoy anything anymore, the very dress that I wear is a badge and I know that everyone knows what I have been through to keep things going.

And Dallas is two connected inclinations with a big hotel in the middle and dark street night of nowhere at all and I sigh relief as we pass through, too much this proximity of death. The baby Rach sleeps next to us on the seat and I am unable to take care of her anymore. Say this is the end.

Hotel in Ft. Worth, paid for by the bondsman of course, who seems to take every opportunity to walk behind me and bug me, as if I had fucked him. The conscience of the whole world is digging my ass. Nancy F says later that this hotel is a center for hustlers, call girls, dope addicts, etc. ... Another ripping cord to my neck muscles, how I am hoping to hold my head up in such a state? Tell the truth, unburden myself and hope that people will stop directing it all back to me, unconsciously? Will that help? I have no trust in any but my own methods to protect myself and they are silence and contempt so my eyes pierce Nancy F as she says this and I hold a permanent grudge probably.

Rachel slept on the floor and we arranged pornographic sessions of getting together again. Arranged? Pornographic? We have been married too many times under too many dubious circumstances, how does it do it to us?

Go back. We both immediately want to go back. My urge is to go back without delay and my first words to Ray when he is out of the Webb County Jail are that I would like to take him to Nuevo Laredo and show him what a real border town is like. I had done some research in the legal library to pass time and found that bail bond is good no matter where you go in the intervening time as long as you show up in court again on the specified date. But we have no money and we are both tired out, as I say, and besides, the bondsman wanted us nearby where we would be in sight of his risk. I am also conscious of our own risk having read that a bondsman can recall his bond anytime he thinks that the risk isn't worth it; since I can read this man's despicable character from his face and his name, I am sure that if an agent from New Jersey were to approach him with a deal he would betray us. I was afraid of another kidnap and maybe I talked Ray into it, or maybe we talked each other into it. I am glad to share the responsibilities again ...

Ask why we got such a disreputable bondsman? It is hard to get someone to take on trust a border case because of exactly the schemes we ponder. Everything is well above board and we are off to meet our patrons to see what above board means to them. And we find that they love art—and that is where Ray comes in, being surely poetry's representative in the flesh. And they loved him, and they loved me, too, but I am too desperately frantic a picture of what poetry can do to the soul to be accepted easily. I have always been shy, maybe that shyness has always been an armor for the great darkness within me, truly matching in fact Ray's Neptunian depths. God, I want to make it all human somehow. Too much dark and light clashing, let me have an even cultivation of the seeds.

I had thought that it was my devotion, that my sacrifice in Mexico had kept us alive, and now in Texas it became clearly dependence on poetry, and poetry has lofty words to describe a purity I had a long time been on vacation from. So where was I to turn for sympathy? Maybe I should distill my own poetry so that I can find a correspondence (and don't think this isn't an enormous drive, look at this book!). I am extremely curious about what has happened to me, even to the point of wanting to sample it all again.

A simple life in Fort Worth, a couple of times I lounged beside a leisurely swimming pool, and divined in myself a quality beyond this mixture of share and exuberance, sense the presence of a growing pride; and when they offer us money to leave, when they offer through Ray this possibility of the baby being taken care of by some rich people where she will be safe, and I will not have the immediate worry that my investigations will be tampering with anyone else's life but my own.

In Fort Worth we couldn't even find a suitable place to score, and my thought now is that if I could have had some vision of the lotus blossoms' vibrations, I could have maintained more unity with Rachel's countenance. For she was conceived and grown in issue of marijuana, and coming away from it is infinitely worse than going to it. And I am still truly an emotional junkie, at this moment, but will not allow myself to be taken through changes in directions unnatural to my wont again. But that is what happened in Fort Worth. It was an exaggerated spread of nothing. Undoubtedly somewhere outside the city limits the red dirt grew soul we needed to distraction. Have you ever been so desperate that your own desperation prevented you from taking care of what was driving you to desperation? That is what I told the doctor the one time that I went for medical advice about a cure, and he told me that I was harboring an illusion— imagine that? So, Fort Worth, you make me sick! And I no longer apologize, but turn myself on in retrospect and regain what was lost, and I will, I will, as sure I am building up to another climax here, and you know what that means. I will make it yet.

iréne lara silva

frontera me viste crecer

you saw me as i was
becoming what i was i want you to see me becoming what i will be
        this last time i was POETA
                        relearning all the
roads listening listening speaking speaking
                        quiero
aprender a cantarte, frontera, como eres y como fuiste y todo lo que
podrias ser—
                te canto te muerdo te aprieto te
pruebo me consumes me incitas me sacudas me quitas el sueno
        —yours is the only tierra i want to eat

        until this year DAUGHTER was the only thing i could call myself
here
                spined word that crashes against
FAMILIA and LOSS DESPAIR and BATTLE
                        you are
and are not what i left *todavia colonias todavia pobreza miseria* and
shame   orange groves uprooted
                                new roads
everywhere la migra and border checkpoints and the building of the
Wall
                blood wall wind wall earthen wall
there is still blood on the wind
                        but there is no sun like yours
anywhere else no boundless skies no rain no
thunder like yours there is no wind
                        no wind like yours
and the scent of ocean and palm trees and fruit stands
                                all my
languages braided and all the music i love the peal of accordions
everywhere
                long green limbs of sugarcane
along the roads and later the ashes of burnt sugarcane in the sky like
spiraling storms of miniscule crows
                        frontera, me
llamas me murmuras me acaricias me agaras de la mano

                                  i stood on your earth again

remembering and forgetting

                                  redefining PAIN
                                          redefining WOUND

redefining

                                          BELONGING

Hector Gomez

Tejanese Prayer

Let us let go of all political correctness,
not with finesse,
'tu sabes,'
but with 'sabor.'
'O sea,' let's rip off our clothes
for this cover itches like a 'colcha' on a hot summer day.
Let's make love with our words,
free flowing 'palabras,'
free flowing poetry.
Tejanese vagabonds in the house,
enthralled in the madness
for madness sake.
Love for love,
'maldicion por cada pinche maldicion.'
Laying naked is the first test of freedom,
my soul-peers,
so let us be readied to hear the world call out our names
'y se ponen de pie—'
'Madre,
Santa,
Dios de mi alma,'
before your thorned eyes bleed for me,
'Hossanna,
o sea,
mi Reyna,'
let me express with my words
and forgive the worst of me,
if only 'pa saber
lo bueno que puedo ser,
que al cabo,'
love begets love, 'que no?'
'Y rogando' goes only so far.
Amen.

Lady Mariposa

Valley Haikus

Las Milpas, TX
In barrios cholas
die lonely waiting for prince
cholo to save them

Under Mesquite
mecanicando
apa tried to teach HeyZeus
what his father knew

Laundry Matt
young girls place babies
on top of high washers as
they talk on cell phones

The Law
el chota es, Juan—
el panson que casi no
acabo high school

Corner
peros roñosos
buscando peras in heat
barrio crack head laughs

En La Walmart
chancla babies en
papers on Sunday mornings
on our way to church

Jardines
Abuelas water
gardens that no one will tend
after they are gone

The Bus Station
On Monday, ladies

drive to El Centro to pick
up the rented mom

Downtown 17th
La Yerberia

won't go, refuses to light
velas for its death

Edinburg Jukebox 1
Women don't love like
Barbra Streisand in the Rain
They love dry, alone

Edinburg Jukebox 2
Willie Nelson con
Sus old blue eyes, no longer
Makes me cry at bars

Edinburg Sports Bar 1
Rats rest in corners
of neon lit sports bars, while
the vatos shoot pool

Edinburg Sports Bar 2
JayLo in mesh net
looms longingly on the wood wall
perfect in silence

Edinburg Sports Bar 3
Gorditas in crews
stalk slowly to restrooms while
las flacas sit still

Pochito Papacito
Corazoncito
con labios que saben a
lenguas quebrando

Amerikana
In my borderland
Mother and Father held close
like America

La Llorona at HEB

La Llorona finally had time to read after she left the children to die in the bathtub. Left. She never believed she did it on purpose. She could not hear them fussing and fighting in the bathtub over her iPod that played "Bad Romance," on repeat.

They met at HEB a local grocery store and sampled quesidillas made with goat cheese and habanero which made Llorona's eyes water.

He called her Laura because he refused to call her by her name. "Laura, why did you drown your children? Do you have any remorse?"

She said, "No. I have decided to accept loss forever."

Ginsberg looked around in his hungry fatigue. This grocery store had a million pinatas, sweet bread of all colors. Candles of all saints and sizes.

He missed Walt more than ever. This woman was a weepy girl, crying over everything from the price of cigarettes to the out-of-season corn.

"So, what do you want to discuss?"

La Llorona straightened her infinity scarf. Women who recognized her did a doubletake and kissed their babies. They vowed no matter how much they loved Lady Gaga they would pay attention to their babies as they bathed.

"Well, I have been reading all your work, all I can borrow from our crappy library anyway. I don't like *Howl*. Everyone says it's your greatest poem of all time. *America*, now that's your best, hands down."

Ginsberg was too busy staring at the checkers. The sacker boys these days especially at this HEB were so out, they were never in.

"I am in agreement with you," he said brushing her off. As he pulled out his iPhone to take a picture of a boy he would try to take home and impress with his amazing collection of Time Magazine that dated way before this boy's mother was born.

Erika Garza-Johnson

On the Road in Texas
(after Cy Twombly)

Sit in the obligatory John Wayne room in
a Texas BBQ joint on 290.
Eat with cliché cowboys in unknown town.

Bass fish ventriloquist in Coldspring
venture then to a picturesque swamp
where Burroughs might've lived or did.
Crows caw by the City Hall, downtown.
Antiques in abundance
because there ain't nothing
but rich folk in these parts.

Rothko Chapel: pray.
Canvases with
black
black
black
green
black
blue
black
paint. Meditate on a Bloody
Mary at the River Cafe,
or wait for a table at Kim Son.

Cy Twombly.

Scribbles ain't nothing but poetry.
Ain't nothing but poetry.

On the way back
Vintage cars at the Continental Club
lost hippies dance Son,
once hippies with too much money buy
Huichol bracelets outside celestial
restaurants serving sour cream enchiladas,
bats fly to their under bridge homes,

bats at sunsets, bat sculptures at dusk
bats that screech, guano under bridges.

Aquarena Springs abandoned
on cold June days
Gruene hall, Americana and
custom boots.
Parents drink Lone Star,
children pitch horse shoes.
Eat Brisket sandwiches.

La Tuna for a Sol.
Salma Hayek on a dozen
life size paintings at the Blue Star.
Resin made petrified wood type benches to watch
cormorants and their young swim
in shallow emerald water in King William.
Old flour mills,
old Pecan Shelling Sheds,
old, old buildings.
Popocatepl and Ixtacihuatl
invite you to eat Ralphie's Special
Chicken tacos with cabbage
in transparent corn tortillas.

Mesquite trees,
brush shade where
illegals rest.
Cactus flowers adorned with
horned lizards on the brink of extinction
sacrificed to modern Gods
during droughts. Quails.
Bluebonnets used to bloom
in bunches. Indian Paintbrush.
Roadrunner roadkill, Bobcat carcasses,
rotting raccoons,
vultures roost on water towers.
Carnivorous bugs and snakes
at rest-stops killing rats that have
overrun twisted oaks and
toilets.

San Manuel chorizo,
Delia's Tamales, Guerra's Tacos,

empanada abundance,
pan de polvo paradise,
parrilladas, pico de gallo,
pan de campo.
Caracaras fly over Delta Lake
Carcasses caught in the branches
in polluted water.

Cy Twombly.

Poetry ain't nothing but scribbles.
Ain't nothing but scribbles.

Edward Viduarre

I Want a

i want a
heart,
-broken.

death
via suicide
via cancer
via drowning
via sadness.

love,
-blind,
with purpose
for no reason,
-estranged

i want all things

lose my mind,
job,
religion,
and self

get a new job
in a field
picking beer cans,
cotton,
even body parts

i will be a rabbi,
priest,
atheist, agnostic,
buy me a tambourine
for i want to be a monk

i want to believe
in God, Buddha,
Muhammad,
and my conscience

i want to be a troubadour,
bohemian, drunk,
a bull fighter,
mariachi for hire,
maybe a poet

i want to own cats,
and let them run my life,
raise kids,
and let them teach
me new things,
i want to go to jail,
and do time with
innocent people,
-broken
and see with new eyes

i want to write a poem
that will be read
100 years from tonight
a poem
that will have a new meaning
every time
it's read,
and be forgotten
for another 100 years

i want to live
and survive
through
heartaches,
death,
and poorly written
poems

and i want
you with me
to witness it all.

Oscar Peña

South Texas Blues Man

He glides through the door
Of the Taco Bell
Heels tapping spit-shined
Tangerine Stacys
His khakis and snap-buttoned
Shirt medium starched.
Name tooled across the belt cinched
'Round a twenty eight inch waist.

A bluesman, a poet, un blusero
Flaco orders supper—

Señorita, un taco e una soda por favor.

Then starts to sing—

    I miss my wife and Lone Star beer
    And making love on Saturday nights.
    Wish I could smoke just one more cigarette
    But I'm getting old
    And I got sugar in my blood.

    She died.
    Who died? My woman, pendejo
    A long time ago. The only one I can cheat on now
    is my doctor so I sneak a bowl of menudo
    Sunday mornings as I make my way to church
    Ain't nobody gonna know, but me and God
    And he's got me talking to myself.

Salsa in his pocket
Coca Cola in his hand
Supper wrapped in paper
Flaco glides out into the night.

Oscar Peña

Desert Fruit

He sits in the cupola of the caboose
on a northbound Missouri Pacific
freight train on the main line that runs
through the Wild Horse Desert
between Harlingen and Kingsville

Waiting on a southbound train
the brakeman looks out, past the horizon
of his straw hat
and sees a man broiling in the sun
trying to hide under scrub huisache

The brakeman saunters out to stretch a leg
and in a moment of forgetfulness
leaves his jug of water
beside a tangle of nopales.

No. 366 arrives in Kingsville.
Engines slowly pulling into the yard
a Border Patrol greets the train,
looking over and under railcars.

Asked if he's seen illegals
the brakeman answers—

Thought I noticed
someone waiting for the night train,
turned out it was just a javelina
rooting prickly pear,
gnashing for a drink.

Katherine Hoerth

"Adan y Eva" in the Rio Grande Garden of Eden

No matter the taste of the tongue—this story
doesn't change. The garden grew glorious

before the fall. Adan watches the pecan branches
reach up the tree's trunk from a crabgrass bed, aloe

awakened. He feels the wind curve the thick stems of Indian
blankets, and watches the pads of cow tongue cactus split

open at the bean pod flavor of mesquite. The faceless
Eva awaits, fading into the backdrop of paradise. She stoops

behind her Adan—his wild chest hair, his open
mouth grin. Eva kneels behind the swaying palm leaves,

shielding her eyes from his erect Adam's apple. It begs
Eva to cast away her veil of fronds, to show her face,

to take a bite. But until her bare toes mingle
among the blue sage brush—the crown-of-thorns

masking the pink spines of devil's head, she'll remain unnamed,
a hidden bloom in the prickly Rio Grande Garden of Eden.

Alan Oak

Gonna Starve!

Gonna starve!
Gonna walk the streets
A madman poet
Hearing angels and demons
And six-inch gnomes
Gonna starve!
Gonna smoke morning dew
And howl at the moon,
Kick little kids
Who get in my way,
Laugh at the people
Who pass-a me by
Why cry?
Gonna starve!
Gonna live in cafes
And sleep under trees,
Eat only trash,
Pee in the snow,
Crap on the street,
And fart in your face
Gonna starve, yeah,
Gonna starve!
Gonna walk in the hills,
Read all the time,
Sing on the corner
– Spare me a dime? –
Say what I think
Though it hardly makes "cents"
Gonna starve,
Uh huh,
Gonna starve!
Gonna BURN, baby, BURN
All of my money
Drive off my friends
Suck all my fat
Till I'm nothing
But skin
And bones

And wrinkles
And an old tattoo
That used to say
"Mother"
In Elvish
And die,
Fucking die
Gonna starve!
Old,
Used up,
Washed up,
Wasted,
Clutching
In this hand
Three perfect poems,
Callin' this, this shit,
A life well lived
Gonna starve!

Alan Oak

Needle

Lick
the Needle
Whir tornado-like

Mother's voice
Screeches

the Witch

Poke
the Needle through
a Hole in her
Head

Diana Dominguez

Howling Geisha
(for Beccie)

She was born on the day
Ginsberg howled
his pain and grief to the world.
The rhythm of the Beats
lulled her to sleep in a backroom
while her mother served
drinks at the Cedar Street Tavern.
She grew up hearing
her mother's boozy
confessions that Kerouac
fathered her, but abandoned
them both for the road.
At seventeen, she found an
envelope full of cash in her
mother's underwear drawer—
a messy scrawl across the front:
for the kid, in case she
really is mine—Jack.
Fed up with her mother's
bourbon and Benzedrine fog,
she bought a one-way ticket to Japan,
seduced by images of
haiku Zen masters under
flowering cherry trees
on every street corner.
She met a geisha one night
who saw ... something—
sad, fierce, yearning—
in her smoky topaz eyes,
told her she should
join the sisterhood.
At the geisha house—
the finest okiya in Tokyo—
the okaa-san took her in
as her newest geisha daughter.
She learned her craft well,
lived long, was much in demand.
They talk of her still in Tokyo;

the round-eyed geisha
who crafted her own Way of Tea:
performed a flawless chaji ceremony
as she howled
her pain and grief to the world.

Isaac Chavarría

contemplating

cultural icons
under a microscope

juan camaney
  [sexist or blue-collar]

switch

 edward james olmos
   [pioneer or mexicano stereotype]

switch

raúl salinas
  [cell mate or poet]

switch

selena
  [idol or adulteress]

switch

Alton
  [barrio-colonia or dumping ground]

switch

Reynosa
  [sister city or travel advisory]

switch

pocho
[identity o identidad]

switch

frontera

to border zone

switch

Chicano/a
to Hispanic

switch

hasta cuando
I'm topsy turvy
y ni se donde
estoy or which
cultura i speak

Irma Guadarrama

River Rain

The rio bravo takes you across to safety
  away from the clutches of jaws and jails;
The rio floats you across into the arms
  of the one that has loved you always;
The rio saves you from the monster
  that you dreamt about when you were five;
The rio pulls you under until
  your remains are deeply buried within;
The rio haunts you in the darkest of
  moments and shatters your dreams;
The rio drives you mad
  until your spirit dies with you;
The rio turns you into a liar
  and thief, a shell of what you used to be;
The rio baptizes you and leaves you
   naked when you think you know its eternal secrets;

Only the thick, mysterious fog can work its
  powerful magic, dragging, stirring
its ghostly spirits, and unveiling the corpses
  washed up on its shores;
The clouds, laden with sadness and anger,
  open, and let the rain burst into tears;

  Rain, rain, river rain.

Christopher Carmona

Keeping the Beat

I found the beat
underneath my feet
pounding like a boombox
with the bass turned all the way up.
It was the beat I had been looking for ...
I first found the beat in a bar
next to three kids
spouting poetry and prose
about those who speak the streets
and have learned the art of bleeding.
One took it on the road
weaving songs of the land made by men's hands.
The second took it to the microphone
and howled from the Brooklyn Bridge
to the Golden Gate
chanting his mantra about friends crashing and burning
and mother's gone mad.
The last one took it to the presses giving it a page
and letting the world hear its birth
while playing a horn full of rhyme
and dimestore junkies.
But the beat did not stop there.
It kept on like all beats do
and I found it on the Venice boardwalk
standing next to a madman with a cranial guitar screaming verses about golden sardines
into parked cars with windows rolled up
and empty passenger seats.
I found it in county lock up with a young pachuco peddling escapism for 3 dollars a hit.
I found it on an Austin street corner
where a red salmon spoke to me
about community and the essence of who I am.
I found the beat in the pocket of a dirty blonde boy
with tattered red shoes and gold disco pants
who wrapped his worries in bugler skins
and dreamed of thinking what had never been thought.
I found the beat bleeding next to revolutionary roses and spilled box wine.
I found the beat waiting with its duffel bag at a bus stop in a town no one will remember.
I found the beat buried in the broken spine of my poetry books thumping over and over again to a

tune as old as the dirt in the floorboards.
I found the beat
buried deep within my wordy heart
pounding in my voice
it was the beat I was looking for ...

                                                    it was the beat to keep.

Beat San Antonio

is a wide sprawling city, the 7th largest in the United States. The town is a bit schizophrenic, with its military bases at the center of its conservative side, and its large Mexican-American population voting mostly democratic. This makes for an interesting dialogue always going on and helps make San Antonio today perhaps Texas' most important literary city, having a respect for both tradition and the new. Many fine Texas writers live in San Antonio and are included here. The city has long had a love for the arts, and that love has made San Antonio a major US tourist center. One editor retains a fascination for the inner city where he lived as a small child, and later worked as an adult at Paperbacks Y Mas, operated by Ricardo Sanchez. When his 81-year old former Republican aunt came to visit in San Antonio from Illinois, the Henry Gonzales Convention Center impressed her because US Representative Gonzales had tried, unsuccessfully, to impeach the second George Bush. One of the town's parks was famous as the only place a person could tour a Japanese Tea Garden and then go for an elephant ride. Wings Press prospers as a long established literary press run by the energetic Bryce Milligan. The press publishes a wide variety of writers while maintaining a focus on Latino authors. No other Texas City supports an arts' organization as large and various as the Guadalupe Cultural Arts Center.

Walt Whitman

Leaves of Grass
Section 34 (1855)

I tell not the fall of Alamo ... not one escaped to tell the fall of Alamo,
The hundred and fifty are dumb yet at Alamo.

Hear now the tale of a jetblack sunrise,
Hear of the murder in cold blood of four hundred and twelve young men.

Retreating they had formed in a hollow square with their baggage for breastworks;
Nine hundred lives out of the surrounding enemy's nine times their number was the price
        they took in advance,
Their colonel was wounded and their ammunition gone;
They treated for an honorable capitulation, received writing and seal, gave up their arms,
        and marched back prisoners of war.

They were the glory of the race of rangers;
Matchless with horse, rifle, song, a supper or a courtship,
Large, turbulent, generous, handsome, proud, and affectionate,
Bearded, sunburnt, drest in the free costume of hunters,
Not a single one over thirty years of age.

The second Sunday morning they were brought out in squads, and massacred ... it was
        beautiful early summer;
The work commenced about five o'clock and was over by eight.

None obeyed the command to kneel,
Some made a mad and helpless rush ... some stood stark and straight,
A few fell at once, shot in the temple or heart ... the living and dead lay together,
The maimed and mangled dug in the dirt ... the newcomers saw them there;
Some half-killed attempted to crawl away,
These were despatched with bayonets, or battered with the blunts of muskets;
A youth not seventeen years old seized his assassin till two more came to release him,
The three were all torn, and covered with the boy's blood.

At eleven o'clock began the burning of the bodies;
And that is the tale of the murder of the four hundred and twelve young men,
And that was a jetblack sunrise.

Jack Kerouac

from *On The Road*

San Antonio

Suddenly we were in absolutely tropical heat at the bottom of a five-mile-long hill, and up ahead we saw the lights of old San Antonio. You had the feeling all this used to be Mexican territory indeed. Houses by the side of the road were different, gas stations beater, fewer lamps. Dean delightedly took the wheel to roll us into San Antonio. We entered town in a wilderness of Mexican rickety southern shacks without cellars and with old rocking chairs on the porch. We stopped at a mad gas station to get a grease job. Mexicans were standing around in the hot light of the overhead bulbs that were blackened by valley summerbugs, reaching down into a soft-drink box and pulling out beer bottles and throwing the money to the attendant. Whole families lingered around doing this. All around there were shacks and drooping trees and a wild cinnamon smell in the air. Frantic teenage Mexican girls came by with boys. "Hoo!" yelled Dean. "*Si! Manaña!*" Music was coming from all sides, and all kinds of music. Stan and I drank several bottles of beer and got high. We were already almost out of America and yet definitely in it and in the middle of where it's maddest. Hotrods blew by San Antonio, ah-haa!

"Now, men, listen to me—we might as well goof a coupla hours in San Antone and so we will go and find a hospital clinic for Stan's arm and you and I, Sal, will cut around and get these streets dug—look at those houses across the street, you can see right into the front room and all the purty daughters layin around with *True Love* magazines, whee! Come, let's go!"

We drove around aimlessly awhile and asked people for the nearest hospital clinic. It was near downtown, where things looked more sleek and American, several semi-skyscrapers and many neons and chain drugstores, yet with cars crashing through from the dark around town as if there were no traffic laws. We parked the car in the hospital driveway and I went with Stan to see an intern while Dean stayed in the car and changed. The hall of the hospital was full of poor Mexican women, some of them pregnant, some of them sick or bringing their little sick kiddies. It was sad. I thought of poor Terry and wondered what she was doing now. Stan had to wait an entire hour till an intern came along and looked at his swollen arm. There was a name for the infection he had, but none of us bothered to pronounce it. They gave him a shot of penicillin.

Meanwhile Dean and I went out to dig the streets of Mexican San Antonio. It was fragrant and soft— the softest air I'd ever known—and dark, and mysterious, and buzzing. Sudden figures of girls in white bandannas appeared in the humming dark. Dean crept along and said not a word. "Oh, this is too wonderful to do anything!" he whispered. "Let's just creep along and see everything. Look! Look! A crazy San Antonio pool shack." We went in. A dozen boys were shooting pool at three tables, all Mexicans. Dean and I bought Cokes and shoved nickels in the jukebox and played Wynonie Blues Harris and Lionel Hampton and Lucky Millinder and jumped. Meanwhile Dean warned me to watch.

"Dig, now, out of the corner of your eye and as we listen to Wynonie blow about his baby's pudding and as we also smell the soft air as you say—dig the kid, the crippled kid shooting pool at table one, the butt of the joint's jokes, y'see, he's been the butt all his life. The other fellows are merciless but they love him."

The crippled kid was some kind of malformed midget with a great big beautiful face, much too large, in which enormous brown eyes moistly gleamed. "Don't you see, Sal, a San Antonio Mex Tom

Snark, the same story the world over. See, they hit him on the ass with a cue? Ha-ha-ha! hear them laugh. You see, he wants to win the game, he's bet four bits. Watch! Watch!" We watched as the angelic young midget aimed for a bank shot. He missed. The other fellows roared. "Ah, man," said Dean, "and now watch." They had the little boy by the scruff of the neck and were mauling him around, playful. He squealed. He stalked out in the night but not without a backward bashful, sweet glance. "Ah, man, I'd love to know that gone little cat and what he thinks and what kind of girls he has—oh, man, I'm high on this air!" We wandered out and negotiated several dark, mysterious blocks. Innumerable houses hid behind verdant, almost jungle-like yards; we saw glimpses of girls in front rooms, girls on porches, girls in the bushes with boys. "I never knew this mad San Antonio! Think what Mexico'll be like! Lessgo! Lessgo!" We rushed back to the hospital. Stan was ready and said he felt much better. We put our arms around him and told him everything we'd done.

And now we were ready for the last hundred and fifty miles to the magic border. We leaped into the car and off. I was so exhausted by now I slept all the way through Dilley and Encinal to Laredo and didn't wake up till they were parking the car in front of a lunchroom at two o'clock in the morning. "Ahh," sighed Dean, "the end of Texas, the end of America, we don't know no more." It was tremendously hot: we were all sweating buckets. There was no night dew, not a breath of air, nothing except billions of moths smashing at bulbs everywhere and the low, rank smell of a hot river in the night nearby—the Rio Grande, that begins in cool Rocky Mountain dales and ends up fashioning "world-valleys to mingle its heats with the Mississippi muds in the great Gulf."

Laredo was a sinister town that morning. All kinds of cabdrivers and border rats wandered around, looking for opportunities. There weren't many; it was too late. It was the bottom and dregs of America where all the heavy villains sink, where disoriented people have to go to be near a specific elsewhere they can slip into unnoticed. Contraband brooded in the heavy syrup air. Cops were red-faced and sullen and sweaty, no swagger. Waitresses were dirty and disgusted. Just beyond, you could feel the enormous presence of whole great Mexico and almost smell the billion tortillas frying and smoking in the night. We had no idea what Mexico would really be like. We were at sea level again, and when we tried to eat a snack we could hardly swallow it. I wrapped it up in napkins for the trip anyway. We felt awful and sad. But everything changed when we crossed the mysterious bridge over the river and our wheels rolled on official Mexican soil, though it wasn't anything but carway for border inspection. Just across the street Mexico began. We looked with wonder. To our amazement, it looked exactly like Mexico. It was three in the morning, and fellows in straw hats and white pants were lounging by the dozen against battered pocky storefronts.

"Look—at—those—cats!" whispered Dean, "Oo," he breathed softly, "wait, wait." The Mexican officials came out, grinning, and asked please if we would take out our baggage. We did. We couldn't take our eyes from across the street. We were longing to rush right up there and get lost in those mysterious Spanish streets. It was only Nuevo Laredo but it looked like Holy Lhasa to us. "Man, those guys are up all night," whispered Dean. We hurried to get our papers straightened. We were warned not to drink tapwater now we were over the border. The Mexicans looked at our baggage in a desultory way. They weren't like officials at all. They were lazy and tender. Dean couldn't stop staring at them. He turned to me. "See how the *cops* are in this country. I can't believe it!" He rubbed his eyes. "I'm dreaming." Then it was time to change our money. We saw great stacks of pesos on a table and learned that eight of them made an American buck, or thereabouts. We changed most of our money and stuffed the big rolls in our pockets with delight.

Allen Ginsberg

Dear Jack

... I am reading about Jim Bowie, who was a great amurican out of the old west. He became a legend in his own lifetime, as a wild knife fighter: people would challenge him to a duel, and he'd set conditions like: stripped to the waist leather pants nailed down to a 3 foot log face to face fight it out with knives; or sword vs. knife barefoot in a dark room; or left hand tied together in a 10 foot chalk circle (the last against Bloody Sturdevant, crazy Natchez gambler feared up and down the Miss.) (The first against pirate Lafitte's lieutenant). He once got involved in a famous duel on a sandbar on the Mississippi, it culminated years of rivalry in land speculation and politics in Natchez, and the principals fired twice without hitting, so the duel was over (he was on the sidelines) all of a sudden one southern Judge shoots another bewhiskered Doctor, and the whole island goes up in blood, about 12 men in a free for all with sword handed canes, shotguns, pistols, knives. Bowie was took by surprise, wounded about six times, worst when this here major Wright sticks cane sword through his chest, and pulls pistol on him. According to story Bowie, all full of wounds in a fit of rage, kills Wright by pulling him down on him with one hand and sticking knife in guts. Wright's famous words on this occasion were "Damn You, Bowie, You have killed me!" He spent a lot of time in New Orleans, also was a big land speculator and slave trader, getting slaves from wild pirate encampment at Galvez-Island, site now Galveston, Jean Lafitte's. However apparently he was also crooked land speculator, fixing up phony titles and selling half of Arkansas to people all over south. He took off for the Texas west when things got hot, represented himself as a great American landholder, learned Spanish, became catholic and Mex. Citizen, married the Mex. Governor's daughter, kept leaving her to live with the Indians for half year at a time, rediscovered a fabulous Lost Bowie Mine, silver, somewhere around San Saba River, but never got to use it and it was lost again, knew Sam Houston and other scouts and rangers, led (on Santa Anna) fabulous fights, death tolls 60 to 1, with crazy Texan groups, etc. Wife dies, gets on year and a half drunk in San Antone, rescued (supposedly by Sam Houston who told him he was a yellow shit), got hung up in Texan Independence war, wound up helping plan and dying in the Alamo, sick of life, Cannastra suicidal. Rushed around like crazy fool in Alamo, getting ready for immolation, fell off walls, got pneumonia and broken hip, killed 3 Mexicans entering his room (with 2 pistols and knife, before being bayoneted) where he was sick in bed, according to one story. According to another was found cowering under a mattress. Alamo incidentally was a great affair, lot of men including Davy Crockett died there. The great immolation place of the early westerners. He had had his own bowie knife made for him, specially to kill people, and soon it was all over the west as chief weapon, until days of six-shooter. Knife was like King Arthur's sword, talisman. Also an intellectual, of a kind, besides change of language, he was friends with Audubon, who was at the time a crackpot French Bohemian in New Orleans. Also a daemonic gambler. Knife at hip like a magic cock, law unto self all over west. Like some preacher in Texas small-town shouldn't get quiet and bowie gets up and says, "Looks to me like youse guys needs preaching too. Shet up and listen or you gets me knife in your evil skulls. M'name's Jim Bowie." I know about all this because I read a historical novel about him for Newsweek and I'm jest practicin up on my review here. Also went to Librry and looked up more on him. If I had time, I'd like to find out about Bridger and Crockett etc. Incidentally he lived with nomadic Indians, and was on the road with them in 1000 mile circle from west Texas to Washita River (Colo?) and down to Texas Colo. river, near sea.

Am putting Neals possalcard with your other old mail, so send me back Joan's letter anyways, er bring it. When you hittin this neck of the woods agin podnah?

> O diddle diddle ipsy fiddle
> Huckleberry pie
> When I shoots mah six gun
> The knives begin to fly.

> An when the knives are flyin
> a cowboys gonna die,
> O diddle diddle ipsy fiddle
> Coconut mah eye.

So much for that. Reason we don't write is we're too familiar with plans and selves already alright. So what? I dimme dam dam don't give no shit wha the hell happen when ahm daid. Frantic bopalive I say, frantic bopalive. Mah haids hip. Mah hip's hooray / mah hoor's heer. Fug dem golden letters, bell dem sacred cows. Bull down the shade. Bubble bubble bubble bubble bub

Allen Ginsberg, Done by hiz hand.

Tomás Rivera

[Caló: "chale"-no, cool it; "nel"-no; "simon"-yes]

On the Road to Texas: Pete Fonseca

He'd only just gotten there and he already wanted to leave. He arrived one Sunday afternoon walking from the little town where we bought our food on Saturdays and where they didn't mind that we came in the afternoon all dirty from work. It was almost dark when we saw this shadow crossing the field. We'd been fooling around in the trees and when we saw him we were almost scared, but then we remembered there was more of us so we weren't so scared. He spoke to us when he got near. He wanted to know if there was any work. We told him that there was and there wasn't. There was, but there wasn't till the weeds grew. It'd been pretty dry and the weeds didn't grow and all the fields were real clean. The landowner was pretty happy about it since he didn't have to pay for weeding the onion fields. Our parents cursed the weather and prayed for rain so the weeds'd grow and we had to make like we cared too, but, really, we liked getting up late, wandering around among the trees and along the stream killing crows with our slingshots. That's why we said there was but there wasn't. There was work but not tomorrow.

"Aw, fuck it all."

We didn't mind him talking like that. I think we realized how good his words went with his body and clothes.

"There's no goddamned work no fuckin' place. Hey, can you give me something to eat? I'm fuckin' hungry. Tomorrow I'm going to Illinois. There's work there for sure ..."

He took off his baseball cap and we saw that his hair was combed good with a pretty neat wave. He wore those pointed shoes, a little dirty, but you could tell they were expensive ones. And his pants were almost pachuco pants. He kept saying chale and also nel and simon* and we finally decided that he was at least half pachuco. We went with him to our chicken coop. That's what we called it because it really was a turkey coop. The owner had bought ten turkey coops from a guy who sold turkeys and brought them to his farm. We lived in them, though they were pretty small for two families, but pretty sturdy. They didn't leak when it rained, but, even though we cleaned them out pretty good inside, they never really lost that stink of chicken shit.

His name was Pete Fonseca and Dad knew a friend of his pretty good. Dad said he was a big mouth since he was always talking about how he had fourteen gabardine shirts and that's why the folks called him *El Catorce Camisas*. They talked about Fourteen Shirts a while, and, when we went to eat beans with slices of Spam and hot flour-tortillas, Dad invited him to eat with us. He washed his face good and his hands too, and then he combed his hair real careful, asked us for Brilliantine and combed his hair again. He liked the supper a lot and we noticed that when Mom was there he didn't use pachuco words. After supper he talked a little more and then laid down on the grass, in the shade where the light from the house wouldn't hit him. A little while later he got up and went to the outhouse and then he laid down again and fell asleep. Before we went to sleep, I heard Mom say to Dad that she didn't trust that guy.

"Me neither. He's a real con man. Gotta be careful with him. I've heard about him. Catorce Camisas is a big mouth, but I think it's him who stabbed that wetback in Colorado and they kicked him out of there or he got away from the cops. I think it's him. He also likes to smoke marijuana. I think it's him. I'm not too sure ..."

Next morning it was raining and when we looked out the window we saw that Pete had gotten in our car. He was sitting up but it looked like he was sleeping because he wasn't moving at all. I guess the rain waked him up and that's how come he got in the car. Around nine it stopped raining so we went out and told him to come have breakfast. Mom made him some eggs and then he asked if there was any empty house or some place he could live. And when was work going to start? And how much did they pay? And how much could you get a day? And how many of us worked? Dad told him that we all worked, all five of us, and that sometimes we made almost seventy bucks a day if we worked about fourteen hours. After breakfast Dad and Pete went out and we heard him ask Dad if there were any broads on the farm. Dad answered laughing that there was only one and she was sort of a loser. La Chata, snub-nose. And they went on talking along the path that went around the huts and to the water pump.

They called her La Chata because when she was little she got sick with something like mange on her face and the nose bone had gotten infected. Then she got better but her nose stayed small. She was real pretty except for her nose and everyone spoke bad about her. They said that even when she was little she liked men a lot and everything about them. When she was fifteen she had her first kid. Everyone blamed one of her uncles but she never told who it was. Her Mom and Dad didn't even get angry. They were pretty nice. Still are. After that, she'd shack up with one guy and then another, and each one left her with at least one kid. She gave some away, her parents took care of others, but the two oldest stayed with her. They were big enough to work now. When Pete arrived, it was just two weeks after she'd lost again. Her last husband had left; he didn't even get mad at her or anything. Just left. La Chata lived in one of the biggest chicken coops with her two sons. That's why Dad told Pete there was only one and she was sort of a loser. We figured Pete was pretty interested in what Dad said, and it seemed pretty funny since La Chata must've been about thirty-five and Pete, well, he couldn't have been more than twenty-five.

Anyhow, it turned out he was interested in what Dad said, because later, when we were fooling around near the pump, he asked us about La Chata. Where did she live, how old was she, was she any good? We were just talking about that when La Chata came down to get water and we told him that was her. We said hello to her and she said hello to us, but we noticed that she kept on looking at Pete. Like the people say, she gave him the eye. And even more when he asked her her name.

"Chavela."

"Hey, that's my mother's name."

"No kidding."

"Honest, and my grandmother's too."

"You son-of-a-bitch."

"You don't know me yet."

La Chata left the pump, and when she was pretty far away, Pete sighed and said real loud:

"Hey, mamasita, mamasota linda!"

Just to make sure she heard, he told us afterwards. Because, according to him, broads like to be called that. From then on we noticed that every time La Chata was near Pete he would always call her *mi chavelona* real loud. He said it loud so she'd hear and I think La Chata liked it because, when work started, she always chose the rows nearest Pete and, if he got ahead of her, she'd try and catch up. And then when the boss brought us water, Pete always let her drink first. Or he helped her get on and off the truck. The first Saturday they paid us after Pete got there, he bought some fritos for La Chata's kids. That's how it began.

I liked it best when he sang her songs. Pete was going to stay and work, he'd say, until everything was over. He went to live with two other guys in an old trailer they had there. We used to go after supper to talk to them, and sometimes we'd sing. He'd go outside, turn towards La Chata's house and sing with all his might. In the fields, too, we'd just get close to her or she'd come along and Pete would let go with one of his songs. Sometimes he even sang in English: *sha bum sha bum* or *lemi go, lemi go lober,* and then in Spanish: *Ella quiso quedarse, cuando vio mi tristeza ... Cuando te hablen de amor y de ilusiones* ... Sometimes he'd even stop working and stand up in the row, if the boss wasn't there, and he'd sort of move his hands and his body. La Chata'd look out of the corner of her eye, like it bothered her, but she always went on taking the rows next to Pete, or meeting him, or catching up to him. About two weeks later they both started going to get water at the truck together, when the boss didn't bring it, and then they'd go behind the truck a while and then La Chata would come out fixing her blouse.

Pete would tell us everything afterwards. One day he told us that, if we wanted to see something, we should hide behind the trailer that night and he'd try and get her to go in the trailer.

"You know what for ... to give her candy ..."

Us and the guys who lived with him hid behind the trailer that night and then after a long time we saw La Chata coming towards the trailer. Pete was waiting for her and she'd just got there and he took her hand and pulled her towards him. He put his hand up under her skirt and started kissing her. La Chata didn't say anything. Then he leaned her up against the trailer, but she got away and told him you son-of-a-bitch, not so fast. Pete was inviting her to come into the trailer but she didn't want to and so they stayed outside. Do you love me, will you marry me, yes I will, when, right now, what about the other cat. Finally she left. We came out of the dark and he told us all about it. Then he started telling us all about other broads he'd made. Even white ones. He'd brought one from Chicago and set up his business in Austin. There, according to him, the Johns would line up at five bucks a throw. But he said that the broad he'd really loved was the first one he married, the right way, in the Church. But she'd died with the first kid.

"I sure cried for that woman, and since then nothing. This fuckin' life now with this chavelona, I'm beginning to feel something for her—she's a good person, if you know what I mean."

And sometimes he'd start thinking. Then he'd say real sincere like: "Ay, mi chavelona ... man, she's a hot one ... but she won't let me ... until I marry her, she says."

Three days after we'd hid, Pete decided to get married. That's why all that week that's all he talked about. He had nothing to lose. Why, him and La Chata and the two boys could save a lot. He'd also have someone to cook his gorditas for him and his nice hot coffee, and someone to wash his clothes, and according to Pete, she could handle at least one John a night. He'd start calculating: at four dollars a throw, at least, times seven nights, that was twenty-eight dollars a week. Even if he couldn't work, things'd be pretty good. He also said he liked La Chata's boys. They could buy a jalopy and then Sundays they could take rides, go to a show, go fishing or to the dump and collect copper wire to sell. In fact, he said, him marrying La Chavelona was good for all of them. And the sooner the better.

A little while later he came to talk to Dad one night. They went out on the road where no one could hear them and they talked a pretty long time. That night we heard what Dad and Mom were saying in the dark:

"Get this: he wants to marry La Chata! He wants to elope with her, but what in? So it's better to get married for real. But— get this—he's got some sickness in his blood so he doesn't want to go into town to get the papers. So what he wants is for me to go and ask La Chata's father, Don Chon, for her hand. He wants me to go right away, tomorrow ... 'Don Chon, I've come today commissioned to ask for the hand of your daughter, Isabel, in matrimony with young Pedro Fonseca.' How's that eh? ... How's it sound, honey?"

"Tomorrow after work, right before supper ..."

Next day all you heard about was how they were going to ask for La Chata's hand. That day Pete and Chavela didn't even talk to each other. Pete went around all day real quiet and sort of glum, like he wanted to show us how serious he was. He didn't even tell us any jokes like he always did. And La Chata also looked real serious. She didn't laugh any all day and every now and then she'd yell at her kids to work faster. Finally the work day finished and before supper Dad washed up, parted his hair four or five times, and went straight to Don Chon's house. Pete met him in the front yard and they both knocked at the door. They went in. It was okay—they'd asked them to come in. About half an hour later they all came out of the house laughing. They'd agreed. Pete was hugging La Chata real tight. Pretty soon they went into Chavela's house and when it got dark they closed the doors and pulled down the shade on the windows, too. That night Dad told us about ten times what had happened when he went to ask for her hand.

"Man, I just spoke real diplomatic and he couldn't say no ..."

Next day it rained. It was Saturday and that was when we really celebrated the wedding. Almost everyone got drunk. There was a little dancing. Some guys got into fights but pretty soon everything calmed down.

They were real happy. There started to be more and more work. Pete, La Chata and the boys always had work. They bought a car. Sundays they'd go driving a lot. They went to Mason City to visit some of La Chata's relatives. She was sort of strutting around real proud. The boys were cleaner now than ever. Pete bought a lot of clothes and was also pretty clean. They worked together, they helped each other, they took real good care of each other, they even sang together in the fields. We all really liked to see them because sometimes they'd even kiss in the fields. They'd go up and down the rows holding hands ... Here come the young lovers. Saturday they'd go shopping and go into some little bar and have a couple after buying the groceries. They'd come back to the farm and sometimes even go to a show at night. They really had it good.

"Who would of said that that son-of-a-gun would marry La Chata and do her so right? It looks like he really loves her a lot. Always calling her mi chavelona. And can you beat how much he loves those kids? I tell you he's got a good heart. But who was to say that he did? Boy, he looks like a real pachuco. He really loves her, and he doesn't act at all high and mighty. And she sure takes better care of him than the other guy she had before, don't you think? And the kids, all he does is play with them. They like him a lot too. And you gotta say this about him, he's a real hard worker. And La Chata, too, she works just as hard. Boy, they're gonna pick up a pretty penny, no? ... La Chata finally has it pretty good ... Man, I don't know why you're so mistrusting, honey ..."

Six weeks after the wedding the potato picking ended. There were only a couple of days more work. We figured by Tuesday everything would be over and so we fixed up the car that weekend since our heads were already in Texas. Monday I remember we got up early and Dad, like always, beat us to the outhouse. But I don't even think he got there because he came right back with the news that Pete had left the farm.

"But what do you mean, Dad?"

"Yeah, he left. He took the car and all the money they'd saved between him and La Chata and the boys. He left her without a cent. He took everything they'd made ... What did I tell you? ... He left ... What did I tell you?"

La Chata didn't go to work that day. In the fields that's all people talked about. They told the boss about it but he just shook his head, they said. La Chata's folks were good and mad, but I guess we weren't too much. I guess because nothing had happened to us.

Next day work ended. We didn't see La Chata again that year. We came to Texas and a couple of months later, during Christmas, Dad talked to Don Chon who'd just come down from Iowa. Dad asked him about Pete and he said he didn't know, that he heard he'd been cut up in a bar in Minnesota and was going around saying the cops had taken all his money and the car, and that the boss had told the cops after all, and they'd caught him in Albert Lea. Anyhow, no one had given any money to Don Chon or La Chata. All we remembered was how he'd only just gotten there and he already wanted to leave. Anyhow, Pete made his little pile. That all happened around '48. I think La Chata is dead now, but her kids must be grown men. I remember that Pete appeared out of nowhere, like the devil himself—bad, then he turned good, then went bad again. I guess that's why we thought he was a shadow when we first saw him.

Kamala Platt

Viaje into the Vortex
(the Geography of Sutraing/ Suturing Out the Spiral)
Epistolary Poem to Allen Ginsberg

You travelled the highway about Meadowlark in '66
and wrote conservative Kansas back into a poetry against wars.
Now, that landscape is twice burned, once by drought
that would bind us to refugees of the earth's rising fever,
were we to ever leave our AC-befuddled rooms.

Your bus-trips probably passed by Leavenworth
where Raúl would be writing reading, listening to languages
that lurk in the crevasses ...
where wise ones masticate their palabras
before being Frankensteined, and walled off
by the mean spirits metastasizing the good earth, herself.

You travelled across Kansas
to proclaim Sutras against the wars ...
that began before my birth.

Before the fires the fires began this summer
I traveled back up from the junction
of the Rio Grande & the Chisholm Trail
following hoof-prints petrified into asphalt
from where now a wall shuts us from the Mexico
the Beats loved. where they loved. where they immigrated to work
returning to the Magic Valley with palabras
that proclaim Sutras against those reoccurring wars
we now worship with our day's work.

ps I heard at the Peabody Farmer's Market that Florence
has no more pure spring water in its tower.

Juan Perez

The Cat from the Other Side of the Tracks

Do you know that cat
That cat from the other side of the tracks
Where the vatos are all down
In all kinds of shades of brown
Where poverty is spread a good mile wide
Like smooth tortillas all around

So you know that cat
Can't put it any clearer than that
Handcuffed and taken downtown
Chicano the verb, not the noun
Because colors speak louder than words
Where lineups make minorities frown

Hell everyone knows that cat
That cat from the west side of the track
Where the madrecitas are all trying to make you fat
With menudo and tamales and that
That cat works every low-paying job around town
Can't really miss him unless you're wacked

That semi-illusive cat
That cat from the other side of the track
Where speaking Mexican is a real fact
And the good life is all that's that
And the sun sun-shines, yes it shines
On all those cats from the other side of the tracks

Juan Perez

El Primo

Para Mi Primo, Jose Arvizo (September 9, 1951-March 24, 2011)

Se murio el primo
Un vato loco
But he was alright

Saw him the other day
Headed down South Estes Street
On his grey and silver motorcycle
With an old stereo strapped to the handle bars
Listening to some lost rancherita
If you can call that crazy

Yeah, se murio el primo

He's cheated death a million times
And la muerte finally got the upper hand
Because of his bad heart
Even though I didn't see anything wrong
With a heart in the right place
But he'd be the first to tell you that
When it's your time to go
It's your time to go, vato

Simon, se murio el primo

Saw him a few years back
Headed down South Luna Street
Where my parents used to live
When my dad was alive
And my mom was still okay in the head
They used to start stories with
Te recuerdas de esto or te recuerdas del otro
Simon, I remember

Si, se murio el primo

Saw him a few months ago

Pumping gas at Roberts
As he yelled out "Hey, White Girl!"
To my wife like he always did
Disregarding all the prejudice that would stop the world from spinning
All the racial tension of those that didn't understand
That these words were some deep terms of endearment
Of relationship, of belonging to this place
Making my girl know what it was like
To belong to my Mexican family

Yeah, se murio el primo

But I'm not gonna worry man
Because I am gonna see him again
Even though his heart broke down
He never gave up on being himself
And that was a good thing
Because mi primo had un corazon grande
And God smiles on that

Simon, se murio el primo
Un vato poco loco
But he is gonna be alright

Manuel Luis Martinez

Tougher Than Us

"I've come to the conclusion that I serve mankind more beneficently as an installer of satellite dishes than as a mediocre, generally unheard of, barely-practicing poet." I say this to Tull with *corazon*, hoping that my friend will disagree.

"Poetry? What have you written lately?" he asks looking through a box of cassettes I haven't listened to since the last time he came through town. Lots of Rush and Boston from our long gone stoner college days. Tull isn't about to grant any undue comfort. He is sitting next to me, the thinning red hair atop his head in a ludicrous Viking puff, an exclamation point to his oft-vitriolic commentary. What should I expect? He is not literary. He likes television. He hungers for instantaneous information despite his Luddite protestations to the contrary.

And yet, I have no answer for his no-nonsense question. Truth is, I have written nothing for months since my mother called with the news that my father, The Evangelist, was dead.

"My fate hangs in the balance," I say. It's supposed to be a joke.

He doesn't answer. He's preoccupied with a map now. He's unfolded it roughly, tearing it along a crease, ripping the heartland in two. Tull does everything with a maddening lack of restraint, going through life as if he's being paid by the package to open Christmas presents for someone else's children. Rip, rip, rip.

We are driving southeast with the express purpose of climbing the Smoky Mountains. Tull believes the trip will bring him a measure of peace. His marriage to Karen has failed and he is at loose ends once again. I want the trip to bring something else, an answer, at least a clue. Hell, I'd call it inspiration if it wasn't such a tired cliché. It's happened before, a trip to someplace unconventional and unhip, even unpleasant. Places like Presque Isle, Maine, or Bustamante, Mexico. The last thing I wrote was on a short trip. I drove south by myself, heading for the border, but I stopped well short:

I would like to steal you away from yourself,
    escape to Mexico
      Then have you come looking for us.
         I
              Bet
                  You
                      Would
                          Stay.

Not much? But it was. Yes, another poem for my ex Zoe that I never sent, but that nonetheless gave me some comfort, as if I was doing *something* instead of just feeling low and insecure, spending a lot of time doing sit-ups and worrying that everything I've done so far, including the poetry, boils down to distraction.

Tull has come to escape soulless Toronto before it devours his will to live. The Smokys and Nashville are supposed to do the trick. He's hoping that peace lies just around the corner in some rustic setting. He imagines something unspoiled, untouched. Virgin land for the Viking with the preposterous red beard grown for our road trip.

There has not been much to do this winter in Indiana except think about The Evangelist and the death of my desire to write. It's been brutally cold and dreary. Tull keeps talking about just wanting a few days where nothing happens. Not me. I want something to happen, anything, something that will spark a poetic response, a thought, a trigger. A signal flare from the depths of my Midwestern hibernation.

Tull has brought a duffle bag and a Coleman lantern. "We are sleeping in a hotel," I tell him. But he counters that we're going into the mountains. "I need nature," he says. "I just know that at the top of the mountain I'll suddenly understand how to once and for all gouge out the eye of the shitstorm."

He can say what he likes, but I'm not going to sleep outside. My people spent hundreds of years doing that involuntarily. Mexicans migrants on the picking trail, sleeping on the cold, hard ground. "We don't do that anymore," I say, the indignant voice of my people.

"At least I'm out of Gog and Magog," he says. "Toronto is Babylon with shittier weather. It's God's horror movie. Everywhere you look, drug addicts, criminals, whores, homeless, the sick, and those are the decent people. Jesus, it's gotten to the point where I can't breathe anymore." He takes a long, violent pull on his baby blue asthma medication dispenser. "There's no fucking human beings anymore," he continues. "I can't stand the shits I work with. They all think life's a fucking bowl of cherries and they're the only ones with spoons. I gave this girl a nice gift. A hammock from Peru. She never called back," he says now taking a purely gratuitous pull on the dispenser. He inhales like he's hitting a joint, breathing deeply as if the fumes not only relieve his clogged lungs, but also his tortured mind. He holds his breath and exhales towards the cracked-open window of the pick-up releasing the leftover pollution from the big city, the gaseous vestiges of his private Gomorrah.

"The weather's going to get better, and I could've hung it up outside," he says. "Besides, she didn't really appreciate it. People don't appreciate things like hammocks anymore. It isn't high tech enough. That," he says with emphasis, "is exactly what's wrong with Toronto."

Heading south on I-65 thru southern Indiana, we approach Louisville, the first town in Kentucky. Crossing the Ohio River, the city is not as impressive as the expanse of the water below us. Tull cranes his neck, nodding in approval.

"I can feel the chain being broken," he says deeply satisfied. "I love rivers. Water makes a place better. Carries away all the bullshit. Not like a lake where everything collects until the stink stifles everything. A river cleans a place right up," he says taking a deep breath even though the windows of the truck are rolled up tight.

We reject the city silently and it disappears as suddenly as it came up, the tops of red brick buildings and Kentucky Derby billboards dropping behind the confused spaghetti of highways pressed against the gray sky. We turn towards Lexington.

"I feel much more relaxed here," he claims. "In the U.S. people are tougher. Better constitutions. Not like in Canada. Example: we had a blizzard and fuckers protested. They picketed the mayor because he didn't clear the streets fast enough." He pronounces his most withering judgment on his fellow Torontoans: "Wimps. Can you imagine something like that happening in Texas?" Tull idealizes the Lone Star state where we went to college.

"That's what I tell them at work—'tough it out like they do in Texas.' Everyone's worried because our company is going to merge with some big conglomerate. 'Don't worry,' I say, 'We're going to get it in the arse. No doubt,' I say, 'No doubt. They'll let us swing for as long as they can, and then, boom, here comes the big chorizo, so pick a hole and open wide.'"

We climb higher and higher, big trees, pecan and oak, flying by as we listen to bluegrass, seeing a circle of Eurofarmers square dance in our mind's eye. I am beginning to get a feel for hillbilly culture. I almost appreciate it. "Imagine coming up here straight out of a crowded tenement in NY or Warsaw or some shanty in the middle of a barren potato field in Ireland, and thinking you've escaped only to find yourself on this cold hard mountain? Nice land, but what to eat? And when the winter hit, if you got so much as a sniffle, that just might be your ass," I say. Tull looks out the window snorting every once in a while in agreement.

"Say son, better stack gramma out with the wood. We'll giv 'er a proper burial when the thaw comes," I say imitating a pioneer. "How many times do you think those words were spoken around here? Say what you will, but they had to be tough."

"But you want to know something, Rafa," Tull says. "Not tougher than us."

We pull over to get coffee. A large mall in Lexington. It is grotesque, with linen stores the size of aircraft carriers and bookstores that hold more than the Library of Congress. We wade through dozens of people waiting for lattes as if we were at some yuppie coffee bar in San Francisco instead of a redneck outback. "Canadians don't like the U.S.; everyone hates you guys," Tull says beginning to get impatient. He's going to take out the long wait on my country.

"This is the motherland, the core of American identity," Tull says. "It's all here: the country with its halfwits and hillbillies, bluegrass and incest, and lots of half-baked patriotism. But they all love Jesus," he says. "Listen, these dummies got no chance of recognizing the Antichrist unless he shows up in a neon suit plugging the Blessed Whore of Babylon in the ass."

While I drink my coffee, I walk around the bookstore. All these road trip books, Kerouac, Twain, Hemingway, Acosta, Kesey, Rivera, Hunter Thompson, all of them crisscrossing the continent, in deserts, on the ocean, over mountains, in the cities, in bars, jails, whorehouses, churches, and none of them ever finding anything much. Well, anything approaching the *It* Kerouac longed for. But I guess that's the point. The artist knows he can't really ever find what he desires, because what he desires most of all is the search itself. The elusiveness of the It is what fuels the search, keeps him trying to invent the vocabulary to describe it. But to find It, to define It, and thus to possess It, would ultimately be tragic. Better to live in its absence, and thus keep desire alive. Keep the muse close, tantalizingly close, but at day's end, impossible to get hold of because that would be The End.

And yet, I thought that somewhere along the line, I'd get an *answer*, goddamnit. I wanted to crawl into the ass of the origin, come out with a hunk of wisdom. But now, I have to confront that poetry hasn't gotten me a fucking thing. Answers, love, refuge? No, and hell no.

I don't want to write about inaction and paralysis anymore. I want to *act* and *then* write about it. The Evangelist, the only person I've ever known who even did anything close to that, is dead now, and his *magnum opus* finally added up to a cryptic warning not to believe anything except that nothing is true.

Back on the road, we spot a motel called the Irish Inn. It's a dump, but it's late and Tull likes the name. The lobby is smelly and dank, a depressing pissy couch the only furniture besides a vending machine selling candy bars only a sugar-fiend would recognize. And then it hits me. This is exactly the kind of place that The Evangelist croaked in, unheralded, unloved, alone.

"Thanks," Tull says taking the key. The clerk says checkout's at 11:00, and we walk out. We climb up three flights and find our room. Tull turns the key and gives the door a shove. The light and television are on. There is a six-pack of longneck beer sitting on the nightstand next to a bed that looks freshly mussed. ESPN blares out hockey scores and generic highlights. We stand there nonplussed but not as nonplussed as the naked guy who walks out of the bathroom brandishing a hard-on. He is hairy with a gut sticking out farther than his rod. "What the fuck," he asks, too surprised to bother hiding his cock. "Get the fuck outta here!" His pecker bobs angrily and Tull and I take a step back. "They gave us the wrong key," Tull says.

"Who the fuck gave you the wrong key!" he roars moving towards us. "You here to suck my dick?" We back out fast and head for the stairs. "What kind of place is this," I say rumbling down the steps. "Let's find a place down the road closer to Knoxville."

"No," Tull says. "Knoxville's even more of a freak show than this place. But we better get a deal now."

He marches into the lobby and heads for the night desk. "Hey man," he says to the clerk. "You gave us the wrong key. We walked in on some guy beating his meat."

Without saying a word, the clerk reaches down and pulls out another key. "This room'll be better."

"Hey, man. I think maybe we should just take our business elsewhere," Tull says leaving the key where it is. "The guy's boner was pointed at me. Give me my money back."

"I can't do that," the clerk says sitting up a little straighter. "This room I'm giving you is better for the same price."

"Throw in some of those snacks," I say pointing at the vending machine. We both choose O'Henrys, the only remotely familiar candy bar selection. "This place is fucked up," Tull says ripping into the candy as he plunges past the night desk, shoulders squared, a mad Ahab in search of an unharshable high. "Jesus, I came here for some peace and things are fucking up already."

The next day, we roll into Nashville and sleep all day. We hit the town that night. We find the Siren Club where the blues music sounds pretty decent. We pay our cover and order a couple of beers. The band is good.

Next to us, a young woman, a dirty blonde, eyes painted satanically dark, chain-smoking is listening to her friend, a heavy brunette with a tight green dress that pulls her belly into two doughy loaves. "Every time Jimmy leaves you, you go off the deep end, Tif. And you say every time that you're not going to take him back, that you're not going to go to bed with the first man you see, and you do it anyway," she says.

"Fuck him," Tif says. "I don't care," and she takes a bewitching pull on her cigarette.

The blonde notices Tull and smiles. Tull smiles back. Before I know it, we're sitting at the table with Tif and Whitney. Drunk as I am, I cannot make Whitney attractive. I squint. I look at her from different angles. None of it works.

"Wanna know your future?" she says to me. "Give me your hand."

She takes it, palm up, using her other hand to stroke the lines that face her. She peers, reading what there is to read.

"Can't see anything?" I ask.

"You might not like it," she says.

"That's okay."

"When you stretch your pinky in this direction, well, that says you'll only have one true love your whole life," she says looking closely.

"And this line, it fades out and that means the lady of fortune hasn't decided what to do with you yet, although I can tell this line here means you better watch yourself around water." She fingers the crease in my hand.

"Why water?"

"Your life line ends here. Death by drowning."

I get up and lumber towards the john. The bathroom floor is tiny red and black tiles that make me even dizzier. I try and concentrate on feeling still.

I stare at the mirror, into my eyes in order to regain my equilibrium. I look old, I notice, old like I remember thinking The Evangelist was old when I was a kid. I see him in the mirror as he swims inside me somewhere, peeking out from the depths of my eyes like he's just waiting for me to become him despite my lifetime of resisting that, of resisting his laugh when it comes out of my mouth, his jabber-walk when I am in a hurry, his meanness when I strike out at the women who have tried to love me. I am a thirty-two year old boy on a fruitless trip, the Evangelist's age when he left my mom, when he had already fathered two children. I am childless, aimless, unsure of myself. "Bet your ass, fear water," I say to The Evangelist as he looks back at me from the glassy surface of a suckass pool. I lean my forehead against its mirrored twin, as if praying to him, to our grave and graven image.

Just then, my Viking friend enters the bathroom. "What are you doing," he wants to know. "Jesus, you are really hammered," he says stepping up to the urinal. "Should've stuck to beer. Mexicans shouldn't drink gin. Can you handle yourself a while? I think Tif is ripe."

The girls help me to my truck. Whitney gets in behind the wheel. Tull goes off with Tif and the two of them get into a white Escort. They follow behind, then flash their lights to catch our attention as they turn into a liquor store.

"Not feeling too good, huh?" Whitney says. She's being nice to me. I am leaning my balloon head against the window. I feel like moaning but resist. We get to the hotel and I manage to get to the elevator before I throw up into a fake plant suspended from a blue wicker hanger. "Good one," Whitney says. She is much nicer than I gave her credit for.

"You got us here," I congratulate her.

"Yup," she says, "got us here." She leads me to my bed where I dump myself, fully clothed. Tull and Tif arrive. They are in a high mood. They have a bottle of Tequila. They have ice and a lime. They are going to do shots. Tull grabs the plastic cups from the sink. He is sure now that he is going to get laid.

Whitney watches them from the other side of my bed. They don't invite her to come over.

"Wanna lie down?" I ask her. "No funny business. Just lie down?" I feel bad for Whitney and her heavy frame and her heavy life. She gets in with me and before I can stop myself I say, "I'm sorry that I said you were fat."

"You never said I was fat, asshole."

"Oh," I say trying to recover. "I meant sorry I thought you were fat."

"Fuck you," she says getting up. "Let's get out of here," she says to Tif and before Tull can even launch into protest, the girls are walking out the door with the bottle of Tequila—

In the morning, we smoke a joint to paper over our hangovers. It does the trick and I'm even willing to have breakfast. We eat waffles at the Waffle House before starting back to Indiana. "On the map it says we're going to go right past Lincoln's birthplace," I say. "We should check it out, see where old Honest Abe was born."

"Sounds good to me," Tull says and we drive until we find the exit. "There's the sign," Tull points. I turn off the highway pulling onto the small farm road that leads to the birthplace. "Think it's a log cabin?" I say.

"Hell yes. We'll take a picture in front of it." He holds up his disposable camera.

Tull starts in with the old stories about his father, the tortured Irishman, the poor drunk who loved his family and his drink in reverse order. "It got to where every night I'd have to go fetch the old man," he says. "Imagine that, having to walk into the tavern and drag your dead drunk da' home. God he was stubborn," he says playing his father's greatest hits as we drive south. "He put up awful fights. Once I found him asleep on the railroad tracks. I had to pull him off before he got cut in half, and the whole time him cursing, telling me 'piss off, runt,' while he kicked at me with his puked-on hobnails," Tull muses. "Jesus, it gets old trying to save someone who wants to goddamn die." He sighs. "All there is to do is to try to pull it together. My pops couldn't do it. Yours couldn't either. Makes you realize you're the next one in line to fuck it all up," he says.

I keep my eyes on the road looking out for the log cabin. It's a distraction, this looking for the origin of something grand, something failed.

We ride on for a long while until Tull breaks the silence. "Listen, Rafa, I was thinking, we're close enough. I get the general idea of where this fucker was born. No need to get too sentimental about it. Lets turn this thing around before it gets dark. I've had enough of this good ol' country time lemonade shit."

"I got an idea," I say stopping on the side of the road. A few hundred yards away, I've spotted an old dilapidated red barn. It is faded and peeling, ghostly quiet, and I half expect to hear the whinnies of phantom horses. We walk up to its opening and as we get there, it begins to rain lightly, its smell making gentle fingertaps that catch me by surprise. In only a few seconds the scenery has become an iridescent green, as if the landscape has come to life. It is disorienting, the grass and trees seeming to have crept up on us while we weren't looking. It's as if we've caught them in the act of growing, something nature does as we while our time away fruitlessly in the gray, concrete city.

"We'll take a picture in front of this thing," I say. "Yeah," Tull says smiling. "Who the hell's going to know the difference?" We bring our heads close together, two brothers who never did find a father. I hold the camera at arms length and aim so that the lens will capture our moonfaces and the barn house backdrop. I snap the picture. We'll claim to all who see it that this is honest Abe's birthplace. That we made it all the way ...

Andrew Hilbert

The Two Midget Twins of San Antonio

The two midget twins of San Antonio liked to ride mechanical bulls. Their names were Red & Peacock. Red liked whiskey and his face was always sunburnt and alcohol dried. Peacock was kind of a prude.

They were sitting at the bar one night, Red with his whiskey and Peacock with his Bud Lite.

Red said, "There ain't never no damn fine midget ladies for us to share."

"Yep. And these leggies don't pay attention when we tell 'em our dicks are relatively big for our size situation."

"It's a sorry life to live in, brother." Red chewed his ice. "A sorry existence. Bartender! One more!"

"When I grow up I'm guna get me the tallest blonde in town," Peacock said.

"No more bathing in cowboy hats when I grow up!"

"Yep," Peacock put the rest of his beer down.

"Bar keep!" he yelled, "One more Bud Lite, please!"

"We should invest in stilts."

"Yep."

"Maybe one of these days I can stand on your shoulders and we can wear a long jacket and when we take a leggy home we can give 'em the ol' two fer one surprise."

"Yep."

"Oh, well. Bull riding, brother?"

"I'll sit this one out."

"You're a motherfucker, you know that?"

"Yep."

The End.

Beat Austin

was described by the late US Senator from Texas, Ralph Yarborough, as "the Paris of Texas." It is unique to contain both state government and the state's major university within easy hoofing distance of each other. Ginsberg would hang at Quackenbush's Coffee Shop on Guadalupe when checking on his manuscripts at the Humanities Research Center. Andy Clausen drove taxi while Hedwig Gorski produced her play in an abandoned house using street people as actors. For democracy to work, legislators must be compromisers—deal makers—not ideologues. That and the fact a major university is located in the city explain, at least in part, why Austin's on the progressive side. It's legal for a woman, and men, to swim topless at Barton Springs pool or to sunbathe in the parks. The beauty of the area's hills, lakes, and streams brought environmentalist beat writers like Jim Cody to the city's sylvan neighborhoods, inspired by Gary Snyder. The outsider political positions of the beats, and of many of the city's singer-songwriters, have been able to find voice and home in Austin, even as rents continue to rise. Resistencia Books carries on the beat.

Thorne Dreyer

The Spies of Texas
Newfound files detail how UT-Austin police tracked the lives of Sixties dissidents

"Even a paranoid can have enemies." —Henry Kissinger

Allen Hamilton kept his files secret until his death in 2005, long after his retirement as campus police chief for the University of Texas at Austin. His son discovered them while cleaning out his father's office. The boxes of documents and photos from the 1960s included records of the most horrific event in Chief Hamilton's tenure—the August day in 1966 when Charles Whitman perched atop the UT Tower with a high-powered rifle, killing 15 and wounding 33. Graphic photos from the Whitman archives were made available to newspapers to mark the 40th anniversary of that bloody day.

But Hamilton's files also provide valuable links to the complex political and social currents that were washing over the campus four decades ago. These documents—made public here for the first time—tell the story of how the University of Texas spied on its nonconformist and dissident students. The records—covering a period from approximately 1963 to 1970—show the extensive efforts that campus police made to identify, watch, and follow students and faculty members whom it found suspicious.

The files include more than 500 pages of department memos, some from student informers; lists of names of campus "dopers" and activists; and photocopies of newspaper articles and leaflets. Also included are over 250 surveillance photographs. The documents reveal that among the subjects campus police were monitoring at the time were Janis Joplin, Jerry Jeff Walker, and Richard ("Kinky") Friedman.

Some notes are jotted on torn scraps of paper. Others are typed memoranda to the chief and reports from Hamilton to campus administrators. And there are names, lots of names, probably close to a thousand. Some typed, some scribbled, some photocopied from petitions and sign-in sheets collected at meetings and rallies.

* * *

Much of the material in Chief Hamilton's files centers on early Austin countercultural figures, musicians and literary types, especially those associated with the "Ghetto"—an old wooden Army barracks in the 2800 block of Nueces on the west side of campus that was home and/or home base to much of the hipster cognoscenti. The police also seemed focused on the activity of the staff of the *Texas Ranger*, the campus humor mag that incubated a number of major artistic and literary talents.

Janis Joplin numbered among those that the police associated with the Ghetto. In one entry, beside her name are scribbled the words "... suspected of bringing in amphetamines, Dexedrine, etc." Other members of the Ghetto crowd mentioned in the files are musician Powell St. John, who would be a pioneer of the San Francisco psychedelic rock scene; cartoonist Gilbert Shelton, who was to create the iconic Fabulous Furry Freak Brothers strip that appeared in *The Rag* and other underground papers all over the world; and the late William Brammer, a former *Observer* editor whose book *The Gay Place* would be recognized as perhaps the finest novel about Texas politics.

Visiting poets Allen Ginsberg and Lawrence Ferlinghetti—invited for poetry readings—are cited in handwritten notes. (Ginsberg is identified as the "hippies poet." About Ferlinghetti, they haven't a clue.) Other names that pop up in various lists: (now U.S. Rep.) Lloyd Doggett; former *Texas Observer* editors Ronnie Dugger (spelled "Deuger") and Kaye Northcott; Spencer Perskin and Kenny Parker of the classic Austin rock group Shiva's Head Band; folklorist Tary Owens; musicians Mance Lipscomb and Jerry Jeff Walker; civil rights leader B. T. Bonner Jr.; numerous lawyers and professors; two rabbis; and Yale University Chaplain William Sloan Coffin.

As for the Ghetto group in general, the files read that they "float from place to place. Start and end at times at Gilbert Shelton's, (or the) Unitarian Church." In another notation: "Peyote and drugs used in wild parties on Fri and Sat night. Most of the wild crowd members of the *Ranger* staff."

The files contain a photocopy of an April 18, 1963, article from the *Austin American-Statesman* that perfectly relates how clueless the authorities really were. The story describes a "shakedown of local beatniks" (this one by the Austin police vice squad) in which "they spotted several, spoke to a few and bagged zero." It reports that "several girls, spotted leaving one of the apartments tagged as a beatnik hangout, scattered in all directions." The article adds that parties were thought to be getting out of hand and informs that, according to the dean of student life, "local beats are currently getting their kicks from peyote cactus," which, as one officer observed, "makes you dream in Technicolor."

One document in the collection describes a female student thought to "use peyote ... and other drugs, very sexually promiscuous and believed to have nymphomaniac tendencies," and another woman is also labeled as "sexually promiscuous."

The authorities' apparent titillation with sex appeared to heighten when drugs were added to the mix. Yet the fascination of the police stood in stark contrast to the attitudes of these precursors of the counterculture to come. For them, sex was seen as open and natural and no big deal. But that wasn't the only aspect of the scene that the cops got wrong.

The Ghetto is characterized on a scrap of notepaper in Hamilton's files as "a haven for Jews." There are several typed pages of historical analysis of the ghettos in World War II (the Austin Ghetto was in fact a nondenominational operation and was in no way related to the history of the Jewish people) and a psychoanalytical take on the Ghetto's denizens, calling them "individuals lost in the world" with "egocentric impulsiveness," "deviant sexual patterns," and a "rejection of authority and discipline." It also grumbles that they were, well, just "irritating and distressing."

Pat Sharpe

[The following article from UT-Austin student newspaper *The Daily Texan* is a portrait of Janis Joplin circa 1960, when she briefly attended the University of Texas. In that same student newspaper, she was voted "Ugliest Man on Campus." Joplin was already used to the abuse. "They don't treat beatniks too good in Texas," she once said, adding about her hometown: "Port Arthur people thought I was a beatnik, though they'd never seen one and neither had I."]

She Dares to Be Different!

She goes barefooted when she feels like it, wears Levi's to class because they're more comfortable, and carries her Autoharp with her everywhere she goes so that in case she gets the urge to break into song it will be handy. Her name is Janis Joplin, and she looks like the type of girl a square (her more descriptive term-a "leadbelly") would call a "beatnik." "Jivey" is what Janis calls herself, not "beat." She leads a life that is enviously unrestrained. She doesn't bother to have her hair set every week, or to wear the latest feminine fashion fads, and when she feels like singing she sings in a vibrant alto voice.

UNTRAINED VOICE

Since she has never had a music lesson and cannot read notes her voice is untrained. But this lack seems to be an asset rather than a liability, for Janis sings with a certain spontaneity and gusto that cultivated voices sometimes find difficult to capture. She is at her best with folk songs, to which she gives an earthy, twangy rendition. Janis' current ambition is to be a folksinger, though she really prefers blues. She has performed at the Gas House in Venice, Calif. and in Port Arthur, her home town. But she really began to think seriously about singing when she came to the University this year as a freshman majoring in art. She says the people in Austin are definitely more hip on folk music than the clods in other cities she has visited. In fact, it was here that a friend persuaded her to take up the Autoharp.

AUTOHARP

This particular instrument is not one that is seen as often as a piano or a guitar. As a matter of fact, it is about as common as a glockenspiel. At first glance, it looks like a zither, but longer and narrower and with fewer strings. At the squared-off end are 12 bars which are depressed to form chords. Right now, Janis' career as a folksinging-Autoharpist is in its beginning stages. She is currently the female member of a local group which styles itself the Waller Creek Boys. The other two are Lanny Wiggins and Powell St. John, Jr.

GHETTO

When they are not in class or at home, the favorite hangout of Janis and her friends is an apartment which they have nicknamed the Ghetto. The walls are decorated with original modernistic paintings done by local cats, and the furniture defies description. For want of a better name, it might be called contemporary American hodgepodge. Password around the Ghetto is "uninhibited." Man, if a person isn't uninhibited, he's sick. Whenever somebody gets the urge to stand up and do a little impromptu jig, he gets up and does it. And if suddenly he feels like dribbling out a piece of modern art,

85

he goes right ahead and dribbles.

COMPULSION

If on the other hand, he feels inspired to write a piece of poetry, beat or otherwise, man, he writes. Why if a person doesn't feel the compulsion to do something crazy at least once in a while, he is a leadbelly. All activities sacred to leadbellies—like bowling, twisting, or rating their hair—are taboo for cats. Consequently, the cats are confined to being uninhibited and singing folk music for whole hours together, which sounds about as exciting as the average fraternity party. Clichés such as "suave," "swinging," and "I just can't beleeve!" are held in the utmost contempt by the uninhibited, but at the same time it is interesting to note the frequency with which "man," "chick," etc. appear in conversation.

In short, comparing the vast majority of University students to the vast minority of University beatniks would be like comparing a large sack of potatoes to a small sack of onions. The onions may be a little spicier, but they are all onions just the same.

Nadine Eckhardt

[In this excerpt from her memoir, *Duchess of Palms*, McAllen, Texas, native Nadine Eckhardt describes the late 1950s Austin bohemian lifestyle led by her and her first husband, Billy Lee Brammer, author of *The Gay Place*. She was later married to U.S. Representative Bob Eckhardt.]

Testing the Waters, Pushing the Boundaries

During this time I discovered F. Scott Fitzgerald and read every book by or about him. I identified with his wife Zelda, an engaging southern girl with artistic aspirations of her own. Zelda, along with Hemingway's Lady Brett Ashley and Michael Arlen's Iris March of *The Green Hat*, were elusive, quixotic, and irresistible to men. They were romanticized in such beautifully written books ... I wanted to be like them, even though they were confused, depressed, and ambivalent about their relationships. The authors, who were close to the real-life counterparts of these characters, wrote about them in an attempt to support and understand them. I too was married to an aspiring writer who wanted to understand me, but like the enigmatic women of these stories, I didn't understand myself.

While our personal and financial problems simmered underneath the surface, Bill's professional life prospered. He moved from writing sports to the editorial side of the paper and won statewide awards for writing features. Everyone loved Bill; he was charming, witty, gentle, and nonthreatening, indulged by parents, friends, and coworkers. Men liked him because he could talk sports and was athletic, intelligent, and naughty. Women liked him because he asked questions about their lives and actually listened when they answered—and because he was naughty. (Later on, I found his intense questioning intrusive and sometimes felt that it verged on voyeurism. Sometimes Bill would set me up in conversation so he could watch me interact with various attractive male friends. If I met someone at a party and engaged them in conversation, he would quiz me on it when we got home. I would never have allowed this if I had been aware at the time of my right to protect my boundaries. Years later, Bill's second wife, Dorothy, told me that he had done the same thing with her.)

Things were going well for Bill, but even though he was advancing professionally, his salary was still fairly low. Newspaper people never made much money. But my salary helped us gain a feeling of being middle-class, and we had a house and a child, so our parents began to accept us as adults. On August 31, 1954, two years after I had Sidney, I gave birth to another baby girl, Shelby. Responsibilities at home increased. Our income was reduced by one salary, since the economics of my returning to work did not play out: if I paid someone to take care of the girls, all the income from my salary would go toward employing that person, with no money left over. The only alternative was that Bill had to find a job that paid more so I could stay home with the girls. Then Bill found a house for $8,500 on a little street near Deep Eddy Pool off Lake Austin Boulevard, where I took Sidney and Shelby swimming most summer days. Around this time I had a Nash Rambler convertible that I loved; it was the first automobile that I ever considered mine. One day Bill came home with a new Plymouth station wagon. When I asked how he got it, he said, "Oh, I traded in the convertible for it." I was furious. He rationalized the purchase by saying we needed it to haul Sidney's playpen. I was learning the hard way about it being a "man's world."

But this was an interesting period in our lives. We were having a great time socially in Austin, but a horrible time financially. We were part of a set of young, sexually progressive married couples who were the Texas version of Jack Kerouac's Beat Generation. We were in love with romance, decadence, politics, and literature. We read competitively with various members of one set to be witty and sparkling in the most esoteric way. The set included law students, artists, legislators, and youngish professors at UT. Austin was small enough for us to know about each other. Everyone had small children and responsibilities, but we managed to cluster at watering holes like Scholz Garden in Austin, at each other's homes, and at house parties on ranches. We wives took the children to swim every day in spring-fed swimming holes and sat on quilts, gossiping and nurturing our tans. We were humanists—we had faith in human beings, not God or "the spirit." We believed in education and knowledge and reveled in health and beauty.

The men in the group didn't want to be The Man in the Gray Flannel Suit—they wanted to fulfill some kind of vague myth, whether it be the myth of the hard-drinking, hard-drugging, womanizing cowboy-landed-gentry, like a John Wayne character (but with a degree in philosophy). They wanted to become whatever fantasies they possessed. Some of these men peaked early, like Willie Morris, who became the youngest editor of *Harper's Magazine* at thirty-two; Bill, whose book *The Gay Place* was published when he was twenty-nine; and Ronnie Dugger, who was editor of the *Texas Observer* at some point. The women in the group simply aspired to perfection—or at least the *appearance* of perfection.

Our sexual relationships were changing along with the times, and we began to experiment in other, more potentially destructive ways—not just to talk the talk, but to walk the walk. We lied to ourselves and to each other, swapped partners, and acted on our own selfish motivations, doing whatever we wanted to when we wanted to, and rationalizing it later with intellectual verbiage. We discussed everything, and whether it was politics or sleeping with someone else's wife or husband, we couched it in clever repartee and witty put-downs, served with plenty of alcohol. If we slept with someone else's husband, we were discreet; we maintained the façade. We were hypocritical and manipulative. At our weekend parties on ranches, we drank martinis and gin-and-tonics before dinner and brandy afterward, argued about politics and art, felt up each other's wives and husbands, and then headed back to town for the week.

Bill and I enjoyed this lifestyle of fun and games for a while, but eventually he became uncomfortable with it. He saw me enjoying myself, taking care of the girls, swimming every day, and partying on the weekends, and he felt the pressure to bring in more money to stay on par with some of our friends, who were either from wealthy families or were making more money in their jobs.

In 1954, a liberal Texas weekly called the *Texas Observer* was founded by Frankie Randolph, a wealthy woman from Houston. The *Observer*'s editor, Ronnie Dugger, offered Bill a job; Bill was intrigued and immediately quit the *Austin American-Statesman*. Thus began our long friendship with Ronnie and Jean Dugger, who later became Mrs. Robert Sherrill. After working for a corporate newspaper monopoly, Bill enjoyed the freedom of writing for a liberal weekly, and he and Ronnie did some excellent work together. They covered politics and the Texas legislature with a different mission: to report on the cronyism and sleazy politics that profited the politicians and their patrons. Consequently, the *Observer* gained the respect of politicians and lobbyists, which remains true to this day.

Later, when I was working in Washington, LBJ requested to see the *Observer* when it arrived. After his heart attack, I joked that I had reservations about handing it over—the *Observer* didn't cut Lyndon any slack. The *Observer* still labors along in its uphill battle, tackling important news that the dailies ignore.

Our financial dilemmas didn't improve with the *Observer* job, however, and Bill began to actively search for another one. After hearing that LBJ was looking to hire a Texas pressman, Bill talked to someone in his office, and was hired. Soon thereafter, I had an interview with Walter Jenkins, Johnson's right-hand man, and was hired as well. Some of our friends gave us a hard time about these new jobs; in our Austin circles LBJ was considered very conservative, which says a lot about the attitude of young Austin liberals in the fifties. But we were excited about our new prospects, and in January of 1955 we packed up, rented our little house to a couple, and the girls and I winged away on a cushy, luxe Brown & Root plane to join Bill, who had preceded us, in Washington, D.C.

C. Wright Mills

[C. Wright Mills, author of the groundbreaking sociological studies *White Collar* and *The Power Elite*, was, as his friend Dan Wakefield says, "a Texas-bred Maverick." Mills matriculated at Texas A&M in 1935 but was pressured out of the school for writing a newspaper column critical of freshman hazing practices (he transferred to Austin). A popular sociology professor at Columbia University in the 1940s and 1950s, he wore blue jeans, plaid shirts, and workman's boots and roared to class on a BMW motorcycle. As was true of the Beat writers—Ginsberg and Kerouac, amateur sociological chroniclers themselves, were his friends—Mills was a radical individualist who believed in collapsing the distance between one's work and one's life. The following excerpt from *White Collar* is one of several essays he wrote on this topic. Although Kerouac complained that "craft" meant "crafty," Mills' ideas on spontaneity and creativity can still be read profitably alongside Jack Kerouac's "Belief and Technique for Modern Prose."]

White Collar

The Ideal of Craftsmanship

Craftsmanship as a fully idealized model of work gratification involves six major features: There is no ulterior motive in work other than the product being made and the processes of its creation. The details of daily work are meaningful because they are not detached in the worker's mind from the product of the work. The worker is free to control his own working action. The craftsman is thus able to learn from his work; and to use and develop his capacities and skills in its prosecution. There is no split of work and play, or work and culture. The craftsman's way of livelihood determines and infuses his entire mode of living.

I. The hope in good work, William Morris remarked, is hope of product and hope of pleasure in the work itself; the supreme concern, the whole attention, is with the quality of the product and the skill of its making. There is an inner relation between the craftsman and the thing he makes, from the image he first forms of it through its completion, which goes beyond the mere legal relations of property and makes the craftsman's will-to-work spontaneous and even exuberant.

Other motives and results—money or reputation or salvation—are subordinate. It is not essential to the practice of the craft ethic that one necessarily improves one's status either in the religious community or in the community in general. Work gratification is such that a man may live in a kind of quiet passion "for his work alone."

II. In most statements of craftsmanship, there is a confusion between its technical and aesthetic conditions and the legal (property) organization of the worker and the product. What is actually necessary for work-as-craftsmanship, however, is that the tie between the product and the producer be psychologically possible; if the producer does not legally own the product he must own it psychologically in the sense that he knows what goes into it by way of skill, sweat, and material and that his own skill and sweat are visible to him. Of course, if legal conditions are such that the tie between the work and the worker's material advantage is transparent, this is a further gratification, but it is subordinate to that workmanship which would continue of its own will even if not paid for.

The craftsman has an image of the completed product, and even though he does not make it all, he sees the place of his part in the whole, and thus understands the meaning of his exertion in terms of that whole. The satisfaction he has in the result infuses the means of achieving it, and in this way his work is not only meaningful to him but also partakes of the consummatory satisfaction he has in the product. If work, in some of its phases, has the taint of travail and vexation and mechanical drudgery, still the craftsman is carried over these junctures by keen anticipation. He may even gain positive satisfaction from encountering a resistance and conquering it, feeling his work and will as powerfully victorious over the recalcitrance of materials and the malice of things. Indeed, without this resistance he would gain less satisfaction in being finally victorious over that which at first obstinately resists his will.

George Mead has stated this kind of aesthetic experience as involving the power "to catch the enjoyment that belongs to the consummation, the outcome, of an undertaking and to give to the implements, the objects that are instrumental in the undertaking, and to the acts that compose it something of the joy and satisfaction that suffuse its successful accomplishment."

III. The workman is free to begin his work according to his own plan and, during the activity by which it is shaped, he is free to modify its form and the manner of its creation. In both these senses, Henri De Man observed, "plan and performance are one," and the craftsman is master of the activity and of himself in the process. This continual joining of plan and activity brings even more firmly together the consummation of work and its instrumental activities, infusing the latter with the joy of the former. It also means that his sphere of independent action is large and rational to him. He is responsible for its outcome and free to assume that responsibility. His problems and difficulties must be solved by him, in terms of the shape he wants the final outcome to assume.

IV. The craftsman's work is thus a means of developing his skill, as well as a means of developing himself as a man. It is not that self-development is an ulterior goal, but that such development is the cumulative result obtained by devotion to and practice of his skills. As he gives it the quality of his own mind and skill, he is also further developing his own nature; in this simple sense, he lives in and through his work, which confesses and reveals him to the world.

V. In the craftsman pattern there is no split of work and play, of work and culture. If play is supposed to be an activity, exercised for its own sake, having no aim other than gratifying the actor, then work is supposed to be an activity performed to create economic value or for some other ulterior result. Play is something you do to be happily occupied, but if work occupies you happily, it is also play, although it is also serious, just as play is to the child. "Really free work, the work of a composer, for example," Marx once wrote of Fourier's notions of work and play, "is damned serious work, intense strain." The simple self-expression of play and the creation of ulterior value of work are combined in work-as-craftsmanship. The craftsman or artist expresses himself at the same time and in the same act as he creates value. His work is a poem in action. He is at work and at play in the same act.

"Work" and "culture" are not, as Gentile has held, separate spheres, the first dealing with means, the second with ends in themselves; as Tilgher, Sorel, and others have indicated, either work or culture may be an end in itself, a means, or may contain segments of both ends and means. In the craft model of activity, "'consumption" and "production" are blended in the same act; active craftsmanship, which is both play and work, is the medium of culture; and for the craftsman there is no split between the worlds of culture and work.

VI. The craftsman's work is the mainspring of the only life he knows; he does not flee from work into a separate sphere of leisure; he brings to his non-working hours the values and qualities developed and employed in his working time. His idle conversation is shop talk; his friends follow the same lines of work as he, and share a kinship of feeling and thought. The leisure William Morris called for was leisure to think about our work, "that faithful daily companion …"

In order to give his work the freshness of creativity, the craftsman must at times open himself up to those influences that only affect us when our attentions are relaxed. Thus for the craftsman, apart from mere animal rest, leisure may occur in such intermittent periods as are necessary for individuality in his work. As he brings to his leisure the capacity and problems of his work, so he brings back into work those sensitivities he would not gain in periods of high, sustained tension necessary for solid work.

"The world of art," wrote Paul Bourget, speaking of America, "requires less self-consciousness—an impulse of life which forgets itself, the alternation of dreamy idleness with fervid execution." The same point is made by Henry James, in his essay on Balzac, who remarks that we have practically lost the faculty of attention, meaning "that unstrenuous, brooding sort of attention required to produce or appreciate works of art." Even rest, which is not so directly connected with work itself as a condition of creativity, is animal rest, made secure and freed from anxiety by virtue of work done—in Tilgher's words, "a sense of peace and calm which flows from all well-regulated, disciplined work done with a quiet and contented mind."

In constructing this model of craftsmanship, we do not mean to imply that there ever was a community in which work carried all these meanings. Whether the medieval artisan approximated the model as closely as some writers seem to assume, we do not know; but we entertain serious doubts that this is so; we lack enough psychological knowledge of medieval populations properly to judge. At any rate, for our purposes it is enough to know that at different times and in different occupations, the work men do has carried one or more features of craftsmanship.

With such a model in mind, a glance at the occupational world of the modern worker is enough to make clear that practically none of these aspects are now relevant to modern work experience. The model of craftsmanship has become an anachronism. We use the model as an explicit ideal in terms of which we can summarize the working conditions and the personal meaning work has in modern work-worlds, and especially to white-collar people.

Albert Huffstickler

Thanksgiving 1985

Some things need to be commemorated:
I was walking to Winchell's for coffee
when four old boys in a dark blue VW fastback pulled up.
"How ya doin?" asks the driver.
"Fine," I said.
"You wanta go smoke some dope and drink some beer and eat
some turkey?"
"Thanks," I told him, "but I've got a place to go."
"Well, we'll find somebody." They waved and wheeled off.
It was warm in Winchell's. Outside, autumn had finally arrived.
Somehow, as you grow older, each holiday becomes a day of
reckoning.
One of the crazes is talking to his girl on the phone.
She doesn't seem very responsive.
His voice grows louder, more urgent.
Finally, he hangs up and stands a moment shaking his head.
The room busies, them empties.
I finish my coffee and leave.
Walking home, a transient stops me, bums a cigarette
and asks if I know if the Salvation Army is still serving.
I can take a hint. I give him three dollars and walk on,
trying to decide whether that evens the score or not.

Albert Huffstickler

The Suit

There's a certain kind of suit that never was new.
Its first memories are of Goodwill or The Salvation Army or St. Vincent De Paul's.
There's nothing you can do to disguise it.
Cleaning may remove the stains but it will not alter the aura.
Color: dark grey or blue with a thin brown stripe;
double-breasted, wide lapels, pant legs wide all the way down to the cuffs,
loose at waist and crotch. Like army fatigues,
not quite fitting any body but adaptable to all.
It reeks of poverty, of sleepless nights in flophouse, dreary aimless days on city streets.
It has never been fully pressed and its wrinkles
are the wrinkles on the faces of destitute men hunched at the doors of soup kitchens
or the wrinkles beneath the eyes of aging whores standing beneath street lamps on cold corners.
This suit has existed since the beginning of time:
Mary's alcoholic brother (never mentioned in The Bible) wore one to the crucifixion
and, contrary to public opinion, Jesus himself wore one at The Last Supper.
It is the uniform of the disenfranchised.
It hangs on a man's body like a shroud, and worse, it anchors him to his status:
to go up in the world he must first get rid of the suit;
to rid himself of the suit he must rise above his condition.
They give them to inmates of asylums and prisons when they release them
to be sure they'll remember what they are and come back
and they are given to old men in homes for the aged to remind them that they're useless.
Accessories: a blue work shirt and faded tie or stained sweat shirt
on the sockless feet, brogans, or worse, someone's discarded dress shoes,
laces knotted and re-knotted, insides lined with cardboard
to protect the feet where the soles have worn through.
There you have it: the ensemble of poverty,
instantly recognized in any country in the world.
Sufficient justification for slamming the door in a face
or demanding to see a person's money before he's served.
The wearer of such a costume will automatically become
the first to be questioned at the scene of a crime and the last to be released.
He is insulted without provocation and punished on a whim
and no one questions that he deserves it.
He's wearing the suit, isn't he?
And obviously the way to cure him of wearing the suit is to punish him by degrading him further.
After all, it's for his own good.
Well, someday there won't be suits like that.
But before that day comes, a lot of things will have happened.

The mighty will have been brought low and the humble exalted.
And for a long time before it vanishes,
the wearer of that suit will be honored wherever he walks,
as though he were wearing the robes of a king.

PW Covington

You Can't Be Beat No More

... And there's this sack-of-shit hipster poet
Sitting near the stage with his Westlake Hills girlfriend
Waiting for his turn at the Open Mic
So that he can spout his shit and leave
(while others read)
Smoking the most expensive cigarettes he could find, and drinking Pabst from a can

You can't be beat anymore, no
They just won't let you, he says
With a Fuck-bomb and a sneer
You can't be beat no more, Man
You can't hitchhike like Kerouac
There are crazies out there
You can't get out there like Kesey, Man
They test you now, you know
And the chicks don't dig it when you fuck like
Cassidy fucked
You just can't be beat no more, Man
They won't LET YOU, Man

And I wonder; did he set the alarm on his car
Before he came into the bar?
'Cause this Cat is right ...

He'll never be Beat

Lowell Mick White

Riff-Raff

At that time I was still making an effort. I was still trying to get my shit together. It was hard, but I was trying. I was driving the cab on a 24-hour shift, hitting the busy parts of the day, hiding in my motel room when it was slower, resting for a few hours before heading back out on the road. When I was awake in my motel room I would sometimes watch television, evangelical preachers in the morning or psychologists in the afternoon, all of them trying to give advice to the poor unfortunates in their audience. All of them spoke at times about *hitting bottom*. They talked about hitting bottom like that was all there was to it—*ker-splat*, bang, you hit bottom and that's that. The end. Afterwards your life changed, or it didn't. But what apparently none of them understood was that hitting bottom was a complicated goddamn process, that when you hit bottom, you *bounce*, like a basketball. Of course you hit bottom again, and bounce again, and again, every bounce up a little lower than the bounce before, every smack against the bottom duller and longer than the previous one. It's a process that can go on for a long, long time, and your life doesn't change ever, not usually.

Me, I sometimes bottomed out a little and thudded by a rock house or a bar, but usually I went back to my motel room and stared at the television. I would sit in the gloom and listen to the psychologists and preachers give advice, listen to the people in the next room argue and fuck, listen to the motel owner's Rottweiler bark at whores and children. I was trying. I drove the cab as much as I could.

One Sunday, near noon, my dispatch terminal beeped and I was directed to go pick up someone named Miller, at the Wilderness Road Inn, a seedy motel just up the street from my own seedy motel. I parked the cab outside the room where Miller was supposed to be and honked the horn. Company policy dictated that the drivers were supposed to get out and knock on the door for customers, but I refused to do that. In some parts of town—at the sleazy motels, for instance—it could be dangerous. It is illegal for cab drivers to carry firearms, so instead I carried a long, black, heavy steel flashlight. It was okay for threatening to bash drunks over the head with but of course would not be weapon enough to take on a maniac with a pistol. I waited for a few minutes, then honked again. I put the car into gear and was getting ready to turn around and leave when the door to the room opened and a man came out. Miller, I guessed.

He was pale, almost an albino, pale and dressed in black, with a red baseball cap on his lank white hair and mirrored sunglasses. He had a fax machine under his arm. He came down the stairs and got into the cab.

"You want to buy a fax machine?" he asked.

"No," I said. I started the meter.

"Man, you got a cold fucking *no*." Miller sat back and laughed. He said, "Listen, pal, I need some extra cash—I need to get rid of this fax machine."

"But you have enough to pay *me*, right?" I looked at him in the mirror, but I could not see his eyes behind the sunglasses.

"Hey, pal, you think I'm stupid enough to get in a cab without any money? Of course I have enough to pay you."

"It happens." I adjusted my flashlight.

"Hey, pal, not from me. Just stop worrying and start driving, okay? I need to get rid of this goddamn fax machine. Let's try that pawn shop up the street."

I pulled out into traffic and went three blocks or so to the World of Pawn store. It seemed like the kind of fare that cab drivers hated: driving some fool to a pawn shop for a $3.50 fare, no tip. But Miller was in the World of Pawn only for a moment or two, and he came back out with the fax machine.

"Fuckers wouldn't give me enough for it," he said. "I'm gonna have to take it back to the store—it's on the north side. I still got the receipt. You think that's a good idea?"

I thought: The north side. Twenty or so dollars up, twenty or so back, maybe.

"That's probably your best bet," I said. I started pulling out of the parking lot. "These goddamn pawn shops don't pay anything."

* * *

The city was quiet that Sunday and traffic was unusually light. I drove north and found the Office Depot Miller wanted. He jumped out of the cab and disappeared into the store. I sat there glumly, hoping that he would be quick. The meter ticked up once, and then again, and again. No Miller. Then an old fat man in a gray jumpsuit came out of the store. He leaned on his cane, looking at me in the cab, then walked over to the Cadillac parked next to me and opened the door. He looked at me again. No one else was in the parking lot—it was as if the streets had emptied and everyone had gone home. No cars, no people, no nothing except the fat old man who was staring at me. I stared back at him. Finally he walked around his car—slowly, slowly—and came over to the cab. I lowered the window.

"You know, you're parked in a handicap parking space," he said. He had a big bald head and round glasses.

I looked at the handicap parking sign and then back at him. I asked, "Yeah?"

"And you don't have handicap plates, or a sticker."

"No," I said. "I guess I don't."

He planted his cane carefully and leaned over, smiling. He had a huge round head. "Well, you know, I'm kind of an activist for handicap parking rights—my friends call me the Ralph Nader of handicap parking rights." He chuckled and looked at me—proud, I guess, of being the Ralph Nader of handicap parking rights—but I didn't say anything. After a moment, he said, "So, I guess I'll have to ask you to move."

"I'm just waiting for a customer," I said. I looked away at the store. "It'll only be a minute or so."

"Well, then, I'm afraid I'll have to call the police. I'm going to have you arrested." He slowly started to turn away, pivoting on his cane.

"Wha-aaat?" I couldn't believe it. I drive some maniac albino around for an hour, and then I get threatened by an old bald man.

"You're parked in a handicap zone! And you don't have authorization!" The old man took a step back toward me. He wasn't chuckling now—his face was turning red with anger, or madness, and spit flew out of his mouth when he said the word *authorization*. "I worked for years for handicap rights in this city and I'm not going to have my rights taken away by some damn—cab driver!"

"Hey, pal," I said, and stopped. When did I start calling people 'pal?' Miller. Jesus, you drive riff-raff around all day, you *become* riff-raff—and it doesn't take very long, either. I said, "I'm just waiting for my customer, okay?"

98

"I don't give a damn about your customer. I'm not going to have my rights taken away by some sleazy cab driver!"

I remembered another driver once telling me that cabs could park in handicap spaces if they were waiting for a customer. So I said, "Ah, fuck you, call the cops."

"What did you say?"

"Call the cops."

The old man's bald head was turning redder and redder. "No," he said, "*before* that."

"Fuck *you*, I said, *call* the fucking cops." The old man staggered backwards with a shocked look on his face. I hit the window button and the glass rose quickly, and I looked hopefully toward the door, willing Miller to appear. That's how bad my day had turned—I was praying for some goddamn weirdo to get in my cab! As for the old man, let him call the cops. The worst that would happen would be that the cops would write me a ticket that I would stick in the glove box and forget about.

But then there was a *bang* on the rear of the car—and another. I looked around and the old man was beating on my left rear fender with his damn cane. Bang! Bang!

I pulled my big, black flashlight from beneath the seat and got out of the car.

Bang!

I said, "Hey, cut it out!"

Bang!

I said, "Hey, pal, leave my car the fuck alone!"

Bang! The old man didn't even look over at me. He was just glaring at my car, red-faced, grimacing, swinging his cane like an axe. Bang! Bang!

I dropped my right shoulder and took two quick steps forward, swinging the heavy flashlight tight and hard, and I popped the old man right on his collarbone, right at the juncture of his neck and shoulder. *Bang!* His fucking dentures flew out of his mouth and he dropped like a dead piece of meat, cane clattering to the asphalt, his glasses askew, eyes pale in his head. I looked around. The parking lot—the store, the street—was still and quiet, silent, empty, as if under some spell. There was no one around. I looked down at the old man. He was still breathing, I think. The black flashlight was heavy in my hand.

"Hey, pal, what the fuck is this?"

I turned and there was Miller. The red baseball cap was pushed back on his head and he had a big astonished smile on his white face. I could see a blurred reflection of myself in his mirrored sunglasses.

"What the fuck did you just do?"

I said, "He attacked the cab, so I hit him."

"He *attacked* the *cab*? Oh, man!" Miller laughed. "So let's get the fuck out of here, you dumb shit."

I hesitated.

"C'mon—get in. Let's go!" Miller got in and shut the door.

I tossed the flashlight onto the seat and got into the car. I put it into reverse and backed up, careful not to run over the old man. Miller scooted over to the window and looked out at him.

"Man, you drilled the fucker. He's droolin and shit. He might die or something."

"He won't die." I pulled onto the frontage road and then quickly darted across three lanes and onto the highway.

"You *hope* he won't die. Jesus! I'm in a cab with a killer cab driver. Maybe I should be scared, huh?"

"He was hitting my cab with his damn cane," I said.

"So you killed him." Miller couldn't stop laughing. "Oh, man."

"Like I'm supposed to let him beat on my cab with his cane?"

"Fuck no! Kill the piece of shit!"

"I'm glad you think this is so funny." I kept looking in the mirror, expecting a fleet of cop cars to come chasing me. But there was just the usual light Sunday traffic.

"Killer, hey—get off here at 11th street—I need to check out something over on the Eastside."

I got off at the next exit and turned left, crossing the highway and heading east.

"I need a woman," Miller said. "Keep your eyes open."

I drove slowly east on 11th and turned left into Crack Alley and went slowly up the block. There were some sullen looking young black men sitting around on the curb watching traffic. Then a drug runner I knew, Wayne, stepped out from behind a car and waved at me. The windows were up but I could hear him yell, "Hey, stop!"

"Friend of yours?" Miller asked.

"I don't know," I said. "Maybe."

"Make a left here and cut over to 12th," Miller said. "There's no chicks here, just a bunch a crack dealers."

I made a left and went up to 12th and turned right again. We went east past Chicon and then Miller told me to make a left. There was an ancient barber shop with a *No Trespassing* sign in front, and a pair of old black men sitting in chairs. They glared at my cab. Miller rolled down the window.

"Hey! Where's the chicks?"

One of the old men said, "Get the fuck out of here."

Miller rolled up the window. He said, "Dumb pieces of shit."

I made another block and there were three girls sitting on the curb on front of a church.

"Stop!" Miller said. He rolled down the window. "Hey, Michelle, get over here!"

One of the girls—tall, very dark, with short slick hair—got up and walked over to the car. She looked in the window at Miller.

"I remember you," she said.

"Then get in and let's go!"

Michelle turned to her friends. "See you!" she said, and she got in the car.

"How you been?" Miller asked.

"I been okay," Michelle said. "Where're we going?"

"Over to my place," Miller said.

"I want a rock."

"Hey, I don't blame you. Life's stressful. My driver here, Killer, he'll take us to get you a rock."

Michelle looked at me. "I know him—I remember him." She reached up and tugged my ear. "I remember you."

"Oh, man!" Miller laughed. "You know Killer?"

"Yeah, I remember him from some house, somewhere." Michelle got up between the seats, almost resting her head on my shoulder. I could smell the hair butter she used—it smelled like coconuts. She asked, "You remember me?"

"Sure," I said. "Some house somewhere."

"Who was the last black girl you slept with?"

I said, "Uh, you?"

100

"Yeah!" Michelle was pleased. She sat back next to Miller. "Right in the back of the cab! Yeah, you're the one!"

"Oh, man," Miller said. "Killer, I'm learning all sorts of things about you!"

"He's a good driver," Michelle said. "He took me up to Round Rock to see my sister and didn't charge me anything."

"Shit, you should've seen him pop this old man a few minutes ago—he drilled the fucker!"

"He beat up a old man?" Michelle frowned. She reached up and tugged on my ear again. "Why'd you beat up an old man?"

"The old man attacked the cab," Miller said. "Killer didn't have a choice. He just drilled the fucker!"

I stopped paying attention. It was like they were talking about someone else—it was just noise. I drove aimlessly—going a block, then a right, a block, then a left, a block, a left, a right down an alley, wherever, whatever. I'd been bad long enough that I knew this part of town fairly well, at least at night. But now, in the daytime, I could see that there were some nice, well-kept homes tucked in along the street, homes probably inhabited by some decent, well-kept people. I also passed three places I knew to be crack houses, full of riff-raff, and a couple more that looked to be full of riff-raff. Finally we came to the house that Michelle wanted, the house I'd seen her in before or something, a big old place with peeling paint and trash bags in the yard. Other trash bags were stapled or taped to the windows and there was a broken plastic tricycle on the front porch. The house was on a hill and you could look west across the highway and see downtown—the capital, the university, the neon-fringed buildings. Civilization. Miller and Michelle went into the house and I sat waiting for them in the cab, the meter ticking up every now and then, ticking up, ticking up. I sat there looking out at the city, the orange sun sinking behind the hills, people driving up and down the highway in ignorance.

Self Portrait With A Goat

Beginning

My senior year at college there was a Halloween party. The Goat was there as nuclear fallout. I was Mary Hartman.

The Goat was widely renowned for dropping out every semester. I'd never met him, though we moved in similar circles.

We went downstairs to his room in the basement. As soon as we got our clothes off he started trembling. I tried to be gentle and calm, but that seemed to make things worse. Finally I gave up and lay still.

One time two truck drivers picked him up hitching and took him to a dark empty place.

He tried not to remember, but whenever someone touched him the feeling was still right there in his body.

I felt incompetent and sad. A ribbon of light from the party fell down the stairs. Then I looked at the Goat with his big broken nose and his fine, wild blond hair. I wanted him to trust me, so I stayed.

We lived together after that except when he got mad at me. I was unfaithful and bourgeois. He left me a note: he had gone to Alaska. I lay on my bed in a coma. Letters arrived with mid-western postmarks. Drawings of my shoulders. Dreams about my thighs. The whole erotic geography between.

But. Coupledom to be avoided at any and every cost. Cold mention of monogamy and Bloomingdale's.

After three weeks he called from Minneapolis. We both knew he should come home right away.

Once I lost the car keys and put out a cigarette in my hand. He sat beside me, frightened but elated.

We were best at each other's furthest extreme.

Middle

After I finished school we left the country forever. But first we drove all over saying goodbye. We put ten thousand miles on the car in a month. I knew I was pregnant the whole time.

I got pregnancy tests in Planned Parenthoods from Saratoga to Las Vegas. Negative, every single one.

"See," the Goat said cheerfully, "no cause for alarm!"

"Yeah," I muttered, watching the highway. "Right!"

I could see us in some godforsaken communist country. Me six months pregnant. Then what.

We got back to the east coast at the end of the summer. I went to my mother's house. The Goat went somewhere else. He and my mother never hit it off, though once he sent her pistachio nuts in the mail.

My mother took it calmly but her doctor was a quack. He gave me hormone pills to "bring on my period." Ha, I thought. I told him I was definitely pregnant. "Oh no dear, you can't be," he said.

This baffled me.

A week later, I was sitting out back on a lawn chair with my mother's miniature dachshund, Noppsie Goose. Finally I went inside and called the Goat. But I think he should have been the one to call.

He said uh-huh. Uh-huh. Then we hung up.

End

We lived in an abandoned factory near the Berlin Wall. The weather was revolting, but we were determined. Then we ran out of money and couldn't get work.

It was not an easy time for the Goat and me. We could hardly hold a civil conversation. Even the simple facts were bones of contention.

I was making coffee. I poured kerosene over a pile of garbage in the middle of the room. The factory was sadly lacking in handy appliances.

"Goat," I said. He was sitting near the window in a broken swivel chair, staring at a six-month-old newspaper.

The windows were ten feet high and stretched the length of two facing walls. The light rolled in all day in tremendous implacable waves which felt gray and swallowed everything in their path. The Goat liked to sit by the window where the backlight made his details disappear.

"Goat," I said. "Answer me."

"Mmm," he said, pretending to read.

"I think we should go home, Goat."

"Home," he repeated.

I poked the coffeepot out of the fire with the end of a broken flute. The milk was out on the window sill, staying cool.

I sat on the floor in front of the Goat where the light from the window poured into my eyes and burned the ends of his hair. His face was a shadow with glasses.

"We don't have any money," he eventually said.

"What about calling your brother?" His brother was a rich psychoanalyst in Los Angeles. He said if we got in trouble just to call.

"I still think we could get jobs," he mumbled quickly.

That was it. I jumped up and took off around the room in a circle, stomping my feet and making rain dance sounds. He watched like a judge at ringside.

Then I came around the curve. There were tears on his face. I fell on the floor with my head in his lap and whispered things into his leg.

He rocked back and forth in the chair.

While he was at the post office making the call, I packed what we still had worth taking. In the beginning there was a ton of stuff, but we never learned to cooperate. Things kept driving off in people's cars.

I saved the notebooks, the maps, and the broken movie camera. Most of our thrift shop clothes I had to burn. The mattress and the coffeepot I left for future residents. When I finished, the Goat was still gone.

By the time he got back it was dark out. He said everything was set. The money would come tomorrow. We were in a relatively jolly mood and built a big fire. The Goat told me about current events in America.

Thousands of people were in a green and white striped tent waiting to get on standby flights from London. In sleeping bags. It was a horizontal line.

The Goat perked right up and was a big social success. He played cards and drank wine with everybody. He tried to get the camera working for a movie about standby life. Unfortunately I wasn't in the mood.

I lay on the ground with my head on the knapsack. I talked when I saw something to eat.

A German girl named Zenzi had a crush on the Goat. She dragged her backpack over by us. She was going to Kentucky and had a very annoying laugh.

Everything was striped green in the tent light. It was impossible to tell the time of day. It seemed we had been there for several months.

"I'm going to Texas to see my sister," I announced one morning. We were close to the front of the line.

"Okay," said the Goat in a noncommittal tone. I didn't know if he was coming or what.

The man from the airline made his daily appearance. We were leaving transcontinental purgatory.

The travelers were saddened by this news. They liked the tent. They wrote their addresses and kissed each other goodbye.

Zenzi was now with us in some more formal way. The Goat asked for three seats together.

A girl falls in love with an aborigine in the outback. Many repulsive reptiles are looking on. The Goat was trying to say something, but I was busy watching the movie. I turned and gave him several mean looks.

At baggage claim he told me Zenzi was hitching with us to Lexington. Why not. It was on the way to Texas.

Zenzi was an airhead and a snake. On the other hand, I shouldn't be so snotty. So what if she was stealing my boyfriend.

* * *

The three of us got rides with surprising ease. Everyone who picked us up spoke fluent English. The United States zipped by looking smug.

Zenzi and the Goat reminded me of me and the Goat. She had been sent to replace me from Central Casting. I smiled fakely, feeling fat and outdated.

The Goat consulted my opinion about practical matters in a kind cheery voice, as if I were mentally retarded. I couldn't wait to get to Lexington and be rid of them.

It was night in Lexington. We were in a Denny's eating two eggs any style while Zenzi tried the phone numbers she had.

"What are you going to do?" I asked, examining my eggs.

"What do you mean, what am I going to do?"

"I mean stay here or come with me or what."

"Stay here? What? What do you mean?"

I gave the Goat a terrible look with my teeth. "Which word didn't you understand?"

"What's the matter with you, anyway?" the Goat demanded in a low voice. "You're acting like an idiot."

"So, I'm an idiot. Big deal."

Zenzi returned from the phone. All her friends were temporarily out of service. She recited the recording in her adorable German accent.

I thought I would puke just from looking at those eggs.

The Goat was describing for Zenzi the many splendors of Texas. The convenience stores. The cactus. The cows.

Zenzi exhibited some interest in my eggs. I graciously insisted that she eat them.

* * *

My sister Stella and her boyfriend Nick lived in a shack across from the cemetery. They had five dogs. He was a plumber, she was an auto mechanic. They had blue uniforms with their names in red script on the pockets.

The dogs heard our footsteps in their sleep. They jumped up barking like trained circus seals. Stella and Nick came out on the porch in their bathrobes. I decided to stay in Texas and look for a job.

I went down to the Safeway to pick up a paper. Stella came along to buy something to eat.

She filled me in on events since my departure. Many of our relatives had gotten mono. Noppsie Goose, however, was in good health.

"Who's that girl?" she asked me casually as we went through the electric doors .

"Just some girl we met waiting for the plane."

"Is she nice?"

"Oh, she's all right."

We were trying to figure out if jumbo eggs were really worth it. Five cents more than extra large, ten cents more than medium. There was a formula which neither of us remembered.

The next day I put my fate in the hands of the Texas Employment Commission. They subjected me to a difficult test. I had to sit in the waiting room for three straight days with nothing but a five-year-old *Sports Illustrated*.

The fourth day they certified me for a federal government project to assist the terminally unemployed. I went on to an interview to be the driver education instructor at a summer camp for teenage delinquents.

I pulled over to call the Goat on my way home from the camp. I wanted to drink a million margaritas.

No one was home. Probably swimming with the dogs.

The dogs were strewn around the lawn like victims of a sneak attack. The day was blue-hot and clear. I pulled into the driveway thinking about buying things. A summer dress. A paperback. A burrito.

The window shades were drawn against the sun. The air inside was dark and thick and sweaty.

Zenzi and the Goat were laughing in the bedroom. I didn't think, I just opened the door.

I shut the door and went into the kitchen. Then I felt breath on the back of my neck.

"Hi, Goat," I said quietly.

"Hi," he said.

"I got a job today."

He put his arm around my waist to pull me against him. For a second I could have shut my eyes and let go. Then it was already too late.

"Don't fucking touch me."

"Oh, God," he said, "You don't even—"

"Shut up, okay. Just shut up."

I turned and stared blindly into his face.

Zenzi walked in. "You can't say anything," she announced. "You knew what was going on and you didn't care."

The little Nazi bitch.

"Besides," she continued, buttoning her shirt, "it's your own fault. The forbidden fruit is sweet."

The Goat was helpless. I walked out the back door.

Two seconds later I walked back in. She was speaking softly with her fingers touching his cheek.

"Get the fuck out of here," I said.

The Goat tried to open his mouth .

"GET THE FUCK OUT OF MY HOUSE, ZENZI. I'M NOT KIDDING." I ran to the bedroom choking and slammed the door.

Low voices continued in the kitchen.

I opened the door and screamed across the house. "Goddammit, there's nothing to talk about. Go with her if you want. I don't care."

I threw her knapsack out into the hall.

* * *

The camp was six miles out of town in a castle built by acid heads out of chicken wire, foam rubber, and spray cement. It looked like a giant seashell made of Marshmallow Fluff.

The campers were all addicted to sniffing paint and eating white bread. They were shoplifters and dope dealers. They refused to participate. Fortunately drivers ed had a natural following.

The other counselors were lovely people in their thirties who knew nothing about running a camp full of hardened criminals. My role as driver's ed teacher was supposed to be very key, since I had each kid out alone three times a week. This was written up at length in all the grants.

After work I'd go home and he'd be lying there. He had a notebook full of lists of Things To Do. He wrote letters to long-lost friends in a 1968 diary, which he tore out and left around for me to read. He ate candy bars. His hair was a rat's nest.

All through May and June he was leaving in two days. He said he was going to Los Angeles. Once a week he'd go down to the Employment Commission for day labor. This was not constructive at all. He'd come home from doing shitwork angry and humiliated with twenty-five dollars in his hand.

Somewhat better than this was the Plasma Center. They paid fifteen dollars a pint.

We kept everyone up all night with our baby talk and hysteria. Stella shot me meaningful eyebrows over coffee.

Well Jesus Christ. I spent the whole day driving around with delinquents and then I came home to the vegetable. I'd spend half an hour trying to get him out of bed. Anything. Mexican food. A walk in the cemetery. "Oh come on," I'd wheedle. "It'll be fun."

The only thing he wanted to do for fun was make love. I didn't want to anymore, hardly ever. He'd touch me in the night and I'd hiss without thinking. Stop. I have to sleep. Lie still.

Some nights he jerked off right next to me in bed. I looked sideways at his profile. He was ugly.

This whole time it was one hundred degrees every day.

* * *

"Change to third, Phil. No, not first, third. Over and up. When the motor makes that noise it wants you to change."

Behind the Sonic Drive-In a creek ran through the woods. We parked the car and went down to wet our feet.

His sisters and brothers were in reform schools and foster homes. His mother had a stupid, violent boyfriend. She was gone for weeks at a time and forgot to leave the food stamps. He was fifteen. He wanted a moped.

"So," he said conversationally, "how are you?"

There were designs on his face and his legs from the sun. They shifted as the air brushed through the leaves. Our toes touched accidentally under the water.

"Hey, can I ask you something and you promise you won't get mad?"

"Sure," I answered, interested. What was this.

"You smoke pot sometimes, right?"

"Well, yeah, sometimes." You asked for it, I told myself.

"Only sometimes?" He sized me up, eyes half-shut, over his animal cheekbones. I almost blushed. "What about now?"

Holy mother of God, I thought, help me. Here I was on the verge of saying yes.

"I really really want to," I assured him. What a professional. "And I would, in a different situation. It's not that—"

"Forget it," he interrupted. "I understand."

I noticed I was touching his thigh with my second and middle fingers. "Let's go swimming," I heard myself say.

"Swimming? Here?"

"Oh, come on. It's hot as hell."

I stood up resolutely and started taking off my shirt.

He watched for a second, then bent to untie his shoe.

He kept checking to see just how undressed I would get.

* * *

The day Stella turned twenty-one we went out to a fancy restaurant. My friend Rain from work came along. I figured somebody had to be there who was on speaking terms with the Goat. And he always had a special way with lesbians.

The Goat and I fought for hours over what he should wear. "Anything but that," I moaned, "please." He kept his clothes in a heap stuffed under the bed.

For Stella's present, Nick had planted grass and flowers in the yard. Also a little fig tree and a birdhouse. I gave her a string hammock from Guatemala. The Goat came up with a miniature plastic lunchbox filled with tiny pastel-colored sandwiches.

The Goat had become a vegetarian. He eyed the menu from a distance like a piece of fascist propaganda.

I was desperate for everyone to get along. I helpfully pointed out items that had no meat. "What about some eggs?" I suggested in a bright voice. "Why not try the huevos rancheros?"

"I can read," he informed me coldly. Rapid eyebrow fire from Nick and Stella. Were it up to them, he would have stayed home.

I drank a number of margaritas and tried to keep up the conversation. Rain and I told stories about the camp.

Then she got in a semi-argument with Nick about the causes of homosexuality. He had heard it was a genetic mutation. Stella joined in on Rain's side. Outnumbered, Nick gave up. "All right, all right. Maybe it's different for girls." The Goat splashed around in his soup.

I split the check with Nick and Rain left the tip. The Goat was insolvent as usual.

We went back to the shack to eat chocolate chip ice cream cake roll. One thing that Goat could do was bake. My mother called from New Jersey to wish Stella a happy birthday. She put Noppsie Goose on the phone to say hello.

I took Rain home in Stella's car. I decided to go in for a minute. Then once I started talking I couldn't stop. His hair, his lists, his nose, his diet. Forbidden fruit. Our sex life. Money.

I tried to add up how much I'd spent on the Goat in the course of the past two years. I had to estimate in several of the categories: rent, gas, planes, food, phone bills. I didn't even include things like laundry and movies. I subtracted the loan from his brother and threw in half the abortion.

It came out to two thousand dollars. I looked at my calculations and couldn't speak. Rain brought over a glass of wine and sat beside me on the couch. She stroked my hair with one slender hand.

I didn't even want to talk about it. But I couldn't stand the thought of going home.

I started kissing her to see what it was like.

* * *

"You owe me two thousand dollars," I told the Goat when I got home. It was late, I had been at a bar since work.

The Goat was a lump under the sheets. He reached for his glasses and stuck out his head.

"Oh yeah?" he said. "Where were you last night?"

"Up late, talking to Rain."

"What did you talk about all that time?"

"Nothing. You."

"What about me?"

"Are you still going to Los Angeles?"

"Why?"

I waded through the wreckage and sat down on the edge of the bed. "I think you should leave, Goat," I began earnestly. "We're driving each other nuts. Just look."

"What do you mean, *we*? I'm the basket case, right? I'm the one who's been in bed since May. You have a job, you have friends, you drive around, you make money, you're as productive and responsible as can be. If your boyfriend gets out of hand, you just tell him to lie still. And he does, right? He lies still."

This was the longest speech the Goat had made in a year. I had to take it in for a second.

"I'm going out of my mind, Goat, I swear to God I am. I'm having affairs with a teenage kid and an older woman. I can't think straight any more, I don't even know what I'm doing. I just know I can't stand it. I really can't."

"Oh great. This is great. All that bullshit with Zenzi and now you're fucking ten other people." He pulled the sheets back over his head.

"I am not fucking ten other people. And it's nothing like the way it was with Zenzi, not with me and them, not with me and you. Anyway, I told you to go with her if you wanted. Maybe you should have just gone."

"Fuck you," he said. "I'm leaving."

He jumped out of bed and dragged his knapsack out of the closet. He started stuffing in all the junk that was on the floor.

"Make sure you don't take any of my stuff," I told him.

"Your stuff. Oh my god. Your stuff. Don't worry, little Miss Bourgeois Hypocrite, I wouldn't dream of touching your sacred possessions."

"I can't believe this. I can't believe you have the fucking nerve to say that. I'm so selfish, I'm so bourgeois, that's why I've spent two thousand fucking dollars supporting you in proletarian bliss for the past two years."

"I don't even know what you're talking about."

"I'm sure you don't," I spat, going outside to sit on the porch. I buried my face in the nearest available dog.

In a little while he came out. He was wearing a black tuxedo jacket and a battered fedora. He had a contraption made out of a seat belt to hold up his pants. "Okay," he said. "I'm ready. Let's go."

I headed out to the northern city limits. I could tell he was trying to talk. "What," I said.

"I need some money for the trip. I don't have enough to get there."

"Oh yeah?" I answered warily. "How much?"

"About fifty would be good."

"Well, let me see." I stuck my hand into my purse and opened my wallet. There was a wad of bills. I had just cashed my check.

I pulled out a five. "Here I can give you this."

He looked. Then he took it.

"You could at least say thank you."

He smashed his fist into the dashboard.

By then the sun was gone. The road was dark. I pulled over and stopped the car in the emergency lane. A ray of neon cut across his cheek.

"I hope you get good rides," I said.

"I hope I get run over."

My voice was broken. I covered my face.

Then we looked at each other through our hair and our glasses. Everything dissolved in between.

I wanted him completely inside me.

I wanted him to totally disappear.

W. Joe Hoppe

Miles to Go
(February in Austin)

Fat drops of rain
staccato the windshield
Water freezes at thirty-two
degrees Fahrenheit
It's forty degrees now
Night's coming on

The radio station
turns from news to
Miles Davis sketching Spain
his horn is warm
I pull my knit cap
over my ears
crank up the heater
roll down the window

W. Joe Hoppe

Junkyard Thaw

This would be spring
in Michigan
earth gone to mud
with a slim skin of ice
flecks of snow
that would be in the shadows
if there were sun enough to make any

But I'm here in Austin
after they've opened schools
and roads back up
from four days of ice
below freezing and nobody
knew how to act

Today's adventure
finds me at the junkyard
where icicles give car grilles
vicious fangs
ice glazes dented fenders
windshields and windows
sliding off occasionally
for weak mimicking
of a real glass crash

The air is thawing moist
misting down
and it's just like back home
though the cars are not so rusty

I'm searching
for a simple piece of chrome
an 8 nestled in a V
to complete a 3-D Valentine
hot rod heart to be auctioned off
benefiting an art gallery downtown
"Baby—you've got my heart
banging on all eight cylinders"

is the idea
distributor cap and wires
and sparkplugs and flame
decals, too
a V-8 would top it right off

But the cars here are too young
to proclaim a mighty V-8 heart
a few minivans admit to V-6s
but the Cadillacs and the Oldsmobiles
even the Camaros and Firebirds
all play it subtle

My only luck is with the Fords
—the company that made eight cylinders
affordable for all—
a Triton V-8 badge on a pick-up
a rectangle V-8 shy on a T-bird

I pry the badges off
with a skinny screwdriver
careful
because they aren't even metal
just plastic brittle
and flaking
like the ice
off of everything

Back inside the office
mud stomped off my boots
orange space heaters roar
wet gloves steam
on hot metal
the guy behind the counter
waves me off

This morning's treasure
comes absolutely free

Lorraine Caputo

para Dora

Ah—
    D-Lady
    dē tejana-Madonna
        swirling
          & shuffling
            around
            through
                the rhythms of the conjunto

Ah—
    D-Lady
    dē tejana-Madonna
        her angelic face
            framed by loose curls
                brushing her shoulders
            & flowing
            bouncing
                on the rhythms of this conjunto

Ah—
    D-Lady
    dē tejana-Madonna
        her heavy-lidded eyes
            ojos de café
        & her smiling mouth
            su boca dulce
        the affection of many lovers' poems

Ah—
    D-Lady
    dē tejana-Madonna
        so graceful
            & poised
        drifts
        twirls
        smiles
            around

through
    the conjunto rhythms of this night
her eyes bright

Lorraine Caputo

Freedom of ...
—a multi-voice poem

I was walking over the bridge
over the Colorado-River-Town-Lake
& heard a brother
tell his companion, yellow-coated
her dark hair under hat

Now this is what you call
freedom of speech
the sun on the water
the ducks
that train over yonder
& people wandering 'round

They leaned against
the green-painted railing
waiting for their friend, back-packed
in a Harley cut-off

Now this is what you call
freedom of speech

His words continued in my mind
making me stop to watch
the train crossing the bridge
in the distance
the green water
rippling
& flowing
carrying a Styrofoam cup away
the white swans, the mallard ducks
fed by a tejana & her children

Now this is what you call
freedom of speech

making me sit down
to write
this poem

Ángel, his wife Josefina
& Butch, his wandering compa
from Mexico
(Missouri)
stop to offer me
today's paper
still wrapped in thirds
with a rubber band

I tell Ángel
You inspired this poem

I never would have thought ...
he says

I wish them
Safe Journeys
Ángel wishes me
Paz

Now that is what you call
freedom of speech

Ricardo Acevedo

Cool

Medicated disorderConcentrated on my own thoughtsOld Snuff containerFound object luminescent finger resinPour on the text, scratching the distressAlways the elements of a hammerPour on the text, scratching the distressThe mysterious aspects of death*OH Dream, Whack the WildOH Dream, Whack the Wild*Blood of red swirl of black historyPreacher juke box talks about cultural resistorsPush pins sins send's trance sistersTransfer of the torch burn gripThe monster man, monster man, monster man, he's got a monster man*OH Dream, Whack the WildOH Dream, Whack the Wild*I Came here this time as a tour guidePlaid pants short of the momentDiscription of OH YEAH rock ball race star From a bar stool where he bobs busy, like a camera, like a camera, lack of camera*OH YEAH ... OH YEAH ...* Click, click, click,

Joy Cole

A Year

Here:
making love with don
eric and i at sunrise trapping a hawk
gathering pomegranates
bathing with krystal
smoking pot in albuquerque
fran and i painting
gambling in las vegas
writing poetry with leta
carol's wedding in sacramento
examining ice crystals in mexico with hal
facing death on a desert in arizona
writing denese's wedding ceremony
putting cosmetics on the beloved dead moliye
sharing the creative daemon with juan
fighting with don
sculpting the sun dancer
getting drunk to drums

Hedwig Gorski

Can't Get Gregory Corso Out 'a My Car

from Liberty Lunch driving Gregory back
to Michael and Niko Wojczyk's.

inside Ford mustang turquoise 1967 six cylinder
on the passenger side, an intelligent creative human being
Gregory, like Al Pacino arrested for burglary.

outside Andy Clausen's
bushy dark eyebrows formidable
more so than the man himself.
A Man so desperate he must have
the smallest penis in the world.
I offered him a lift from the show now
I can't get Gregory Corso out 'a the car.

Sticks like glue to the turquoise vinyl.
Did not want a penis Gregory
despite his poem about a pure soul smelling the bathroom.

I slid out of the aqua naugahyde in front of typical wood frame Austin house university 1980s town
intimate enough
where people left front doors unlocked.
Did you ever live in a town as sweet as that?
Tiptoeing through Clausen children's bedrooms
toward the lighted bathroom
planning for minutes before taking each next step.
Gregory got lonesome
in pulchritudinous night filled with sultry longing.
He followed.

Suddenly free, I peeled away down 5th street
across I-35 freeway
east toward love.

Hedwig Gorski

There's Always Something to Make You Happy

Opposites in pairs get dressed up to go out.
The address is blurred.
Blinking colored lights.
I know people
who have mastered abstraction,
talents for knowing ghost language,
non-linear ideas without tongues.
THIS IS THE PLACE,
a detour into dreamland,
a party of un-monogamous conversation.   Friends pour in
from rhinestone cities,
people showcased in cement.
Block parties downtown spiraling
spiraling with entertainers,   fun like
opium,   winking
collectively:
"There's a paradise you haven't tried."
"There's a paradise you haven't tried."
Couples drinking whisky go dancing.
Tower bells ring as if holy.
Under there, thieves and prowlers
would like the writers to tell   their
histories to strangers.   They think their survival is
noble
but their integrity unused.

Their lies sealed with   impeccable
kisses.
They imagine being attractive
to the ladies who undress for the night.
FLAWLESS IN THE WORLD OF SILHOUETTES.

Her legs massaged by secret
angel eyes, like a racehorse.
The pile of clothes near her bed
looks like a pile of diamonds,
a pile of roses,
so beautiful,
so perfect,

they're going to evaporate
any day now into spirit and bliss.
A pile of racehorses.
A pile of liars.

Spirits charging a lot of money
can tell you:
"There's always something
that can make you happy.
There's always something
that can make you happy."
         Never forget.

My sister
discovered
how to
make
fire
and ice
out of nothing.

Too many friends
have been
litter
on the floor
where
the carpet is melting.

Thom the Worldpoet

i will be a hummingbird

a song with thin wings, slim to the sounds
always in motion, flitting around
even when still, above the ground
i will be a hummingbird

like she who threw a starfish into sea
saving one stranded starfish minority
it starts with the art of one/eternity
begins /one moment @ a time

one step towards an unattainable goal
one line of a well remembered poem
one life/one breath/one planet /one home
it always starts with one ...

so i will be what you cannot see
until every one of us is winged
with alacrity/levity will be suspended
by deep weighted ground gravity

if you hear wings within the wind
look for movements sharpening within
we are all learning new words to sing
i will be a hummingbird!

Thom the Worldpoet

Recycled Reads and Half-Price Books

Dumpster diving behind Half-Price books brings poetic treasures
Chris shows me a BEAT author thrown out by BORDERS when they closed
He rescued that kitten even when the rest of the litter was tossed
Recycled Reads sells used Austin Library books in much the same way
If you examine Half-Price shelves carefully there is a CLEARANCE area
where Ovid and Sophocles vie with cooking and self-help tomes from the 70s
Garage Sales yield contemporary treasures—especially MOVING SALES!
Libraries once loved need be liberated when shelf space becomes non-existent
Most libraries have a FREE MAGAZINES stable outside awaiting your eyes
More sell off old books @ $1 paperback, $2 hard cover—cheapest lovers for your eyes pleasures!
Bibliophiles rejoice when text is valued more than antique status—
when first editions are signed and in well read condition
Books are more than cults—they are doorways to other worlds
and we often return to old texts to re-acquaint ourselves
with the Lawrences and Laings, Orwells, Hesses and Castanedas
we grew to love, and treasured them like gifts of poetry
Rilke, Rumi, Rimbaud ring treasures on our shelves
Until, one day, we must release them
and thereby be released ...

Steve Wilson

Poem for Allen Ginsberg

It is a simple equation. You are
either in or out of the stream.

Check your feet for moss.
Check your shoes for river

mud. If you step into a current,
it is yours. Change your name,

an instant becomes centuries. Moments,
white pebbles. Where are the limits,

then? The children calling after
their father in the fields, his hands

cupped under a drink of water?
One is within or without. Think,

like a fish swimming lazily
into its self. This, or the other.

Susan Bright

Sweet Bird of Revolution

A Golden-fronted Woodpecker
slips his long black beak deep into
water from the yellow flower cup
of a cactus. Gently,
in air empty of clatter, he
stops for a drink,
an ordinary being all dressed up,
zebra coat, sweet faced bird,
soft eyes, earnest soul.

I have seen him,
hour after hour after hour,
bang his head against our telephone pole
banging, banging, tap, tap-ú-
like me, bang, bang, tap, tap
bang, bang, tap, tap—
all day, all day, and the next,
and the next.

There must be nourishment in it,
or a place to nest, regenerate, set
a few eggs in a hole, sleep.
He is trying to collapse
the infrastructure. I
drill holes into the grid,
change the essence.
Our whole lives,
we work at it.

The utility will bring
another pole next week.
The letter carrier brought a card.
They'll be here Tuesday
sweet faced bird
with soft brown eyes.
You'll have to start again,
poke through bitter black pitch,
or find another home.

The aura of a migraine
scatters silver spots
across the way I see.
Today, your golden crown,
red hat full of rhythm,
grey shirt,
long beak, pointy claws
balance just so
above Mimosa bursts.

Soon we will return
to relentless banging.

Today, you bring me such quick
joy I almost stop wondering
if it's worth it.

Gregg Barrios

Confessions of a Counterculture Past

Growing up in the south Texas town of Victoria in the 1950s, my future seemed bleaker than that of the teenagers in *The Last Picture Show* or the nameless young Mexican narrator in John Rechy's *City of Night*.

But the public library and the movies sustained me. Later, military service allowed me to physically escape. As Doug Sahm in his Chicano persona of Doug Saldaña would later lament, "It takes a lot of soul to live in Texas."

My father, a photographer by day, moonlighted as a movie projectionist. My favorite theater was the Tejas-Aztec outdoor twin. My brother and I sat on its outdoor projection tower waiting for the nightly wide-screen Texas sunset's fade to black. Face north, the screen filled with Hollywood noir; turn south and Spanish language comedy with Cantinflas or Tin-Tán flickered brightly.

All those trips to the library paid off when the librarian asked me to review books for the Sunday newspaper. My parents were incredulous. No person of color had ever written for the paper. I was 16 and would receive five dollars a review and all the new books I could carry. Within a year I had reviewed books by J.D. Salinger, John Steinbeck, Grace Metalious (of Peyton Place fame) and Billy Lee Brammer. The review of Brammer's now-classic novel *The Gay Place* came with a graphic of the Governor's Mansion in Austin and a headline that asked, "Is this the gay place?"

When I got out of the service, I enrolled at the University of Texas at Austin. It was the fall of 1964, and I was eager to join what was then a new experiment in university housing, something called College House. In contrast to the dorms, which were still segregated, College House pioneered integrated housing. Men and women, beatniks and sorority members, locals and foreign students, as well as students from diverse ethnic backgrounds, we all lived together.

Later that semester, the University regents voted to integrate the dorms. For some of us, it was a late-in-the-game effort to save face: LBJ had signed the Civil Rights Act of 1964 while his daughter was still living in a segregated dorm. Meanwhile, those of us living in the barracks-style building on Rio Grande imagined ourselves to be taking part in a 20th-century incarnation of Brook Farm, the literary commune where Hawthorne, Emerson, and so many others tried to create an intellectual community in 19th-century Massachusetts.

In 1965 we started a film society, which became Cinema 40. We petitioned for more film courses and the hiring of film teachers for what was then a nascent department that would become today's department of Radio-Television-Film. As a result of our efforts, the University hired New Yorker and *Esquire* film critic Dwight MacDonald. Soon, Rod Whitaker (the novelist Trevanian) joined the ranks to teach filmmaking classes. We held a series of lectures open to the public: William Arrowsmith on Antonioni, Roger Shattuck on the French New Wave (we brought Alain Robbe-Grillet and Godard to the campus), Peter Soderbergh on Hollywood World War II films. (He brought his then 4-year-old son along with him. Now an Oscar-winning director, Steven Soderbergh busied himself coloring his program notes while his father spoke.)

We nearly got busted attempting to screen Jack Smith's polymorphous perverse *Flaming Creatures* at the University Y. When we screened Kenneth Anger's controversial underground film cycle

[Magick Lantern Cycle], critic MacDonald prodded the audience by asking if they had indeed followed the edict in the program notes to drop acid before the screening. When no one raised their hand, MacDonald brought the house down by retorting, "What a bunch of squares. But I forget this is LBJ country."

During Thanksgiving break in 1965, several of us from College House piled into a car and drove practically nonstop to Washington, D.C. for the Vietnam Peace March at the White House and the Washington Monument. We got as far as the Arkansas side of Texarkana when the mother of one of the students in the car—an African American—asked us to leave her son behind. She was worried about what would happen if a carload of ethnically mixed college kids was stopped while driving through the deep South. We honored her request. About some things, we were still realists.

After the rally, I came back to Austin inspired to join SDS [Students for a Democratic Society], while remaining immersed in cultural life as well as cultural politics. In the fall of 1966 there was a new publication in town—*The Rag*, Austin's first underground newspaper. I wrote about film and reviewed new titles from Grove Press—Burroughs and Rechy, Che and Jean Genet. Among the later *Rag* adventures that I remember well was a benefit for the paper, a screening of the Beatles' *Magical Mystery Tour*. We had been led to expect a large share of the gate from three sold-out performances. Instead, an emissary from the Beatles informed us that our share came to less than $100. Incensed, *The Rag* responded with a long commentary. Forget "All You Need is Love," it proclaimed. The Beatles' new mantra was "All You Need is Cash." I wrote a long letter to George but only received a reply full of Maharishi Mahesh mumbo jumbo.

Eventually *The Rag* folded. The Sixties and the "Counterculture" would soon be over. We would be left to fend for ourselves.

Disappointingly, so many stories of Austin and the 1960s are about a place and a time and a movement perceived as all-white and all middle-class. That, of course, was never the whole story. As for me, I had come a long way from Victoria in the 1950s. But clearly not far enough. Armed with my dog-eared copy of John Womack's *Zapata and the Mexican Revolution* and a battered Super 8 movie camera, in late 1969 I moved south to Crystal City, where Chicano students had walked out demanding more representation, Chicano teachers, bilingual education, and classes about our role in American history. La Raza's struggle for civil rights had begun. And I was right where I belonged.

Raúl Salinas

Shame on the Shaman

West of this here freeway …
Far beyond Osten
City limits
cramps my style.

Smilin' rimester screams:
"Ah got a bone to pick wid y'all.
No explotation of the mastodons here, bo-ey,
but a sacred, most
ancestral Bone
to pick wid y'all."

We got a litter "sorta" airy set in town
no cause to get me down
but up it don't
won't, for damn sure
ensure a cure from
puritanical poetics.

Canticles to confused clones
prone to parrot/
garroting in the pro sez,
beating of the baldhead
within the belly of the drum
strummin' 'n hummin'
a git-down tune
by the light of the
artificial moon.

Claustrophobic cabbies
sway
down Eastside alleyways
chasing Cassady & Corso dreams
that scream in the orgiastic nights
of Peter hung
on Ginsberg lungs
amid sights of a long ago
almost never, never-land

where the Real Beat lived
neatly ensconced
in the heart of a
Golden Sardine.
"Will the real Mr. Kaufman
please come to the counter for your
dental plates. The County paid
for these you know, oughta consider yourself lucky."
Pluck his poems out as he sleeps!
weeping for those who never had a poem
unto themselves, and therefore
doomed to gloomy garbage-rummaging
for lost-found poems to call
their own.

The "shaman" sang a song
no sacred Shaman sings.
Shame on the "shaman!"
Sha ... man?
Shah ... mahn?
The man was shammin'.

Raúl Salinas

Letter to Lefty

Say, Man:
Just wanted to let you know
it sure was a drag when you left us.
All those people who never understood.
Good thing someone got popped,
they were jammin' me with the charge.
Made bail
straight from the jail
to the mortuary
to carry
your bones through the stones
to the end of the trail.

Sirens and saxophones wailed
as i sat there thinking
your death sinking in
lives lived lavishly
too soon come to an end
friend, brother, comrade, and confidante
of underdoses / overdoses
of jazz, junk,
yen-shee, O, & mud
ashes of the Phoenix
Arizona pirate's cave
in the middle of the desert.
Rebels without a cause
just 'cause we didn't give a damn.

Hit smack dab in the jibs
Mary Lucas ... ruca loca
in the San Jo
of our cherrypicking youth.
Truth of the matter is ...
Burnt spoons and wet cottons
not soon forgotten
we was close to being grown
by then, man,
when teenage gunsel

gunshots
got you
Blown away!

Andy Clausen

Enough About Me

Enough about me, I am hopeless
    as I should be
Everyone knows hope is a desperate heave
    from the half court line
A phony virtue gestating incapacity
I am getting old, hell, I am old
I get a discount no one asks to see my ID
Hurt, take medicine, try not to talk about it
I'm left cold by a thousand young wiggling buttocks
When the camera close-ups cheer leader legs
    and the panties I go make black coffee
I honestly don't get a vicarious experience hearing
    the voices of the courageous doing what it takes
    to mend a disaster on the 10 o'clock news
I'm not inspired by the unmellow dramas of celebrities & billionaires
    gosh they got troubles too

The masses disillusioned with this enlightenment
All this virtuality they see has charneled faces
    that just get by, whose time is short
    whose destiny is a fathom unknown
The value of human life has become chemistry & numbers
    in a placebo formula that abstracts life & death
Amazing information, astral travel machinery, and yet
The life has trumped A life
Misery is compounded in the eyes that only glimmer
The imaginary no longer sparkles
Prices rise, Labor goes down
Perhaps when they no longer can afford art & music
    they'll make their own
On the Sunny Side of the Street
They can see the brightness, they'll learn from the mustang
    the renegade the outlaw the Beat poets
    who did it for years and the Poor who've done it
    since they been around

Meanwhile all those guns and bitter confused dumbed
    down consumed bodies ready to fix blame

Doing so do the dirty work for peanuts
They are bombarded by the most insidious culture
    ever devised, every product, near every display
    every media diversion, a pick pocket's ploy

When the most sacred becomes a way to amass wealth
When we are told to go shopping
    as a response to Terrorism
We are told the Truth

The masses, are they like the Eloi?
    or the end of the Weimar Republic?
The president moves his speech on why there's not enough jobs
    to not conflict with the first quarter of a football game
The pull is strong, buy something and be happy, just watch
    something far away, go on vacation, say it's all good
Very little warrants trust, very little truth is not
    buried in lies and the bitterness of a job
    reached dead end is not easily smiled away
Nor strong drink, nor the whorehouse of the street
    and Internet cheer the uttered uncertainty
The jokes have punch lines groaning from lack
You'll never get your old job, your old whatsup back.

Lyman Grant

290 West

So I'm driving down 290
west thinking what a day hot bright
dazzling I'm lucky s o b
saying to myself you ought to be
sitting beside me windows down
to hell with the AC today
imagining your beautiful
eyes looking at me little beads
of sweat along the curving line
of your gorgeous lips geez you're hot
I'm hot and I'm saying to myself
everybody's driving around
probably heading off to the pool
or the movies maybe the mall
just so it's cool and it's proper
and all I want to do is step
on it ease it into high take
you with me down 290 west

doesn't even occur to me
it's Thursday you dope these people
are working making cold calls or
picking kids up from mom's day out
doing chores getting stuff for home
this ... even though I'm working too
just stepping out of the office
to buy you a little something
like a card with a poem on it
by someone who knows how to say
the things I'm feeling ... finally
I realize they don't make cards
saying what I'm feeling at least
which is where I was aiming when
I stop in the heat remember
I'm you're married and no one's
cutting out on 290 west

today

Beat Dallas

Did you ever see Big D from high in the airplane night? The city is a jewel; the city is a lovely skyscraper sight. But Dallas, she's a jungle too—to roughly paraphrase Jimmy Dale Gilmore. Dallas is a city where stories of accidents on Central Expressway can be routine tales you hear. It is a city where poverty is met daily walking central city streets or heard as tattered old folk sing hymns on the buses. Ginsberg came to town to read on the radio with Karen X in the wee AM with gunshots in the background. Dallas has money too, as well as an arts district, wonderful writers' organizations, and great museums. Its sister city west, Fort Worth, hates to be mentioned secondarily to the big D. It has artistic venues that Dallas does not have. The original beats stayed overnight with a Dallas bookstore owner friend. Dallas and Fort Worth have long been home to artists and musicians on the fringes making a living by hook or crook. The Metroplex has always burned with its own rhythms of beat.

Allen Ginsberg

Thoughts on a Breath

Cars slide minute down asphalt lanes in front of
      Dallas Hilton Inn
Trees brown bare in December's smog-mist roll up
      to the city's squared towers
beneath electric wire grids trestled toward country water tanks
distanced under cloud streak crossed with fading
      vapor trails.
Majestic in a skirt of human fog, building blocks
      rise at sky edge,
Branches and house roofs march to horizon.

I sat again to complete the cycle, eyes open seeing
      dust motes in the eye screen
like birds over telephone wires, curve of the eyeball
      where Dallas and I meet—
white motel wall of the senses—ear roar
      oil exhaust, snuffle and bone growl
      motors rolling North Central freeway
Energy playing over Concrete, energy
      hymning itself in emptiness—
What've I learned since I sat here four years ago?
In the halls of the head or out thru the halls of the senses,
      same space
Trucks rolling toward Dallas skyscrapers
      or mind thoughts floating thru my head
vanish on a breath—What was it I began
      my meditation on?
Police state, Students, Poetry open tongue,
      anger and fear of Cops,
oil Cops, Rockefeller Cops, Oswald Cops,
      Johnson Cops Nixon Cops
      president Cops
SMU Cops Trustee Cops CIA Cops
      FBI Cops Goon Squads of Dope
Cops busted Stony Burns and sent him to
      Jail 10 years and a day
for less than a joint of Grass, a Citizen
      under republic, under Constitution, of Texas?

We sit here in police state and sigh, knowing
        we're trapped in our bodies,
our fear of No meat, no oil, no money, airplanes
        sex love kisses jobs no
        work
Massive metal bars about, monster machines
        eat us, Controlled by army
        Cops, the Secret Police, our own thoughts!
Punishment! Punish me! Punish me! we scream
        in our hearts, cocks spurting alone
        in our fists!
What thoughts more flowed thru our hearts alone
        in Dallas? Flowed thru our hearts like oil
        thru Hilton's faucets?
Where shall we house our minds, pay
        rent for Selves, how
        protect our bodies
from inflation, starvation, old age, smoking
        Cancer, Coughing Death?
Where get money to buy off the
        skeleton? If we work with Kissinger
Can we buy time, get off on parole? Does
        Rockefeller want Underground
Newspapers printing his subsconscious mind's
        nuclear oil wars?
Will 92nd Armored Division be sent to seize
        Arabia oilfields
as threatened December's *US News &*
        World Report?
What'd we remember that destroyed these armies
        with a breath?
How pay rent & stay in our bodies
        if we don't sell our minds to Samsara?
If we don't join the illusion—that Gas is life—
        How can we in Dallas SMU
look forward to our futures?
        work with our hands
like niggers growing Crops in the field,
        & plow and harvest our own corny
        fate?
Oh Walt Whitman salutations you knew the laborer,
        the sexual intelligent horny handed
        man who lived in Dirt
and fixed the axles of Capitalism, dumbed and
        laughing at hallucinated Secretaries

    Of State!
Oh intellect of body back & Cock whose red neck
        supports the S&M freaks of Government
        police & Fascist Monopolies—
Kissinger bare assed & big buttocked
        with a whip, in leather boots
scrawling on a memo to Chile "No more
        civics lectures please"
When the ambassador complained about Torture
        methods used in the Detention Stadium!
And I ride the planes that Rockefeller gassed
        when he paid off Kissinger!
Stony Burns sits in jail, in a stone cell in
        Huntsville
and breathes his news to solitude.
                            Homage
to the Gurus, Guru om! Thanks to the teachers
        who taught us to breathe,
to watch our minds revolve in emptiness,
        to follow the rise & fall of thoughts,
Illusions big as empires flowering &
        Vanishing on a breath!
Thanks to aged teachers whose wrinkles
        read our minds' newspapers &
        taught us not to Cling to yesterday's
        thoughts,
nor thoughts split seconds ago, but
        let cities vanish on a breath—
Thanks to teachers who showed us behold
        Dust motes in our own eye,
        anger our own hearts,
emptiness of Dallases where we
        sit thinking knitted brows—
Sentient beings are numberless I vow
        to liberate all
Passions unfathomable I vow to
        release them all
Thought forms limitless I vow to
        master all
Awakened space is endless I vow to
        enter it forever.

                Dallas, December 4, 1974

Edwin "Bud" Shrake

[Edwin "Bud" Shrake was a reporter living in Dallas at the time of the Kennedy Assassination. The morning of the assassination, Jack Ruby came to his offices at the *Dallas Morning News* and accused him of having an affair with his headlining stripper, Jada. It was true. Jada is "Jingo" in *Strange Peaches*, and Shrake's alter-ego in the novel is an actor named John Lee, who stars in a TV Western called *Six-Guns Across Texas*. John Lee wears his hair long for the part and keeps it long when he's back in Dallas; he thus looks like a "freak" but can pass as a good old boy because he plays a cowboy. This allows him to travel both in the ultra-conservative world of the rich Dallas oilmen (H. L. Hunt is "Big Earl") as well as in the underground of Jack Ruby's Dallas. In this excerpt from *Strange Peaches*, John Lee is on an airplane with "the Colonel" and talks with him about politics and about the Colonel's daughter, who is a beatnik junky living in Venice, California. The novel is set on the eve of the Kennedy assassination.]

Strange Peaches

We went to the first-class section in the rear of the Electra. With the bag in his lap, Franklin sat beside Gretchen. Billy Bob scurried into a seat beside Jerre across the aisle. That left the Colonel and me to take a double several rows farther back. I had hoped to read or sleep rather than be prisoner to a conversation, but we had scarcely cleared the river on the alarming takeoff from National when I understood that the Colonel definitely intended to talk to me. So I thought, well, Colonel, if you want blabber I'll have to give it to you, and I swallowed another Bennie with the first drink the stewardess brought.

"John Lee, I've never heard you mention politics," the Colonel said.

"I don't care about politics."

He seemed worried and thoughtful. "You're an actor," he said. "Those stories you do on TV are full of politics. The rancher wants to protect his cows and his land from the sheepherders, and so he gets the mayor and the sheriff on his side. That's politics. Suppose the rancher needs more land for raising beef cattle, and he asks his congressman to get the army to chase off the Indians. Politics. If the farmers get together and elect their own mayor and sheriff and run off the rancher and the sheepherders, too, that's politics, John Lee."

"You don't really need to relate everything to Western movie plots," I said. "Besides, in our show we don't fiddle around with politics, we shoot."

"Shooting can also be a political action. In this world you can't exist outside politics," the Colonel said. "You're a natural politician, John Lee. The way you get along with Francis and Little Earl and me one hour, and the next hour get along just as well with some of those left-wing friends of yours, or theatrical people, that's practical politics on a personal level."

"I try to have a good time. You take care of the politics, Colonel."

"I do my damndest," he said.

He looked as if he meant it. Among the things I had begun to understand was that many people mean the grotesque things they say, and think of them as important. Often I used this knowledge to my advantage, and in that respect I suppose I often played with people as a politician does. Of course, to accept their ravings as meaningful made my own life nonsense. It could be comforting at times to assure myself that everything I did was nonsense, but it was not satisfactory to dwell upon.

"Young men like you need to be involved," the Colonel said. "You know the saying—there's no such thing as an innocent bystander."

"I don't believe that's true, Colonel. I'll eat and drink and fool around, and not hurt anybody if I can help it, and when it's over I'll be as dead as you will be after you have connived for a lifetime in politics. It's all out of control, anyhow. Anything that's not a mystery is guesswork."

"If you'll pardon me for saying so, that's a whelp's philosophy. Irresponsible. Men are not angels. They're not very intelligent on the whole. They're not even decent in large numbers. Their thinking has got to be done for them. Their moral positions have to be set. Not to accept this responsibility is as great a crime against mankind as to be a Hitler."

We were finishing our second drinks. Both of us had refused lunch, a rare thing for me to do. I was on the aisle, and I watched the twitching rump of a stewardess going toward the galley. I was wondering how to reply to the Colonel with appropriate sincerity, and whether to ask for a third drink, when a face poked around the edge of the seat in front of me and looked back with a conspiratorial grin.

"Fellow up there said to pass this to you," the face said.

He handed me the flight bag with the bottle neck protruding from it. By the weight, I could tell the two hundred thousand dollars was still inside. With the Colonel holding both glasses, I tipped the bag and poured more drinks. The man in front looked around again.

"Want me to pass it back?" he asked.

"Take a drink yourself," I said.

"What is it?"

"Scotch."

"Never learned to like it."

He took the bag to relay it back to Franklin. I saw it pass above several rows of seats, being handed along in good humor by the passengers. Colonel Burnett allowed himself to smile before settling back with his drink and assuming a serious expression.

"John Lee, I'm terribly worried about Papa Doc," he said.

"Who?"

"I'm afraid they're going to kill him," said the Colonel.

"I didn't catch who you're talking about."

"Papa Doc. Duvalier. I know he's a bastard in the eyes of the world. Many of his own people don't exactly love him. But I don't want him killed. What would become of Haiti?"

"Who gives a damn?"

A small ghost passed across the Colonel's eyes.

"The Republic of Haiti has four million people," he said. "It may be true that under the rule of Dr. Duvalier they aren't allowed all the freedoms we spoiled whites are accustomed to. But the Haitians are smiling, gentle people. If our government murders Papa Doc, what will become of the Haitians? Chaos would overwhelm them. Did you realize most of America's baseballs are made in Haiti?"

"Come on, Colonel. I've heard about Haiti. They've cut down the trees and strip mined the hills. The country looks like a bulldozer park. A camera crew I worked with that had been to Port-au-Prince told me the room maids at the hotel dried them after showers and sucked their cocks for tips. How would anarchy hurt those girls?"

"Some people are the same regardless of the system," said the Colonel, smiling and sipping his drink. "If you would suck a person for money, it wouldn't matter to you what grander political schemes your betters might have in mind."

"That girl up there next to Billy Bob might argue about that," I said.

The Colonel looked out the window for a moment, the purple ripples beneath his eyes shivering as if breathed upon. Besides the fact that he could drink a quart of Scotch and still say Washington, what I knew about the Colonel was that he had been born somewhere in New England, had gone to Dartmouth and had won a battlefield promotion to captain in World War II. During the Korean War he was recalled and given a big job in the Quartermaster in Tokyo. By figuring out the procurement of supplies, he wound up involved with sugar, meat, coffee and God-knows-what-else on an incredible scale, and he came to know a number of important people in those areas.

Now he lived alone in an apartment building occupied mostly by upper-level civil servants. His ex-wife had married a college regent and lived in Denver, and his sixteen-year-old daughter was a heroin addict who lived in a beatnik house around North Beach in SanFrancisco, when she could escape from behind the walls where her father periodically locked her.

"That girl up there next to Billy Bob is not a political theorist," the Colonel said at last. "She is being paid two hundred dollars a day and expenses and is supposed to do what she's told. That doesn't require thinking. "

"So who would kill Papa Doc?" I said.

"Bobby."

"Which Bobby is that?"

"That goddamn Bobby Kennedy."

"I guess he'll slip down there and put a golf tee in Papa Doc's taco."

"With your typical lack of understanding, you are making light of a very sinister man," the Colonel said.

"Well, he's your client."

"Not Dr. Duvalier. I mean Bobby Kennedy is a sinister man. He'll do anything to get what he wants. He has power, too, real power. I don't know how he can be stopped."

"Sounds like you're going to have one dead black rascal down there in Haiti," I said.

"You can hardly blame Papa Doc for what he recently did," said the Colonel. "He put a voodoo curse on the Kennedys. He swears—Baron Samedi will call on them." The Colonel chuckled, "Imagine believing magic will protect you from enemies."

"I've asked them not to kill him," said the Colonel. "I've asked Bobby personally, and I intend to ask Jack personally. I don't think you can trust either one of them, but I have to do what I can. I've told them if they won't kill Papa Doc, I'll promise to have him out of Haiti and into a Swiss villa by this time next year."

"Can you do that?"

"I think so. If I can talk Papa Doc into being scared enough. You know, besides his magic, he's surrounded all the time by mean niggers with guns, and he thinks nobody can get close to him. But they got Trujillo, didn't they?"

I nodded. The Colonel flipped the top of his gold lighter back and forth.

"Bobby can be a very vindictive person," he said. "He's persecuting poor Billy Bob Teagarden out of low-down spite. He wants to hurt Big Earl. Hell, Big Earl gave the Kennedys money! Big Earl likes Catholics! Now Bobby wants to kill Papa Doc, and he wants to kill old Diem over there in Vietnam."

"In Indochina?" I asked.

"That's what it used to be called. Little yellow bald-headed Buddhist sons of bitches, they kneel down out in public and burn theirselfs up with gasoline. What the hell kind of a way is that to act?"

"I worked in a film in Hong Kong, Singapore, Bangkok and Kuala Lumpur. Sure saw a lot of Americans over there."

"If Bobby wants to kill some repressive dictator prick, he ought to shoot Castro," said the Colonel. "That sorry Communist is executing thousands of good people on the Isle of Pines right this minute, and we don't do anything about it!"

"There was the Bay of Pigs," I said.

"Sabotaged from within! Castro is laughing at us. First thing you know, he'll have troops in Mexico."

"We can hold them at the border, Colonel. They'll never get past Laredo, if I know my Cubans."

"Goddamn Castro," the Colonel said bitterly. "Batista might have had failings as a person, but at least he was our friend."

"I guess you lost a few clients in Cuba."

"Good men, too. Damn good men. Big Earl, good Christ, what he lost! One of the finest ranches in this hemisphere! Swarming with Communists now! Come out of every damn thatch-roof shack and mud hut you ever saw, thicker than the cows used to be! Cigars! Good Christ, think of the cigars!" He was flicking the lighter lid madly. "Fine, dark Havana cigars—all gone."

"The Cubans can't smoke them all."

"You can't deal with a sonofabitching Communist." The Colonel had become agitated. He pinched the gold lighter between the thumb and forefinger of his left hand and spun it with his right. When the lighter stopped spinning, I saw that it was engraved "A Gift from Jimmy Hoffa."

"All over this world today they're pushing on us. Pushing, prodding, probing, testing. Indochina, Peru, Honduras. Open terrorism in Venezuela. Stirring up the niggers in Alabama. What's Jack Kennedy doing? Talking about selling wheat to Russia! I ask you, John Lee! His own wife out there in a bathing suit on that damn Greek's yacht, and Jack's coddling the Russians and wanting test-ban treaties. We need a man on horseback to lead this country. I fought and bled! I helped raise the flag. It's goddamn frustrating to see rich boys like the Kennedy brothers giving this country away to the devil. I know this much about Westerns like you're always showing up in, John Lee. If you don't have a tough, horny-looking stranger ride in to save the town from losing its balls, you got no god damn Western anybody will care about!"

Uninterested in politics as I was, this kind of talk nevertheless made me begin to squirm. As opposed to other lobbyists I had encountered, the Colonel dressed with a diplomat's taste—dark blue Savile Row suit, gray silk necktie, an inch of white linen showing at the cuffs. Most lobbyists looked like college football coaches. Billy Bob Teagarden, in his green silk suit and green Argyle socks, with his reddened steam-room face and a manner that was obscene among his own kind and groveling in the presence of little girls and powerful old ladies, could easily have passed for the mayor of Cotulla, Texas, his home-town. Were it not for the odd purple marks beneath his eyes, Colonel Burnett would have looked quite dignified, until he began spinning his gold cigarette lighter and clicking his false teeth.

So I interrupted and asked about his daughter.

"Why do you want to know?" he said.

"I saw her once. She was a nice girl. I wondered if she'd got straight."

"I don't know how much you've heard about her," the Colonel said. "You couldn't really care. But I'll tell you this—she's back out in California with that beatnik trash, sleeping on a mattress on the floor, shooting dope in her arms, smoking marijuana. Probably getting screwed by a different bastard every night. She brought one of them to Washington with her last summer. Some peach! He had a beard and sandals and wore blue jeans and smelled like a wet horse. I said 'kid, let me remind you what happened to Jesus,' and I ran his butt off, I can tell you that. He couldn't leave fast enough. Then the girl lied to the doctors, lied even to me, sat around the house looking at television all the time, and finally she stole a couple hundred dollars from my billfold and took off again. I count myself lucky. This time I don't care if she ever comes back. I care about her about as much as you do."

"Hell of a waste," I said.

"Tragic."

"Think about all those dancing and piano lessons."

The Colonel looked at me as if he had never seen me before. He looked at me two or three times above his glass, all rather rapidly, and then he said, "John Lee, you're kind of a freak."

Did Beatniks Kill John F. Kennedy?

[Testimony of U.S. Secret Service Chief James J. Rowley regarding reports of Secret Service agents drinking at a Fort Worth, Texas "Beatnik" club called The Cellar the night before the assassination. Excerpts from The Warren Commission Hearings, Vol. V, pp. 451-460.]

Mr. Rankin.

    Did you learn in connection with the trip when the assassination occurred that certain of the Secret Service agents had been in the press club and what is called the Cellar, at Fort Worth, the night before?

Mr. Rowley.

    Well, that came to my attention through a broadcast that Mr. Pearson made, that the agents were inebriated the night before at the Fort Worth Press Club. I immediately dispatched Inspector McCann to Fort Worth to investigate the report, and to interview the agents.

Mr. Rankin.

    What did you learn?

Mr. Rowley.

    I learned that there were nine agents involved at the Press Club. And I might say this—the agents on duty throughout that day had no opportunity to eat. When they arrived at Fort Worth, they were informed that there was a buffet to be served at the Fort Worth Club. This is what I ascertained in personal interviews. Upon going over there, they learned there was no buffet, and some of them stayed for a drink. Three, I think, had one scotch, and others had two or three beers. They were in and out—from the time they arrived, I would say roughly around 12:30, until the place closed at 2 o'clock. Now, after that some of them went to the Cellar. This is a place that does not serve alcoholic beverages. They went there primarily, I think, out of curiosity, because this was some kind of a beatnik place where someone gets up and recites, or plays the guitar.

* * *

Mr. Rankin.

    Can you tell the Commission how many men were involved in these trips to the Press Club and the Cellar, where these things were done?

Mr. Rowley.

    There were 9 men involved at the Press Club, and there were 10 men involved at the Cellar.

Mr. Rankin.

    Now, how many men, of those 10 men, were in the Presidential motorcade on the day of the assassination?

Mr. Rowley.

    Four—four men were in the follow-up car.

* * *

The Chairman.

... Chief, it seems to me that on an assignment of that kind, to be alert at all times is one of the necessities of the situation. And I just wonder if you believe that men who did what these men did, being out until early morning hours, doing a little even a small amount of drinking—would be as alert the next day as men should be when they are charged with the tremendous responsibility of protecting the President.

Mr. Rowley.

Well, we checked on that, Mr. Chief Justice, and the agent in charge reported that they were in good physical condition. I don't condone these late hours; no. This is not a rule. This case is an exception. However, because of the activities of any travel such as the Presidents today make from one place to another, to maybe seven States in a weekend, there is constant going. I don't condone this at all. But these men are young. They are of such age that I think that they responded in this instance adequately and sufficiently as anyone could under the circumstances.

The Chairman.

Well, I am thinking of this. As you go along in the motorcade, you have men who are scanning the buildings along the way, don't you?

Mr. Rowley.

Yes, sir.

The Chairman.

... Now, other people, as they went along there, even some people in the crowds, saw a man with a rifle up in this building from which the President was shot. Now, don't you think that if a man went to bed reasonably early, and hadn't been drinking the night before, would be more alert to see those things as a Secret Service agent, than if they stayed up until 3, 4, or 5 o'clock in the morning, going to beatnik joints and doing some drinking along the way?

Mr. Rowley.

If I remember that witness testimony—and that was one of the first statements that he made, that witness was with his wife, and he happened to look up there, and I think he said, "There is a man with a rifle, it is a Secret Service man," and let it go at that. He didn't inform any of the authorities.

The Chairman.

No; nobody did. But I say wouldn't an alert Secret Service man in this motorcade, who is supposed to observe such things, be more likely to observe something of that kind if he was free from any of the results of liquor or lack of sleep than he would otherwise?

Mr. Rowley.

Well, yes; he would be. But then, on the other hand, Mr. Chief Justice, in some instances the men come in from a trip at 1:30 in the morning, which there have been cases on travels that I have made, and have to be up at 3:30 or 4 o'clock, and out in time for a 5 o'clock departure. Then you go all that day until 1 or 2 o'clock the next morning. This is what has happened in the past.

The Chairman.

I am not talking about the past. We are talking about nine men here who were out until rather unusual hours of the morning.

Mr. Rowley.

Yes, sir.

The Chairman.

They were to be on duty the next day. The next day—or if not sooner. The next day they were supposed to be alert to anything that might occur along the line of march. Don't you think that they would have been more alert, sharper, had they not been doing these things?

Mr. Rowley.

Yes, sir; but I don't believe they could have prevented assassination.

The Chairman.

Isn't it a substantial violation of these rules to do a thing of that kind?

Mr. Rowley.

Yes, sir—on the basis of this section here.

The Chairman.

Yes. Now, Chief I noticed, also, in reading some of the reports that three of these men whom you speak of, were actually on night duty, protecting the life of the President. And around 4 o'clock in the morning, when they were protecting him at the Texas Hotel, they said that they had a coffee break, and they went from the hotel over to the beatnik joint. Now, is that consistent with your regulations?

Mr. Rowley.

In this case, I talked to these three agents. They were relieved at different times—because their posts are in the corridor of a stuffy hotel—

The Chairman.

Of the what?

Mr. Rowley.

The corridor that they were on post outside the President's suite was a stuffy one, and they went downstairs to get a breath of fresh air. And they walked—it was a block—and out of curiosity they went into this place. One fellow looked in and left, he didn't buy any coffee. Another fellow went in and felt, I suppose, when he went in that he would buy a cup of coffee. But they were on what we call reliefs, the same as we relieve them around the White House. There are only so many posts, but you have a group of men in one of the rooms of the hotel where they are available, like an alert squad, and relieve everyone on post every half hour. It is a part of the rotation of positions we have.

The Chairman.

Do you have any regulations concerning where they shall remain when they are relieved for this short period of time?

Mr. Rowley.

No, sir.

The Chairman.

They can go any place they want?

Mr. Rowley.

No; not any place. They usually stay within the immediate confines. That is understood. The hotel or the residence.

The Chairman.

Well, they didn't do that here, did they?

Mr. Rowley.

No, sir.

The Chairman.

They went to the beatnik joint.

Mr. Rowley.

Yes, sir.

The Chairman.

Now, is that consistent with their duty?

Mr. Rowley.

No; it is not consistent or inconsistent with their duty. But as they explained to me, they wanted to get a breath of fresh air. If they are at a residence in a remote place, and they want to walk around the area, they might walk maybe a city block or so, which is what they do on a lot of these assignments— particularly in hotels. This was not an air-conditioned hotel.

The Chairman.

It would seem to me that a beatnik joint is a place where queer people of all kinds gather anyway, and that the mere fact that these men did leave their post of duty might be an indication to someone that the President was not being protected, and might leave an opening for them to go there and try to do something.

Mr. Rowley.

They were relieved, Mr. Chief Justice. They didn't leave their post of duty. They would not leave their post of duty until they were relieved by someone.

The Chairman.

As I understood the report, they said they left for a coffee break.

Mr. Rowley.

Well, it is an expression. They left to have coffee, sir.

The Chairman.

Was there any place for coffee in the hotel?

Mr. Rowley.

I think there was a coffee shop in the hotel; yes, sir.

The Chairman.

That was the only place in town, as I understood, from the reports, outside of the beatnik place they could. But they went down to the beatnik place. Did they do that by prearrangement with the other agents?

Mr. Rowley.

No, sir; it was curiosity on their part.

150

Terry Southern

[William S. Burroughs once called Terry Southern "the funniest man on the planet." In fact, Burroughs' most famous book, *Naked Lunch*, owes a clear debt to Southern's darkly comic novel *The Magic Christian* (1958). Southern was born in Alvarado, Texas, and graduated from Sunset High School in Dallas. In Paris in the late 1940s, he became friends with Alexander Trocchi and other Beat-generation associated writers. The following is an excerpt from an essay recounting his experience writing the screenplay for Stanley Kubrick's *Dr. Strangelove: Or How I Learned to Stop Worrying and Love the Bomb* (the subtitle of which was inspired by "Bomb," a poem by Southern's friend Gregory Corso).]

Doctor Strangelove: Outtake: Notes From The War Room

The Corporate, that is to say, studio reasoning about this production affords an insight as to why so many such projects are doomed, creatively speaking, from the get-go. It was their considered judgment that the success of the film *Lolita* resulted solely from the gimmick of Peter Sellers playing several roles.

"What we are dealing with," said Kubrick at our first real talk about the situation, "is film by fiat, film by frenzy." What infuriated him most was that the "brains" of the production company could evaluate the entire film—commercially, aesthetically, morally, whatever—in terms of the tour de force performance of one actor. I was amazed that he handled it as well as he did. "I have come to realize," he explained, "that such crass and grotesque stipulations are the sine qua non of the motion-picture business." And it was in this spirit that he accepted the studio's condition that this film, as yet untitled, "would star Peter Sellers in at least four major roles."

It was thus understandable that Kubrick should practically freak when a telegram from Peter arrived one morning:

Dear Stanley:
I am so very sorry to tell you that I am having serious difficulty with the various roles. Now hear this: there is no way, repeat, no way, I can play the Texas pilot, 'Major King Kong.' I have a complete block against that accent. Letter from Okin [his agent] follows. Please forgive.
Peter S.

For a few days Kubrick had been in the throes of a Herculean effort to give up cigarettes and had forbidden smoking anywhere in the building. Now he immediately summoned his personal secretary and assistant to bring him a pack pronto.

That evening he persuaded me, since I had been raised in Texas, to make a tape of Kong's dialogue, much of which he had already written (his announcement of the bomb targets and his solemn reading of the Survival Kit Contents, etc.). In the days that followed, as scenes in the plane were written I recorded them on tape so that they would be ready for Sellers, if and when he arrived. Kubrick had been on the phone pleading with him ever since receiving the telegram.

* * *

The shooting schedule, which had been devised by Victor Linden and of course Kubrick—who scarcely let as much as a trouser pleat go unsupervised—called for the series of scenes that take place inside a B-52 bomber to be filmed first. Peter Sellers had mastered the tricky Texas twang without untoward incident, and then had completed the first day's shooting of Major Kong's lines in admirable fashion. Kubrick was delighted. The following morning, however, we were met at the door by Victor Linden.

"Bad luck," he said, with a touch of grim relish. "Sellers has taken a fall. Last night, in front of that Indian restaurant in King's Road. You know the one, Stanley, the posh one you detested. Well, he slipped getting out of the car. Rather nasty I'm afraid. Sprain of ankle, perhaps a hairline fracture." The injury was not as serious as everyone had feared it might be. Sellers arrived at the studio shortly after lunch, and worked beautifully through a couple of scenes. Everything seemed fine until we broke for tea and Kubrick remarked in the most offhand manner, "Ace [the co-pilot] is sitting taller than Peter."

Almost immediately, he announced that we would do a run-through of another scene (much further along in the shooting schedule), which required Major Kong to move from the cockpit to the bomb-bay area via two eight-foot ladders. Sellers negotiated the first, but coming down the second, at about the fourth rung from the bottom, one of his legs abruptly buckled, and he tumbled and sprawled, in obvious pain, on the unforgiving bomb-bay floor.

It was Victor Linden who again brought the bad news, the next day, after Sellers had undergone a physical exam in Harley Street. "The completion-bond people," he announced gravely, "know about Peter's injury and the physical demands of the Major Kong role. They say they'll pull out if he plays the part." Once that grim reality had sunk in, Kubrick's response was an extraordinary tribute to Sellers as an actor: "We can't replace him with another actor, we've got to get an authentic character from life, someone whose acting career is secondary—a real-life cowboy." Kubrick, however, had not visited the United States in about fifteen years, and was not familiar with the secondary actors of the day. He asked for my opinion and I immediately suggested big Dan ("Hoss Cartwright") Blocker. He hadn't heard of Blocker, or even—so eccentrically isolated had he become—of the TV show *Bonanza*.

"How *big* a man is he?" Stanley asked.

"Bigger than John Wayne," I said.

We looked up his picture in a copy of The Players' Guide and Stanley decided to go with him without further query. He made arrangements for a script to be delivered to Blocker that afternoon, but a cabled response from Blocker's agent arrived in quick order: "Thanks a lot, but the material is too pinko for Dan. Or anyone else we know for that matter. Regards, Leibman, CMA."

As I recall, this was the first hint that this sort of political interpretation of our work-in-progress might exist. Stanley seemed genuinely surprised and disappointed. Linden, however, was quite resilient. "Pinko ..." he said with a sniff. "Unless I'm quite mistaken, an English talent agency would have used the word 'subversive.'"

Years earlier, while Kubrick was directing the western called *One-Eyed Jacks* (his place was taken by Marlon "Bud" Brando, the producer and star of the film, following an ambiguous contretemps), he'd noticed the authentic qualities of the most natural thesp to come out of the west, an actor with the homey sobriquet of Slim Pickens.

Slim Pickens, born Louis Bert Lindley in Texas in 1919, was an unschooled cowhand who traveled the rodeo circuit from El Paso to Montana, sometimes competing in events, other times performing the dangerous work of rodeo clown—distracting the bulls long enough for injured cowboys to be removed from the arena. At one point, a friend persuaded him to accept work as a stunt rider in westerns. During an open call for *One-Eyed Jacks*, Brando noticed him and cast him in the role of the uncouth deputy sheriff. Except for the occasional stunt work on location, Slim had never been anywhere off the small-town western rodeo circuit, much less outside the U.S. When his agent told him about this remarkable job in England, he asked what he should wear on his trip there. His agent told him to wear whatever he would if he were "going into town to buy a sack of feed"—which meant his Justin boots and wide brimmed Stetson.

"He's in the office with Victor," Stanley said, "and I don't think they can understand each other. Victor said he arrived in costume. Go and see if he's all right. Ask him if his hotel is okay and all that." When I reached the production office, I saw Victor first, his face furrowed in consternation as he perched in the center of his big Eames wingbat. Then I saw Slim Pickens, who was every inch and ounce the size of the Duke, leaning one elbow to the wall, staring out the window.

"This place," I heard him drawl, "would make one helluva good horse pasture ... if there's any water."

"Oh, I believe there's water, all right," Victor was absurdly assuring him when he saw me. "Ah, there you are, dear boy," he said. "This is Mr. Slim Pickens. This is Terry Southern." We shook hands, Slim grinning crazily.

"Howdy," he drawled, as gracious as if he were a heroine in an old western. "Mighty proud to know yuh." I went straight to our little makeshift bar, where I had stashed a quart of Wild Turkey specifically for the occasion, which I was ballpark certain would meet his requirements.

"Do you reckon it's too early for a drink, Slim?" I asked. He guffawed, then shook his head and crinkled his nose, as he always did when about to put someone on. "Wal, you know ah think it was jest this momin' that ah was tryin' to figure out if and when ah ever think it was too early fer a drink, an' damned if ah didn't come up bone dry! Hee-hee-hee!" He cackled his falsetto laugh. "Why hell yes, I'll have a drink with you. Be glad to."

"How about you, Victor?" I asked. His reply was a small explosion of coughs and "hrumphs."

"Actually, it is a bit early for me in point of fact," he spluttered. "I've got all those bloody meetings I poured a couple and handed one to Slim.

"Stanley wanted me to find out if you got settled in at your hotel, Slim, and if everything is all right." Slim had this unusual habit of sometimes prefacing his reply to a question with a small grimace and a wipe of his mouth against the back of his hand, a gesture of modesty or self-deprecation somehow. "Wal," he said, "it's like this ole friend of mine from Oklahoma says: Jest gimme a pair of loose-fittin' shoes, some tight pussy, and a warm place to shit, an' ah'll be all right."

We were occupying three of the big sound stages at Shepperton: one of them for the War Room set, another for the B-52 bomber set and a third that accommodated two smaller sets, General Ripper's office, including its corridor with Coke machine and telephone booth ("If you try any perversion in there, I'll blow your head off"), and the General Turgidson motel-room set. The B-52 set, where we were shooting at the time, consisted of an actual B-52 bomber, or at least its nose and forward fuselage, suspended about fifteen feet above the floor of the stage. They were between takes when I climbed into the cockpit area where they were doing "character shots": individual close-ups of the copilot scrutinizing a *Playboy* centerfold, the navigator practicing his card tricks, the radar operator wistfully reading a letter from home. Short snippets of action meant to establish the crew as legendary boy-next-door types.

Conspicuously absent from the lineup was the bombardier and single black member of the crew, James Earl Jones, or Jimmy, as everyone called him. A classic thespian of high purpose, Jones was about as cultured and scholarly as it is possible for an actor to be, with a voice and presence that were invariably compared to Paul Robeson's.

Kubrick came over to where I was standing, but he remained absorbed in what he called "this obligatory *Our Town* character crap that always seems to come off like a parody of *All Quiet on the Western Front*," a movie that took an outlandish amount of time to focus on the individual behavioral quirks of every man in the regiment. "The only rationale for doing it now," Kubrick said, "is that you're making fun of that historic and corny technique of character delineation." Just as he started to go back to the camera, I saw that his eye was caught by something off the set. "Look at that," he said, "Slim and Jimmy are on a collision course."

Slim was ambling along the apron of the stage toward where Jimmy was sitting by the prop truck absorbed in his script. "Why don't you go down there," Kubrick went on, "and introduce them." It was not so much a question as a very pointed suggestion, perhaps even, it occurred to me, a direct order. I bounded down the scaffolding steps and across the floor of the stage, just in time to intercept Slim in full stride a few feet from where Jimmy was sitting.

"Hold on there, Slim," I said. "I want you to meet another member of the cast." Jimmy got to his feet. "James Earl Jones—Slim Pickens." They shook hands but both continued to look equally puzzled. They had obviously never heard of each other. Somehow I knew the best route to some kind of rapprochement would be through Jones. "Slim has just finished working on a picture with Marlon Brando," I said.

"Oh well," he boomed, "that must have been very interesting indeed ... Yes, I should very much like to hear what it is like to work with the great Mr. Brando."

As if the question were a cue for a well-rehearsed bit of bumpkin business, Slim began to hem and haw, kicking at an imaginary rock on the floor. "Wal," he drawled, his head to one side, "you know ah worked with Bud Brando for right near a full year, an' durin' that time ah never seen him do one thing that wudn't all man an' all white."

When I asked Jimmy about it later, he laughed. His laugh, it must be said, is one of the all-time great laughs. "I was beginning to think," and there were tears in his eyes as he said it, "that I must have imagined it."

Ken Lopez
bookseller extraordinaire

I'll Be Seeing You, Ken Kesey

KESEY, Ken. *Sometimes a Great Notion*. NY: Viking (1964). Kesey's second novel, the presumed first issue, with Viking ship logo on first half-title, in the first issue dust jacket with photo credited to Hank Krangler instead of Hank Kranzler. Inscribed by Kesey with a full-page drawing on the front free endpaper—a drawing of a shelf of books, the titles of which comprise the inscription, above a record player, the music of which is represented and gives the message "I'll be seeing you/ Ken Kesey." The inscription reads as follows: "For Bill & Ann... - / [The following as book titles on a shelf] So/ until/ more/ time or place/ when face to face/ we try one/ other scene/ or what I mean/ is/ when again/ we see/ what then/ ?/ and lock/ our horns/ in trial and/ laff and/ talk .../ [As music] I'll be seeing/ [As knobs on an amplifier]/ YOU/ [signed] Ken Kesey." The image also contains what appears to be a supersonic jet flying over the bookshelf, with the annotation "ROAR" trailing behind it. The recipients were Bill Gilliland and his wife, Ann. Gilliland was a Texas friend of Larry McMurtry, who worked in a bookstore with McMurtry in the early and mid-1960s and who, as a result of his friendship with McMurtry—who was a good friend of Kesey's—hosted Kesey when he came to Dallas in 1964, shortly after the publication of *Sometimes a Great Notion*, to give a reading and talk at the Wellesley College Club Books & Authors luncheon. McMurtry and Kesey had become friends at Stanford University, where they both participated in Wallace Stegner's Writing Workshop, and McMurtry hung out with Kesey at Perry Lane, where an early psychedelic scene flourished, which later moved to La Honda, where the Merry Pranksters were born. McMurtry's Perry Lane time was recounted in his novel *All My Friends Are Going to Be Strangers*. Kesey's talk at the Wellesley College Club was controversial and in some respects famously unsuccessful. He was invited because he was a promising, up-and-coming young author of a critically acclaimed second novel, just recently published; but Kesey was already embarked on the trajectory that would lead him away from the literary life and toward becoming an icon of the counterculture, having recently completed his cross-country trip with the Pranksters in the school bus they called Furthur. Instead of simply giving a reading as everyone expected, Kesey turned the occasion into a piece of performance art, engaging the audience—largely made up of wealthy, rather formal Dallas matrons—in unexpected and provocative ways, tossing rubber balls at them unexpectedly and generally disrupting any sense of decorum that might have prevailed on the occasion. Afterward it was made clear he would never be invited back; it wasn't clear if he would even receive the agreed-upon fee for his speaking, and when he returned home to Gilliland's house he got very stoned, if he wasn't already, and drew the inscription in this book. Gilliland described all this later, and a Dallas newspaper apparently covered the occasion as well. An early, unique inscription by Kesey, roughly contemporary with publication of the book and perhaps the closest thing to a poem that we have seen Kesey write. Probably the best Kesey inscription we've ever encountered.

Pat Littledog

News from El Corazón in the Composing Room

We all know how sleazy street is
it's up in the mornings with too many kids
it's too many men coming in the back door
and not enough time to sweep the floor
it's coffee in the pot and a dirty sugar spoon
it's towels on the floor of a dirty bathroom
and a smell like me and a smell like you
all mixed together in sleazy street stew
sleazy street stew oh sleazy street stew
it smells like me and it smells like you
gimme gimme gimme that sleazy street stew

— especially composed for paula footloose & her 5-piece baby-band

NOW LEO SAYS that of course we will get together again. He calls me on the telephone from seven-eleven parking lots long-distance and says that he loves me and he sends me a hundred dollars a month to keep his name on the mailbox, he in fact spends great parts of his poet-in-the-schools money to drive from galveston to dallas for weekends of love-making and whispered reassurances and barbequed chicken crowded around the little kitchen table with me and the three kids like he is simply a commuting husband and this family is really his. And at first he comes almost every weekend and his hundred-dollar share of the rent comes on the first of the month. But as the fall wears into winter he doesn't come so much, and the money still comes but it's coming later and later, too late to cover the rent, so that by spring I realize that I have got to stop counting on it, the rent is going to have to come from me. Me the sometimes writer. Me the new-born bookstore clerk. And me the mother with the asset of morgani the working son, he does pay his part of the rent, too. And so the household lurches along paying its bills on minimum wage and money that sometimes appears in the mail—homage to love from leo and occasional checks from newspaper accounting offices rewarding me for using my time to write commercially viable articles on choosing melons in the supermarket and growing indoor palms instead of wasting my skills on stories and poems which do not sell.

But life is not grim. I like this upstairs apartment I find myself in. Even with rats in the walls and weeds in the driveway, it has its advantages. There is a room for each of us, and my kids are electronic age kids, so each room has its own kind of electrical noise: second-son playing stereo, daughter playing radio, son-morgani playing electric guitar, him playing the loudest and longest, wanting to be a rock musician so much so he won't have to work at the car wash anymore that he practices his guitar all the time. But the rooms are big and somewhat apart from each other because of a central hall, so it is only at certain peak times of voltage overload that I finally have to let out some kind of yell or scream or politely pointed question /would you please turn it down/ which never stops the mix of noise for good of course, only long enough to give a little quiet time in the evening, a little peace, so my head can come to rest and my thoughts settle down before the sound-level starts building up again.

And then best of all features in this apartment is a white door in my bedroom, a magical device. So the kids can be rocking and rolling, shouting jokes at each other through the walls, they can be rolling the bicycle up the stairs and down the stairs and bringing home friends to play pool on the pool table we found in the alley and placed in second-son's room, and all I have to do is to open this door in my bedroom and step outside. And just like that the lights are out. The electronic noise is far behind me. I am standing on a second-story balcony supported on crumbling colonnades and embraced in the clutch of massive oak branches surrounding the upper part of the house. In the daytime I am in the company of blue jays who soar down through the leaves and squirrels running the branches, and at night I am in the company of stars. And I can sit in my used-to-belong-to-grandmaw rocker out there in the evening and put my feet up on a nail barrel I use for both table and stool and turn my own little radio to the country and western station that none of my kids can stand listening to and smoke a joint. Oh sing it, dolly! Listen to the man play that fiddle! I look down through the tree branches at the cars and bicycles and people passing on the street below who rarely look up long enough to spot me in the leaves—the vietnamese grandmother who comes down the sidewalk every morning with her cluster of children collecting cans, the black man with the twenty braids and red ribbons who rides his bicycle every day, the regular joggers and the dog-walkers, the couples shouting angry words at each other while they walk and the couples with arms around each other, the friday night drunks and the saturday morning whistling mailman—I study them like I study the pigeons who prance and flutter through their various bird rituals along the rooftop of the house next door, composing stories for each one of them and like a benevolent director assigning them roles.

Now in the apartment downstairs lives simon-polli. And when I first take up my observation post on the balcony, I see him coming and going on the walk below me with an array of thin, young and lacquered women on his arm. He is enrolled in the downtown community college with plans for becoming an accountant/male-model & masseur, and he says that the electric guitar playing above his desk keeps him from studying very well. But morgani learns to turn the decibels down when simon-polli knocks a broom handle against the ceiling. I don't like simon-polli too much, I don't like his black pompadour and little twitchy mustache, and I don't like the endless photographs in the simon-polli portfolio he wants to show me with every invitation to his apartment for a beer—simon-polli lounging in a bikini on a broken brick wall, simon-polli dressed in a black gypsy outfit smoldering at the camera-eye, close-ups of simon-polli with his nostrils flared and his pores open. But I do occasionally like to hear his stories. So when he stands in the front yard waving a poorly rolled joint and looking up at me on my balcony perch, I invite him up sometimes to sit with me in the branches. Because simon-polli, see, came from eastern europe somewhere, his earliest photographs he says showed him a skinny kid with a shaved head, symbol of lice control, standing in front of a tent in a refugee camp with his father because when they were released from the concentration camp where his mother died there was no place for what remained of his family to go. He spent five years after the war going from one camp to another, traveling on trains that stopped in towns and villages where constables blocked the doors so that no refugees could get off. Then finally to america with a handful of family jewels which his father parlayed into a decent living selling used cars in chicago. I don't know why simon-polli came to dallas—that is one of the mystery stories he doesn't tell. To go to a community college to study massage? That's what he says.

And simon-polli has a european-sentimental streak at least as strong as that streak in me that keeps my radio tuned to the country-and-western station. His eyes get teary when he talks about his father. He fulminates about the coldness other students exhibit toward him in the college halls. At times he grabs up his guitar and brings it up to the balcony with him and croons out oily love songs from dean martin albums to the passing joggers. One evening he comes with his guitar, full of emotion.

I'm going to be a father again, he says, my four-year-old son is coming from new york to stay with me because his mom doesn't want him anymore.

Well, I didn't even know he had a son or an ex-wife, but I say wow simon, that sounds pretty exciting.

I wrote a song, he says, I'm going to sing it for my son when he gets off the airplane. And then simon starts singin—oh matthew, I love you, you are the sky's blue, you are a bird of a beautiful hue, my son, my matthew—simon-polli singing with his eyes closed his lips pursed up to the moon above the balcony like a jewish coyote.

And then the son does come and he is the most scowling worried and mean little kid I have ever seen. He has thick black eyebrows that meet at a permanent seam between his eyes. But for the sake of good neighbor-relations and in exchange for simon not complaining too much about my own noisy kids, I agree to babysit the son from time to time for free which in fact does make simon very happy, and he invites me to come down anytime I want to and smoke grass with him, his stash box kept full by generous checks from his chicago-father.

So one evening I'm sitting out on my balcony when I see simon-polli coming up the front walk carrying a large over-stuffed chair followed by matthew who is picking up little rocks and throwing them at his father's ankles.

Cut it out! simon is shouting.

No! matthew is shouting back.

When simon sees me on the balcony he calls up. See this great chair? I bought it from this lady down the street who's being evicted. It's okay, it's got some broken springs, she was asking seventy-five but I talked her into taking fifteen.

Sounds like a bargain, I say.

Oh I just felt sorry for her, not that I wanted the chair, he says, although it looks okay, just the springs a little bad.

Matthew lobs another stone.

I said cut it out! simon shouts.

I said no! matthew shouts.

They go on in and there is the sound of whopping and screaming and crying, and I look up the street in the direction the two of them came from to see what is going on. Sure enough, I see daughter standing with some more kids around a pile of stuff along the curb about six houses down. And the sun, I also notice, is almost gone. So I lean across the balcony rail and call down the street for daughter to come home. She comes running, in a minute she's coming out on the balcony. There's a girl with her about the same height, long brown hair like hers, same budding build with almost-boobs making little bumps under her blouse and hips gathered ready to begin making curves.

This is fran, daughter says, she's fourteen, her family's the one that's being evicted.

Hello, fran says, very polite, the same as if daughter had said fran's family owned every house on the block.

Hello, I say, do y'all have a place to sleep tonight?

Fran frowns a little bit. Oh I don't know yet, she says. My mom is trying to call some people. She starts squinting down the sidewalk back at the pile of stuff on the curb. Oh I better go back and see what my little sister is doing.

Well you tell your mom you can sleep on the floor here tonight, I tell her, if nothing else turns up. And I'm thinking that blankets thrown down for them on a bare floor in the apartment of strangers isn't much to offer, they will have to be pretty desperate to accept an offer like that. But then if they don't know where they're staying yet, when it's already dark, then they must all feel pretty scared, pretty bad, and any invitation is better than no prospects of a bed for the night. So daughter and fran run back down the stairs and back down the sidewalk. The streetlamps are on, and I can see a pick-up truck parked along the side of the pile with its door open. There's a black man leaning on the side of it, there's some little kids playing around the pile, and then fran and daughter are there, standing, talking, but too far away for me to get what's going on. I go into the kitchen and start washing the dishes when daughter and fran come back. You need to talk to her mom, daughter says, but they don't know yet where they'll be staying.

So I stop the water and walk down with the two girls. The black man is still leaning on the truck. He is watching two men speaking loud spanish to each other. One is holding up a pair of pants to himself he picked from the pile and he is laughing, and the other is nodding his head up and down like those pants fit him just right, and there is this little blonde woman tottering around the two men on tiny-three-inch spike heels made out of clear plastic and wearing a white nylon skirt like she just got finished drinking daiquiris at some country club pointing her finger emphatically saying put that down! you put that down!

Hey man, put that down, I say while I'm walking up, and when he doesn't, I tap my chest a couple of times and say, a little heart man, a little corazón—CORAZÓN, I say up close to him clenching my fist and shaking it over my heart (this is a chicano charm I learned in el paso, since corazón is something no good mexican man ever wants to be caught short of). Sure enough he puts it down and the two of them snicker, swagger away, saying things I don't try to translate, and the little woman is picking up the pants from the sidewalk and trying to fold them up. I was just telling your daughter, I say to her, that if you didn't have a place to stay you could come stay at our place for the night.

Oh! she's all full of emotion suddenly, shaking my hand. Didn't I tell you? she asks the black man, who has been leaning on the truck in the same position through the whole encounter, the lord provides. And I don't correct her there, we will resort to abstracts like that the rest of the night to cover up our shyness at this strange situation: stranger asks other strangers to move into her house, a city act as strong as street sex, more easily talked about when veiled in euphemism and depersonalized, so that paula isn't really paula but the voice that cried out, the one in need, the little-lost-lamb, so that pat the person came down from her balcony and entered the story as the lord and pushed the wheel of paula's crossed stars and wrote the address down for the next installment of paula's karma.

What are you going to do with all of this stuff? I ask her. She just looks puzzled, looking at all the pile of mattresses and black plastic bags, piles of clothes and shoes and papers already beginning to blow away. So I say maybe you can put it all in my back yard for right now.

The black man suddenly unbends, smiles and says all right, like he's been waiting all this time for just those words. And he starts throwing things into the back of the truck.

I'll go down and get my sons to help, I say, so I trot back to the apartment. Morgani's out, but second-son is there and the two of us walk back to the truck. Paula is running back and forth, up and down the sidewalk, first lifting a bag, putting it down, herding fran and the little sister out of the way, talking in explosive sentence fragments. He stole the television, she says, I'm going to sue him, she says, not suitable, she says, now that's the way he puts it, and look at this! She tucks her chin in at me and points over her shoulder, it took me three days to pack it all up.

Sure enough, I can see that there are lots of things which have been put in black plastic bags and that now are half-dumped, the tops of the bags coming untied. So we all start putting things on the back of the truck, and the black man drives the truck down the block and into our driveway where we unload it, and we do this two or three times until nothing is left on the sidewalk anymore.

So by this time it's about ten o'clock. The black man (whose name is bennie and whose position in paula's story is never quite clear except that his truck has been made an instrument-of-god) wants a joint after we make the last load, and I tell him that I'm out but I'll go ask simon-my-neighbor for one. So I knock on simon's door. Simon's mustache is twitching over the chain latch on the second knock. I stick out my tongue and make a face like I'm all dogged out, which in fact I am.

We've just got finished moving a family upstairs, I tell him.

Oh no, he says, you moved that woman and her kids in with you that got evicted?

She didn't have a place to stay, I tell him, it'll just be for a night or so, until she can figure it all out.

Oh no, he says, I don't mean to sound like a bastard, but I can't take it. She can't move in. There's agencies to take care of people like her. I'm about to go crazy, pat, he says. I'm studying and having to get up early to take matthew to daycare. Shit.

Look, simon, I say, it's just going to be for a little while. Listen, do you have a joint?

Bennie-the-black-man's come up on the porch and is standing right behind me now.

Simon looks over my shoulder significantly, then looks at me again. For you? he asks.

I smile, shrug, guilty as hell suddenly because I'm asking simon for a joint for everyone.

You come down later, he says, I'll give you a joint anytime, but nothing for them.

Does he have any grass? Bennie asks me while simon closes the door.

Not really, I say. Paula comes shuffling up in her little high heel shoes, and we go on upstairs. When we get to the top, there is paula, there is bennie, there is fran the teenage daughter and her little sister, but then there is another baby, too, one I've never seen before, and there is also a german shepherd and a little black puppy. Paula is looking apologetic.

This is cody, she says, pointing to the strange baby boy, dirty faced, in dirty shorts, no more than two years old, slightly smaller than the baby sister.

So okay, I am thinking, there are three children, a woman and two dogs, but this wheel is set in motion now. And they will only be here a few days, they really will not be here very long.

Someone carries up some mattresses from the pile of stuff in the back yard, someone gets sheets, pillows. Then morgani comes in with two joints he's gotten somewhere. So we sit down on paula's mattress and everybody smokes, and we start talking about dallas, whether we want to stay here or not. Bennie the black man says he wants to live in dallas all his life and become a well-respected gangster, morgani says he wants to be a rock musician but maybe somewhere else, and I don't say because I am too busy taking this new landscape in to think of another one, and daughter and fran are already in dreamland falling asleep together on the floor, and cody the little boy-kid is walking around without his pants on, little baby penis peeking out from under round little baby belly, standing in the middle of marijuana talk with a big self-confident baby grin, taking for granted that wherever he is doesn't matter, he owns it all.

OF COURSE I SAY it will only be one or two days, but it won't be just that, it will be one or two weeks or maybe it will be one or two months, even when I am moving the stuff into the back yard, even when I am talking to simon downstairs, I know that saying one or two days is stupid. It is unrealistic. If a single person becomes down and out and gets evicted, then maybe it would only take one or two days to get things straightened out. But a woman with little children is something else again. First, this woman needs some money, she needs either welfare or a job. Then she needs to get herself a place to stay, and then she needs to get some day care for her little kids so that her big kid fran, who is now their all-the-time babysitter, can go to school. Welfare tells her they'll pay her rent for a house, but first she has to get one. Then they will need to inspect it and approve it and file papers on it, all of which takes about six weeks. So she either gets a job and saves her money and pays the rent for that time and the deposit, or she talks a landlord into waiting almost two months for his money. And so where in the meantime can she stay? On the streets, at the salvation army, here with me.

Then there are other problems, there are the problems that made this elaborate system collapse in the first place, paula tells me these other problems in little pieces of sentences that she tumbles out while her eyes roll and her voice goes higher and faster with emotion. Paula is very scattered—she is a woman who has been under heavy fire and is freaking out. So when I ask her a question the answer tends to be so complicated with names and events and history I've never heard of that I quickly lose track of what she is talking about. But she is very angry and when she finds out that I am a writer, she thinks I will be able to tell the world what she is angry about. First, she wants to sue the landlord who kicked her out. She also wants to sue the landlord who kicked her out before that. And then she wants to expose the texas parole board for not letting her old man out. An eight-year-prison term, she says, is too long for burglary. Sometimes she tells me it was a first offense, but sometimes she says he had been a thief, was always a thief, although she hadn't asked him about it, she didn't know it. But these things, she says, that were up in her attic in highland park— the television sets and stereos and what-not which hadn't even been stolen by her old man, he had been framed, of course—they had been stolen by her EX-old man, who was in cahoots with her teenage son by that marriage (fran's brother) who was now in juvenile prison himself, just like her old man, serving time.

This is the way they had it, she tells me as her voice gathers low and intense for a slow build while she's waving a pancake spatula over the skillet and I'm drinking coffee, they had ME in the newspaper as the head of some burglary ring in highland park! ME! And I didn't even know anything about it! Oh, we sold a little tape recorder because it was there, but what could we do! There it all was in the attic! And I told that police officer he was taking an innocent man, we had been framed by my EX-husband, who is a FIEND, he is a DEMON, he is the devil himself, laughing up his sleeve while we're spending time in jail. I even went to jail myself! For five days! She lifts cody the boy-kid up onto the chair by the table. You want some pancakes?

And this ex-husband, she says, you don't know what he is like. He put a rifle down my throat, here I was NUDE, see, and he puts a rifle down my throat and says SUCK-ON-THIS-BITCH! She glares at me with her jaw stuck out like it is him saying it. SUCK ON THIS BITCH! And there I was crawling out the bathroom window NUDE, bloody, because he beat me up—see right here! She shows me some lumps on her head. So I was screaming for help NUDE at the door of some neighbor's.

I'm eating my pancakes, watching her act this all out. There's lots of details I'd like to know that she's leaving out, but she's going too fast to stop her, and I'll hear it all again anyway, she'll tell me over and over SUCK ON THIS BITCH! she'll tell me exactly how he said it, SUCK ON THIS BITCH! until I have the story almost memorized just the way she tells it, with how she gets away left out, with how he got in left out, with what house it happened in left out, just the nude woman against the bathroom tile and the EX-old man with the rifle in her mouth.

SO EVERY MORNING paula gets up, gets herself together, makes breakfast for the babies, and when she leaves she looks great. She is a trim little woman with lots of fluffy blonde hair, who can make herself look like a perfect little doll when she puts on her job-hunting outfit and spends some careful time on her face in front of the bathroom mirror. She always wanted to be a model, she says, but it never quite got off the ground, although she shows me a certificate she once got in 1961 in a miss teenage america contest held in fort worth, and she wants to get enough money sometime to straighten fran's teeth so that the daughter can be given more opportunities to be a model than her mother was. She does have some connections in the movies, her babies could be movie stars, they're so cute, if she could just get hold of this guy she used to know when he first started shooting film, but she thinks he's in California. In the meantime, she throws the i ching several times a day and gets conflicting answers, and goes by all of them, and changes her mind each time about what kind of job she will get or where she will live. She can do secretarial work, and in fact she does get a job, but it only lasts two days, and then she gets another job doing telephone work, but it's at night and she can't work out the transportation, and she gets another job and it lasts for a week but then they lay her off, the cloud of paula's complications always quickly evident to any employer—a woman whose answers to the simplest questions are too complicated, who is already late or missing work the first days of the job because she has no adequate transportation and too many babies at home.

Fran babysits for her mother but she doesn't like it. She's calling her mother at work whenever she can telling paula to talk to the babies on the telephone to make them behave, and the babies like talking to paula but it doesn't make them any better. Although they aren't bad babies, they are simply babies, lively and into everything, and then maybe even livelier and happier than some because whatever problems paula might have, she nevertheless loves her babies and doesn't discipline them much, so they are lively healthy babies who have never been beaten up. And fran has learned child care from her mother. She never hits them, she never hurts them, although she doesn't know what things to do to make them mind, sometimes simply becomes a baby herself laughing and rolling with them on the floor. But then paula calls at five-thirty or six-thirty or seven and says she met a friend or stayed for a drink until rush hour was over and that she'll be home soon, and fran hangs up the telephone and says shit! shit! and smokes cigarettes and yells at the babies and slams doors and drawers until paula comes home.

And then on sundays paula has to decide if she'll take the salvation army bus to huntsville to visit her husband-framed-by-her-ex or take the bus to gainesville the juvenile prison to be with her son. Fran is freaking out from babysitting, she babysits all week and she doesn't want to babysit on the weekends, too, so paula leaves so early in the morning that fran is still asleep and doesn't find out until she wakes up that she is babysitting again. Then whatever time her mother comes in, whether it's five o'clock in the evening or one o'clock at night, she runs out of the house right off, she drives around with the older boys in the neighborhood, she goes to the apartment houses where the older boys live to get high to listen to records to let them feel her up, whatever trade-outs she can do just to get away from the babies for a little while and her mother. Paula yells at her when fran pushes past her heading for whatever is out there—where do you think you're going, young lady? she says.

Fran yells OUT.

Paula yells well you better be home in half an hour!

Then the door slams and paula comes into my room and sits on my bed. Daughter is glum because she can't go with fran. I just don't know what to do with fran, paula says.

Well paula, I say, she's just babysitting too much, she's too young and she's bound to be freaking out.

Well still, paula says, she shouldn't talk to her mother like that.

When paula leaves daughter starts up—why can't I go with fran? she asks me. I'm almost as old as she is, she invited me to go.

Daughter is sitting up in the middle of my bed pouting a little lipstick and blue eye shadow on her face that fran let her use and she's already looking like a young woman, but I don't care I don't care she's not old enough to be in this story fran's beginning to plot out. Look, I tell her, you've seen those gangs of men on the next block hanging out of the windows of low-riders yelling propositions at girls even younger than you, you've seen those old men with their brown bags sitting on the curb in front of the seven-eleven store, you've seen those drop-out boys inside at the video machines whispering about the size of your boobs when you're waiting to pay for your bubble gum, and I squint my eyes and wave my arms like mothers have done for hundreds of years conjuring these images up until daughter finally says all right, all right, even though fran comes in after midnight and she's all right, she hasn't been beaten up, so what's there to worry about?

And sometimes daughter does help fran babysit, she plays with the babies and helps with their baths. And sometimes when I get home from working at the bookstore I tell fran she can go down to the corner and get herself some cigarettes while I look after the babies a little bit. But mostly I don't help, instead of helping I make rules. I mean after all I am the lord, right? I am the lord of the house! So I get home from working at the bookstore all day and I am very tired, and if I have any energy at all I want to spend it talking to my own kids or even doing some of my writing, I don't want to spend it changing diapers and watching little babies beat each other up and cleaning up dog-shit the german shepherd and the little black puppy have laid down. So I say to paula now there shouldn't be any babies up after ten o'clock because me and my kids have got to get to sleep, see. And also I say now paula, having these dogs upstairs has got to stop because the puppy pisses on second son's mattress every chance he gets so you need to make a fence or get a rope or something so that you can keep them out in the back yard. And I say now paula no more babies in my room okay? Because they get into my papers and tear them up. And paula says okay. And I tell the same rules to fran, and fran says okay. But you all know the rule about rules, so I don't help but my rules don't help either and so stew stew stew bubble and brew, dogs shitting on the beds, babies pissing on the kitchen table, stereos, chairs, dishes, everything breaking and nobody knows what to do.

Well simon-downstairs stops daughter in the hall, he tells her to tell me that he is going to call the landlord if I don't throw that family out. A couple of days later he stops fran, he says he is going to call the police if her mother doesn't leave. Then after all that he stops morgani, he says he is going crazy from all the upstairs noise, that he is going to hold me personally responsible if he flunks school. And finally one evening I am getting home from the bookstore just as he is driving up with matthew's scowl peeking over the right side of the dashboard. When I see that we are going to meet on the porch, and just when his eyes begin to narrow but before he can get his words out, I say hi, simon, how's it going? That's a nice shirt you have on, you sure look great in red, you want to send your kid up to play a little bit tonight?

And he says oh! all right! while his eyes are opening up again and his heart is leaping involuntarily like any mother's heart will at the thought of free babysitting. Oh you can't believe what has happened to me, pat, he says while I lean against my door and give him a little allowance of attention, you know I put an ad in the student newspaper for massage by the hour? Well this woman with this incredible voice called! And she asked me if I did massage, like my ad said, and I said yes, and she asked if I would mind coming to her house, and I said not at all, and then she said well, can you pick me up where I work? And I said maybe, it depended where it was that she was working, how much gas it would take, and she said well I work at the playboy club! Can you imagine that, pat? he's shaking his head like he's having a hard time imagining it himself, me massaging a bunny!

Well good luck simon, I say, you send matthew up in his pajamas and he can spend the night.

Thanks, pat, he says, I didn't know exactly what I was going to do with matthew. I wave, and he's fumbling with his door, he can hardly wait to slap on the aftershave and depart, obviously he's not thinking about the noise upstairs, and if he hears any thumps or cries while he's taking his bath and fluffing his chest hair and flexing his fingers, he might think just when he hears it well next time I see that pat I'll say something, I'll give her a piece of my mind, but not tonight, not right now not when I'm so tired of being a mother, and then goes back to the story of his playboy evening already unfolding in his mind.

THE NEXT MORNING is saturday. Paula's told fran she's going to be home this weekend but she's up early with a red bandana around her hair and already down the street in barbie-doll levi's to bring us back donuts from winchell's and a morning newspaper. I hear a knock on the door and think it might be matthew come to get his houseslippers and teddy bear he had left lying on the blanket where he had slept, I had heard him early in the morning before anyone else was up, tiptoeing down the stairs, pounding on his daddy-simon's door and yelling let me in! let me in! mad and worried-sounding like he always sounds until I hear the door open and know that simon did get home after all.

But when I open the door, it isn't matthew, it is a young woman who looks to be still in her teens with a broad country face and yellow hair and a belly about seven months long.

I'm looking for paula knight, she says when I open the door, looking at me like she thinks I'm the one she's looking for.

Well I figure this is more of paula's trouble, so I say what do you need her for?

My name is angela moore, she says, I came all the way from tennessee to talk to the woman who put my husband in jail.

Look, I say into her wide country blue eyes, paula does not live here. She is only staying temporarily until she finds other quarters. I don't know what your business is with her but you're going to have to deal with her somewhere outside of this house.

Is she in right now?

No.

Well, she says swinging her heavy body around, I'm just going to sit on this porch step until she comes.

Now I have no idea how long she's going to be, I say.

Oh I'll just sit here and wait, she says. She's sitting on the front step, her girth spread out around her nesting hen-style taking up all the space between the two porch columns. Unbudgeable. She smiles up at me, heavy with child as they say. So I try, but I can't think of anything to say to her. Not really. So I don't say anything. I go on up the stairs. Fran and daughter and the babies are sitting in the middle of the bed with the television on. I make myself a cup of instant coffee and walk out on the balcony in my houserobe. Blue jays have built a nest within two feet of the rail. One of them is sitting in it. The other one is squawking and dive-bombing the dog from next door. The dog is trotting through the yard with her tail down. I feel sorry for her because she really can't do anything, she can't climb a tree, but then I can relate to the watchful mother bird in the nest worried about the hatching eggs and the father-bird full of paranoia, but then the father-bird relishes his dive-bombing role too much, I think, when he keeps dive-bombing the dog all the way to the end of the block, finally soaring up again through the branches squawking at the mother-bird full of his own glory. I hear some voices from the steps below. It's paula with the donuts talking to angela moore, but I can't hear what they're saying. I sip on my coffee for a while and then go into the house to make some orange juice. Pretty soon paula comes in. She's making her agitated paula sounds like hunh! and whew! and well! like she has been overwhelmed by too much information to spit out in logical sentence forms.

Now who was that? I ask her.

Well! she says. Angela moore! she says. And to think that guy had a wife! she says. Paula is pacing around the little kitchen letting her jaw drop open like there are no words to express her surprise, and I can see that here comes another paula story, and sure enough, she starts telling me another incredible one while I fish a lemon-filled out of the donut bag.

One day she was over on gaston avenue, it was raining and she had just missed her bus. So along comes this guy in a truck, she says, and he asks if I want a ride and I say sure and so I hop in. He asks me where I'm going and I give him the directions. But pretty soon I can see he's not going where I told him to go. So he pulls into an alley and falls on top of me and suddenly he's pulling at my clothes! And I am screaming! So I guess, I don't know, I think he's just nuts, but I guess he gets scared or something, and I'm grabbing at the door handle trying to get out, so he revs the engine up again and takes off. But all the time he's trying to drive and punch me and tear at my clothes all at once, and I'm screaming and he's yelling you cunt! you cunt! And then we're on the freeway and we're going about forty miles an hour and I finally get the door open and jump out—

On the freeway?

She nods solemnly. In the center lane, she says, of north-central expressway, cars coming from everywhere. First I just hang onto the door as much as I can and then I drop off. The car in back of us sees me hanging on the door first and then when I come down onto the pavement he stops and picks me up and takes me to the hospital. And I don't have any broken bones, only pavement burns.

So this angela moore is the truck driver's wife?

Paula nods again. She's mad because I pressed charges. I saw the truck's license plate numbers and the police put him in jail. I mean I'm not a vindictive person, pat, but I think that man needs to be in prison. I mean he is crazy, he could do that to anybody!

Well of course! I say.

But that's not what angela moore is saying. She wants me to drop the charges against him. She says he's not that kind of guy, he was just too lonely being away from her so long. She says I'm ruining her life.

That's ridiculous!

Oh I don't know, paula says. She's sitting down at the table. She's pressing one hand over her eyes. Angela says she'll give me some money.

How much!

Two hundred dollars.

Tell her to go away, I say. I get some eggs out of the refrigerator and scramble them up. Cody-the-baby comes in when he hears the grease popping with half-a-donut still in one hand. He comes tugging on my pants. Paula is quiet, staring out of the kitchen window. The eggs sizzle and simon-polli's voice comes rumbling through the pipes shouting at matthew to take his pants off so that he can be given a bath.

I hate you, matthew shouts!

I hate you too! simon shouts back.

Then there is the sound of crying and simon-polli shouting shut-up! shut-up! while I shovel eggs into a bowl for cody and paula leaves the table to go into the back hall off the kitchen where her mattress is on the floor, shutting the door between the rooms. And cody and I eat the rest of our breakfast to the clicking of paula's i ching coins thrown six times on the other side of the door.

SO IT IS GETTING TO BE close to easter time. And paula is like mother nature herself flitting in and out of the house while her household grows effortlessly around her, the house vibrating with an enthusiasm for its own fecundity which I do not share. Babies come up and down the stairs from all over the neighborhood wanting to play with the two babies at our house. Paula's german shepherd turns out to be pregnant and due to deliver in a matter of weeks. And a blonde girl shows up in morgani's bed, causing him to curtail somewhat the evening practice hours of his guitar, another daughter of paula's a big-boobed teenage girl who's been living with some aunt who wants to kick her out. The phone is always ringing for paula—employment agencies, collection agencies, welfare, foodstamps, the prosecuting attorney's office for depositions, the texas parole board for statements, and angela moore quoting bible passages about mercy and love. Paula says one day hey pat, what do you think about the bunch of us rooming together, after I get a job, then I could start giving you some money for rent, that would help you out. But no no, paula, no deal and no dice no wise and no way baby, I mean even in the bible-story jesus only had to furnish one or two meals at the most out of his baskets of loaves and fishes, the multitude didn't just decide to move in and stay.

Leo is calling long-distance and making plans for coming up from galveston for the holiday. He says is that woman still up there?

I say yes but she's going to be gone pretty soon.

By easter? he says.

I say maybe, but of course I know it probably won't be as soon as that. So after I hang up, I start worrying about leo coming, and I worry that he isn't going to be liking this situation very much at all, since telling him over the telephone that I have been having some house guests doesn't really convey the flavor of the scene. But I figure that I will fix the latch on the bedroom door one of the babies tore off and cook a large turkey, maybe that will be something at least.

So on ash wednesday while I'm on my balcony watching the kids walking home from school, all the chicanos with grey ritual smears on their foreheads, I suddenly notice a man who is standing in the yard looking up at me. Is paula knight up there! he asks.

I say no she's out.

Well when she comes back, he says, tell her roy wants to see her.

And I am thinking oh-oh, oh-oh, is this who I think it is? And sure enough, when paula comes in, and I say that someone named roy came by, she says that's him! That's my EX?

And I say I thought you said he was in california.

Oh no, she says, he came back and he's got an apartment about half a block from here.

I say well how did he know you were here?

But she is vague, she's not sure, or maybe one of the kids told him. Oh and she is worried she is agitated she paces around the apartment telling me about the rifle again, oh he is bound to kill me, she says, you don't know what he's like, he is bound to do me in.

Now paula, I say, don't project, maybe he's in a different mood now, we won't let him in the house, we'll get a peace bond, we'll call the cops.

Oh that's nothing, she says, nothing will stop him! just you wait and see!

166

So that night when everyone's finally asleep and daughter is tucked in beside me, I can't get to sleep myself, I stare at the moonlight coming in through the balcony door, I listen to the wind in the branches outside the window, I look without looking at the darkness hanging between me and the ceiling. Finally I get out of the bed. I stand in the middle of the bedroom in my underwear. I breathe in and breathe out. I make my arms go around in a circle. I make my spine relax. I imagine my arms are going in a circle around the house, making an imaginary line, and I imagine all of us inside of it and roy out. I call out to roy in the name of every power I can think of—in the name of mary and jesus and father peyote and electrical power lines and the rio grande river—making my arms swing out in a large circle ROY ROY ROY ROY DON'T YOU CROSS THIS POWER LINE. Then for a few minutes I stand and don't think of anything, just listen to the sound of all the babies and children and animals in the house breathing in and out.

So the next day after paula comes home from the temporary secretary's job she has been working, she asks me if roy can come over for supper.

You've got to be kidding, I say.

Well he's feeling better, she says. You told me to be calm, so I was calm and we had a drink together, and he's feeling better.

Not a chance, I say.

But he's missing fran, he wants to see her.

No way.

Not even so that fran can see her father?

Tell him to meet her somewhere, not here. Look, I say, you've spent the past several weeks letting me know what a terror this man is and I can't change my mind that fast.

Oh, it's just roy, she says, that's just the way he is.

Well look, paula, I finally say, you tell roy I said there is a line drawn at the first step up the stairs, and I do not want him to cross it. And I tell her this in such a way that she doesn't ask me what kind of line, she knows that I did draw a line and that whether or not she can see it herself she can be sure it is there. So tears come to her eyes, but she goes to her room and throws another i ching and then starts running bathwater for the babies.

I come home from the bookstore on good friday an hour early so that I can do a little cleaning before leo is supposed to come in. Roy is sitting on the porch in one of simon-polli's lawn chairs with fran sitting on the wooden arm talking to him. Roy has on a palm-tree shirt and pressed slacks, his hair is slicked back and his face is still pink from a close shave like he has worked hard to be clean for this visit, and when I walk up on the porch he leaps up standing first on one foot then on another with his hands deep in both pockets.

Well hey, he says, smiling at me, thanks a lot for what you're doing for paula, for my family—but his eyes are everywhere except on me, up and down and over my shoulder, and I think oh-boy he is indeed a squirrelly one, and I don't smile, well really, I say, it's just between me and paula. Then I walk past him as stiff as if I am encased in clacking armor and step over the invisible line at the front step like it is a foot high.

The apartment is rocking upstairs like a john cage concert every dial turned to ten in every room punctuated by shouts and crying buzzing voices.

Get out of here! I yell out randomly. Everyone get out of here for a while!

Second-son comes out of his room and thumps the bicycle downstairs, morgani and paula's stray sex-kitten daughter come out of morgani's bedroom with their faces flushed and their arms around each other, I give the babies a little push down the stairs, go play with fran on the porch for a little while, daughter asks if she can eat supper down the street with a friend and skips down every other stair when I say yes. I start sweeping and picking up my dirty clothes. In a little while fran comes upstairs, but I don't say anything to her. Then she goes back down the stairs again with two glasses of water. Pretty soon I hear paula's laugh outside, too, and fran comes upstairs and goes down with another glass. I begin to make up the bed. The apartment is quiet and the voices on the porch seem far away. I run bathwater, lie underneath the soap bubble surface and listen to the sudden quiet which has settled on the house. My flowered robe leo bought for me in laredo is hanging on a peg on the back of the door, and when I get out of the tub and towel off, I put it on. When I open the bathroom door, there is only slight light in the hallway, the last of the sunset coming through the doorpanes downstairs. Even the voices from the porch are gone and I feel quiet—a few minutes when I am completely alone. But just as I start from the bathroom to my room, I hear the downstairs door click open and I pause on the landing. I peer down the dark stairwell ready for anything and flick up the hall light. A beard and a broad-brimmed hat peek around the downstairs door—leo! Hello baby! he says.

NOW I TELL YOU THE TRUTH, when leo comes home from galveston after him being gone so long, I just want to fuck him that's all I want to do, I want to screw-with-him, I want to love him, lie on top of him, lie underneath him or lie right beside him, and I want to lick him, I want to kiss him everywhere, it's a truth whether it's evil or good, it's all I want to do. And if I had my way I would fuck leo outside under every bush and in every creek and vacant lot and flower bed along swiss avenue and howl like a banshee. But I am civilized and leo is civilized and so we simply go into this quiet bedroom alone together for the first time in a month and put the latch on the door and take our clothes off and get into bed and fit ourselves into one connected self as quickly as possible. So we start wrestling around in the bed together and kissing and me moaning in leo's ear and leo saying unintelligible things when someone tries to open the latched door.

I've gone to bed, I yell out, leo's here and he's going to sleep, too.

It's daughter. She knows what I mean. Oh, she says. Okay.

You can get yourself ready for bed can't you?

She says yes and goes away from the door. Leo starts tentatively pushing up and down again and I push back but it's not quite so much fun. And every time leo pushes up and down the noise level outside the door grows a little more. Lights come on in the hallway. Music comes on.

Finally leo stops. What's that? he says.

What's what? I ask listening with him to the footsteps up the hallway and one of the babies crying, paula talking to fran, fran shouting at paula, second-son switching his stereo back on, simon-polli's television up from the floorboards and outside the bedroom window above our heads of course the cooing of pigeons nesting on the roof of the house next door.

What's all that noise? leo asks as we listen together lying in each other's arms as the house turns up the amps to higher and higher levels.

Oh, I say, that's just the kids coming home.

Well leo's visit goes downhill from there. The babies are crying before the sun comes up in the morning. The telephone rings constantly. Second-son and morgani won't talk very much to leo, daughter talks too much, simon-polli calls up and talks to leo over half an hour telling him the worst all the worst news of what is going on upstairs in that apartment which still has leo's name on the door, and babies in their worst and most crying moods. Egg dye, green cellophane grass, bunnie chocolate bits, egg crumbs and handel's messiah blasting out frank zappa on the stereo. Easter morning and paula is awake before the sun rises making dressing with the turkey already in the oven.

When I come into the kitchen she says see? There's going to be enough for all of us!

And I say who's all of us?

And she says can't roy come up? Just for today?

And I say no.

Even though I'm cooking the turkey?

She starts crying. Leo comes in. Paula runs out.

There's a friend of paula's at the door, leo says. I told him he could wait for her inside.

I walk past leo to go see if it is who I think it is. When I see him sure enough in the hall—over the invisible line!—I stop and glare. Roy you'd better go on out I say.

I just wanted to use the phone.

I don't even say no, I just shake my head. He goes out. But I am suddenly confused. There is a line for roy but leo is in the house. Why am I refusing to have dinner with paula and her ex-old man? And if I have three children and an ex-old man, too, and then if I have leo and some fun with leo, then why can't paula have some fun on easter too? And then it is easter after all! the truce of spring! And why all these rules? But in the middle of the fog I remember it's because of the rent—because paula doesn't pay it, although she has wanted to, but I don't want her to, I just don't. And then the utilities, too, I gather up all the money and pay the utilities, too, I write the checks myself, and I name off the utilities one at a time— gas, electric, water and telephone—like saying a line of beads in a rosary, until the confusion clears and I can move again out of the empty hall.

Leo doesn't want to eat easter dinner in the apartment, so we make a big sack of food, and second-son, morgani, daughter, leo and I carry all the stuff downstairs to load it in the truck. And we do have a good meal at the park and lie in the grass listening to an outdoor band, and then we head back home. Outside on the porch roy is sitting on the lawnchair with a big piece of turkey paula brought down for him, and angela moore has come and she is sitting on the steps talking to paula looking ripe as a two-month nesting egg, and the babies are scooting and squealing around roy's legs. We walk through them and say something about easter and the weather. And I think well it is a pleasant day, they are making happy sounds, leo has had a good time after all, he hasn't said anything one way or another. But when we get upstairs leo shuts the door to the bedroom and explodes.

Didn't you tell me once, he says, that the trouble with your first marriage was that you were always inviting people to live with you? Didn't you say that one of the reasons the marriage fell through was because of that?

Well, I tell him, it wasn't the reason why that marriage fell through—

You'd better get that woman out of here, leo says, she'd better be out of here by the end of the month or I'm not going to pay my part of the rent anymore.

Oh she's going to be out the first of the month ...

I mean it, pat, he says, the idea! you moving all these people in while I'm away!

Well at least it keeps me from getting lonely, I say.

But leo doesn't think that's a bit funny, he's packing up. He kisses me good-bye but he is very angry. Happy risen christ getting the hell out of here hitting the road again to single-man heaven.

So leo is gone. He hasn't even stayed long enough to leave his smell on my sheets. Squashed eggs in the hall. Even my used-to-belong-to-grandmaw rocker has come loose at one of its legs so that when I sit out on my balcony watching leo back out of the driveway, I sit half-sliding out of the seat. And I think leo shouldn't have tried to threaten me, it doesn't matter whether I have his money for the rent or not. But I don't blame him, I want this paula story to end myself, I don't want to be around when the husband gets out of prison and finds the ex-husband on the front porch or when fran finally finds what she's looking for when it's stuck up her body, I don't want to hear what happened this time on paula's way to work, I don't want to walk through the house anymore through broken toys and stereo-sets and spilled milk and dog piss and I don't want to deliver any half-german shepherd puppies! And why should leo finally take his name off the mailbox because of this whim of mine to come down from the balcony one evening dressed in god-clothes forgetting to bring a change of costume? And why can't I be the salvation army? Why doesn't anyone ever listen to MY rules? Why do the goddamn babies keep coming into my room and painting themselves with liquid paper? And I sit and brood watching the nesting pigeons under the eaves of the other roof. I mean, how can they sit there so long when the sky is blue, how do they know when to give up if the eggs aren't hatching?

AND THEN ONE DAY just like in the old movies the news finally comes, the dust of the rescue squad appears on the horizon, the sun comes through the clouds, the late chicks hatch out of their eggs late for easter but still in time for life, and paula has gotten herself a house.

Paula has gotten herself a house! Somehow in the midst of dealing with babies and dogs and checking out want ads and showing up for various jobs, and getting fired and getting hired and going for drinks with friends when the going got too heavy, and trying to find where fran is going at night and trying to keep roy out of the house and visiting two prisons in two different towns every week, paula has managed to find a house, paula has managed to find a house, paula has done all of that. With a little bit of help— angela moore is going to share the rent. Roy is going to live in the garage until the husband gets paroled. Whatever. Still, paula is on her way out.

And the night paula comes home with the news is the night simon-polli comes to deal with me straight out. He's squinching his forehead up and shoveling his moustache up his nose trying to look his most pitiful. I'm going crazy, he says, I stopped at a stop light this morning and put my head on my arms, pat, and I just cried—I just cried!

Well simon (I pat him on the back) you don't have to worry anymore—paula has gotten herself a house! Pretty soon she's going to be moving out!

He looks a little stunned, a little confused when I say that. But then he slumps down again. Oh it's not just paula, he says, it's my son, he's so hateful, I tell him to do things and all he says is no. And my friends won't have anything to do with me anymore because they're all single and I have this son.

Well still, simon, I say trying to cheer him up, not everybody gets to massage playboy bunnies—

His face crumbles with pain. Oh pat, he says, it was just a joke! There wasn't any playboy bunny! I went to pick her up and gave her name at the desk and there was nobody like that working there!

You want to smoke a joint? I ask him.

You got one?

Sure, I say. I take him out on the balcony where a light breeze has begun to come in through the branches and we light up.

It'll get better, I tell him.

How's that?

It just will, I say. Behind us I can hear simon's son laughing with cody-the-baby over something, but with the door closed I can't hear what they're talking about. We pass the joint back and forth for a while, and then we just sit on our balcony perch watching out through the leaves at the street traffic passing, listening to the cooing and chortling coming from the eaves of the rooftop next door, simon and me quiet, for tonight letting the pigeons have the last word.

Echoes and Reverberations:
Allen Ginsberg's East Dallas Drive-By

Driving through East Dallas the other day I had the odd impulse to swing by the old KNON studio. Kind of depressing to see an empty lot taking up that space now.

The studio was formerly located upstairs in a wooden 50's-era two-story house at the corner of Carroll Ave. and San Jacinto Street. The Dallas chapter of ACORN inhabited the downstairs portion of the building. Bearded hippies wearing panchos and sandals had keys to the place. Climbing up the patchwork stairs was like ascending to a teenager's secret tree house. The house on San Jacinto was kinda like a freak Alamo; the last stand for the ghetto underground in Dallas.

It was a rough neighborhood back then. Warring territorial drug gangs pulled brazen drive-by shootings in broad daylight. Hookers did biz in the driveway and Jamaican pimps rolled blunts on the hoods of the cars in the back yard. Vatos and Rastas ruled the roost; I was but a mere suburban visitor on a weekly three-hour pass.

My radio show came on in the middle of the night, so I was literally taking my life into my own hands every time I carried my records back and forth to the car.

"Life Is Hard" was just that—the sound of bad people doing terrible things. Whether it was Slayer, Eazy E, Peter Tosh or the Butthole Surfers, the show could have just as easily been called "High Anxiety." My rabid fan base was well into the dozens.

Most nights, I was pretty much on my own; that meant I was the only one in the building. Most of the time I would have the monitors cranked up so loud in the control booth I couldn't hear what was going on downstairs. No central heating or air at this house, either; just an old window unit upstairs and a tiny space heater under the console.

That night the air conditioner went out and it was just burning up in the booth. I pulled the broken unit out so there would at least be some air coming through the lone window that looked out over San Jacinto Street. You could hear the cars driving by in the background as I back-announced song titles and band names.

The request line buzzed and I picked up. A female voice on the other end inquired if she could bring "Mr. Ginsberg" up to the station to "go through his books." For some reason or another, I got the impression she was talking about KNON's accountant.

As a culturally retarded 23 year old, I had never heard of the legendary '60s Beat poet Allen Ginsberg.

That woman on the other end of the line was longtime Dallas poet, author and frequent WordSpace Dallas performer Karen X. Minzer.

I'll let her explain how we all hooked up.

"Allen was in town for the SMU Literary Festival," Karen recalls. "And someone asked us—I can't remember if it was a student, professor or punk devotee of his, if Allen would be willing to read on our community radio station ... and then suggested Jeff Liles' program. Allen never turned away a gig that represented a 'happening,' and they said KNON was the real voice of the people, so I convinced Allen it would be cool."

Improvisation was an everyday thing at KNON back in the day. Bringin' it by wingin' it. This night was certainly no exception.

Ginsberg was also here recording selections from his album *The Lion For Real* for Island Records during that week. After the SMU performance was over, it was time for their entourage to head for the ghetto radio station.

More key backstory from Karen X: "His reading at SMU that night was magnificent and moving. Allen, Michael Minzer and I had also been generously wined and dined by the inner circle of the academics there. So we then drove over to the KNON studio, tired and still dressed from some 'professor party' (those professors can be pretty wild!), and we knocked and knocked until somebody finally came to the door. Jeff didn't seem very appreciative that we had even gone to the trouble to be there."

As the Lit pack piled through the front door, Karen glared at me and then set the tone for the next few minutes.

"How could you just leave us standing out there for so long?" she said impatiently.

Of course, she had a point; they looked rich and important, and it was the middle of the night in the heart of the 'hood. In my macho-oblivious bliss I had no idea that they were even outside trying to get in. It could have turned out bad. I had the Beastie Boys' first album cranked up so loud in the control room that I didn't even hear them knockin'.

I apologized and headed back upstairs to pick a new record.

I figured they were heading into the office to go sort through some bills and paperwork. When they came into the control room and started getting comfortable, I started to wonder what in the world was up. Why was this woman staring at me? What was that old guy doing with all of those notebooks in his backpack?

"Can I get you anything?" I asked Karen. "Do you need me to let you into the office?"

She wasn't tryin' to hear all that. Apparently she and I had some unfinished business that I wasn't aware of.

"I knew Jeff's name from Theatre Gallery, where I'd been beaten up while performing on stage a few weeks prior to that," Minzer remembers. "And I thought, 'Oh, maybe he'll apologize.' But maybe he didn't know. People getting beaten at rowdy punk scenes isn't exactly Breaking News; except that it was me, baby."

It was impossible to keep track of everything that happened at Theatre Gallery in those days. Her performance art had apparently inspired some sort of unpleasant audience reaction.

"Those were the days of my contact-improvisational spoken word and movement pieces (translated: obnoxious and confrontational presentation). Problem was, when I went back on stage that night, the band that had performed before me began beating me up. It was a pretty humiliating experience."

I had no idea what she was even talking about that night; I was just trying to pick records and do my DJ thing.

"Are you ever going to let him read?" she asked impatiently.

Me: "Who?"

Her: "Allen."

Me: "Who is Allen?"

She nodded towards the old guy in the corner going through all of the notebooks.

Me: "He is reading. He doesn't need my permission to do that."

Her: "On the air, you idiot!"

What was she talking about? Why would our accountant read our "accounts payable" over the air during my radio show?

From the Minzer account: "Liles, the blonde dreadlocked DJ on duty, wasn't open to discussing it when I brought it up, nor did he even acknowledge Allen! I began to get a little impatient waiting for Allen to finally go on the air. We were actually supposed to be somewhere else official and this fool DJ at KNON was making us wait and totally completely ignoring us the whole time."

Chalk it up to blissful ignorance and a head full of boo.

Karen pulled me aside and let me have it: "Jeffrey, this is Allen Ginsberg, the WORLD FAMOUS POET. He is here to read some of his work on the radio. Would you please be so kind as to let him bless your show with his work?"

Me: "Yeah, well, if you put it like that, sure."

Ginsberg sat down directly across from me and pulled up the other microphone. I had no idea what he was going to do or say. He got about 10 seconds into his first piece when he was interrupted by an unmistakable sound in the background.

POP. Bang. POP POP POP. Bang. Bang. POP.

The sound of East Dallas Gangsters playing "Gunsmoke" was indelibly audible through the open window of the control room.

When the shooting finally subsided, there was about a three second pause, and then Ginsberg said, "Shall I continue?"

Me: "Uh, sure. Welcome to East Dallas."

Allen continued his piece, read a couple of other shorter poems, and then called it a night. On his way out the door, he reached out to embrace me. I didn't really expect that sort of thing after what we had just been through.

"On the way out of the studio that night, I was holding Allen's hand, when he leaned over to kiss Jeff in the traditional 'Beat Poet' inner-circle acknowledgment," Karen says.

"Jeff recoiled and sort of pushed him away, his body language was very obvious. I was just like, so insulted, I can't even tell you how I had to restrain myself."

Karen X hated me for years after that night.

"I mean fuck this homophobic, full-of-himself, unappreciative, you-gotta-be-kidding-me disrespectful asshole," writes Minzer. "And that's how I felt for a long time. I was mad about it for so long that years later, at Roxy and Judy Gordon's house one night, I threw a jar that I was drinking out of at him!"

No one disputes that I probably deserved it. Over the years Karen and I eventually buried the hatchet and became friends. Thankfully, we can all laugh about this now.

Fast forward to a decade later: It was June of 1996 and it was hot as fuck in New York City.

Cottonmouth, Texas was booked as the opening act for Tripping Daisy and The Figgs at Brownie's on the Lower East Side. TD drummer Mitch Marine and I had made plans to go grab something to eat at an Indian restaurant on St. Marks Place before the show.

As fate would have it, I was a writer and spoken word performer myself at this point now, and these shows were my first weekend gigs in Manhattan. Of course, by this time, I was fully aware of Allen Ginsberg and his enormous contribution to the American literary landscape. One can only remain an oblivious idiot for so long.

As I sat on the front stoop of Brownie's and waited for Tripping Daisy to finish their sound check that night, I saw a familiar figure coming towards me on the sidewalk. It was Allen, flanked by his longtime male companion on one side, and a younger female assistant on the other.

They stepped closer and closer in my direction. Somehow I screwed up the courage to stand up and ask Mr. Ginsberg if he still remembered his bizarre visit to my radio show in Dallas.

With maybe three seconds hesitation, he looked into my eyes, put his arms around my neck, then said, "Oh, of course you beautiful boy. You never forget the first time someone opens fire with an automatic weapon during one of your poems."

Allen Ginsberg passed away a few months later. At least our odd personal journey had come full circle beforehand.

Karen X Minzer with Allen Ginsberg

This is What You Need

The needy needy need so much!
They need beds in homes instead of sleeping on park
      stones.
They need their rose-covered metropolitan homes
      relocated outside Indochinese-Middle Eastern war
      zones.
They need to keep his rain from flooding their soybeans
      and barley grains.
They need to get refrigerators, old Fords, new Jaguars
      running again!
They needn't leaders abusing Nigerian, Hassids,
      Palestinians and their shoeless children.
They need their civil rights proclaimed by Klansmen in
      rural and industrial suburban prejudice dens.
They need old friends to come back to life, share old
      strife.
They now need new friends, husbands or wives.
They need a first chance at fish in the marketplace now
      and then.
In their neediness they are tearful with shame,
      defamed, near their skimpy tents.
In humiliation they are terrified of the police down the
      cobbled street.
In terror, some emerge terrorist and riddle mankind and
      airplanes with shrapnel of their feelings in order to
      complain.
Smoking hashish, they hate us.
Smoking hashish, I HATE that!
And in hatred, I appeal to you sexually to get down to
      your knees.
Sex is needed, the cosmetics tray rattles constantly.
Sex needn't be tragic, but hunger pinches stomach and
      panics the brain.
Who'll serve the world soup, who can?
These people are under grass and sand.
Even if I didn't remember them in their Palestinian,
      Mexican, Ugandan, Ethiopian hovels, they died,
      fevered.
Yesterday I couldn't get this name off my mind, "Chris

Isherwood."
Never heard of him before. Next day New York Times
     says,
     "CHRIS ISHERWOOD DEAD."

Karen X Minzer

Dharma Broad

Music of a thought stirring
Music of the bowels churning
Chirpy beats of eyelids blinking
Synthesized hum of the blood in my veins
and up the chakras with the grrrrraahhuhhhaaaahhheeeeiiiiiii of my truth

I need a backup band for this random rant
Get me going like an Indian drum machine raving!

Music made me pregnant.
Music is the reason my soul is sound
and that's why I put in my needle every time I shot up heroin and cocaine.

Your music sucks and so do you!
I'd rather listen to the sound of a washing machine.
At least it's clean.

The soft and mute button on a voice
does not drown out the loud buzz of disrespect or disregard.

Non-profit.orgs (.uptight) diplomatic email—blah! makes me wanna urp,
so I won't be passin your petition or coming to or for your benefit.

You sound like a commercial—are you trying to sell me YOU?
Well, I'm not buying.

People who get mad because you tell them the truth
and that creepy crawley silent music, like small pox invading my Indian tribe.
Ahhh ya ya ya ya ya ya yay yay yay!

Quit yelling at me with your off-key music
or at least add a beat for me to dance to
because I'm cutting your tracks and adding a screachy guitar.

Got something mean to say?
Say it with mellow melomelo melopoeia!

My favorite artist-in-residence is the one who put out his thumb
or hopped a railcar, got a job where he was dropped off

and talked like a human being to the other human beings.

So go go go Jack jack jack Kerouac
Disembodied lackey of virtue!
and Allen Allen, your music in my ears when we sang
BirdBraaiiin! BirdBraiiin!
I declare BirdBrain to be victor of the poetry contest!
She hates my guts now and stabbed me in the back.

Betrayal is my least favorite offense.
It hits me in my still open childhood wounds—
treachery of sexual molestation.

Music just sounds like a headache
when it's so full of the precious lies one sings to oneself
while everyone else is listening.

I'm not listening, but I'm feeling you baby!
Ma ma ma ma MAMA!
But I'm not your mama!

Judgmentalism begins with the harshest indictment of oneself, but that
non-musical voice in tight lips holding your breath while you speak—
No you can't event breathe right. If you could you wouldn't be talking so much or writing so much bullshit
to add to the drone of your already painful-to listen-to Greatest Hits.

Blame me?
Yeah, I'm an asshole—at least I'm a flexible asshole.
and your nose is just out of joint from trying to stick it up there!

I AM NOT YOUR GURU.
My guru was a SCREW YOU.
and I am, too.

Got me going like an Indian drum machine.
This is not a love song and I'm beginning to sound like
MC I-HATE-YOU-ALOT-Are-You-Still-Listening-To-My-Take-This-Rhyme-and-Shove-it-Rant?

Actually I'm a yoga teacher and therapist. I prescribe breathwork and poses to help people process their
held grief and anger, but I'm the one holding on now.

I always say that two hours of yoga is the only thing that separates me from every other lunatic on the
street. Over five hours and I'm full circle back there with them.

I also have a special ritual for discharging people's residual or excess psychic energy in my house after they've made it clear that they hate my guts.

It's a kind of yogic exorcism technology:
I take every single item they've ever given me and put it in DIRT—I have it on good authority that it's the best repository of clinging toxic relationship energy.

So, I took out the stereo I'd bought from them and the fucking table it was sitting on and rolled it out to the curb's front garden. The Cure, Beck and Dandy Warhol buttons and CDs, I carefully laid out like dead flowers next to the fence.

The sandals went too—didn't want them kicking me while I'm down. They were already stomping on me hard. Yeah, I put my foot down.

The mirror—well, mirror feng shui is pretty complicated but I knew I didn't want their perception of me bounced back in my face while I was just trying to see if my underwear was showing.

In the middle of the night I remembered that complicated vegetable cutting thing—Sharp EDGES!! oh no!!! And they must have felt smug knowing they'd placed something with me that could slice right through my subconscious and into my very dreams! I got up and tossed it right out the door and double locked it behind me.

Then, in the middle of the fireworks on the 4th of July, my chest began tightening as I remembered their super glue I'd not returned, but my celebrating friends were beginning to grow weary of me wanting to keep running back to my house for chi cleansing and I had to stay there the rest of the night still bonded like plastic to my toxic relationships.

Today I began, revisited the Bhagavad Gita, and paralleling it with my weaknesses in warrior pose and my life.

In the BG, Arjuna and Krishna survey the battlefield and sees that many of Arjuna's best loved family make up the enemy army. Krishna instructs Arjuna that it is still necessary to destroy them or truth and love are lost, but it could only be done with a totally open heart full of love and compassion.

The obvious parallel is that we have to be willing to go to battle within ourselves to destroy our close kinship with our illusions and attachments or trauma-based emotional agenda—neither of which are our friends or relatives—dig?

I also found a great underlying *fear* in standing up in conflict with others that I love, realizing that *I* could be destroyed, and ... I was—but well, that was meant to happen and I was suddenly okay with it.

I looked around my home and saw all the items remaining of my beloved enemy's hate and realized how I was stalling taking it out because I was actually still using some of that stuff! and its parallel into all our lives when we keep using the same old tools even when they're working against or poisoning us.

And the challenge of facing this or facing illumination and the dharma of our self-actualization is only *equal to* our willingness to thoroughly clean our toilets and dishes when we dirty them.

And if we put those things off, we are most assuredly putting off other pieces and chores toward truth and self-understanding.

What's outside of you is inside of you and vice versa.

It's not exactly a new philosophy, but I had to actually *experience it*—which was quite a different feeling than just knowing it or reading about it—also not exactly a new concept, but I'm slow and don't remember having been here before in other lifetimes.

Anyway, I'm over my chi paranoia and washed the mud-caked mirror to bring on back in so I could get dressed tonite.

I remembered that heh, I've actually hung deep with some REAL armed and dangerous characters!!! Like the time I pissed someone off so bad they shoved a loaded and cocked gun in my mouth. What I then figured out to say with my tongue wrapped around a gun barrel in order to save my ass, I now credit as my first awareness of positive chi possibilities. It was also advanced preparation for dealing with requirements of literary non-profit diplomacy and other high or similarly out of balance individuals.

But I get out of balance too. Hello! And I get this recurring rotator cuff injury that feels like and literally represents an emotional stab in the back. The rotator cuff, tightness in the shoulder and rest of the muscles in the area of the heart tell us that our thoughts and beliefs around love are not working for us. It usually means someone can't feel loved unless it's reflected back to them in the form of another person or taking on other people's emotional garbage to feel useful and lovable.

Then some traitor stabs me in the back and blows my mind and I'm injured and depressed.

Who doesn't *fight* mental depression.
With the *Joy Army of the Third Eye*?

Nothing is working for me.
My lover's not coming back.
No one is coming back.
I believe I've exceeded my relationship allotment quota.
Love was divided by the numbers involved.
I have damaged myself—and I have damaged.
Diminished, cut myself off from self-love—
The tears and muscle tears, emotional scars and physical scars—
Scars on my veins, scars on my womb
Scars from falling dead drunk, yet dead to celebration.
The suffering and damage to my children and family!

And it can't be changed.
I can't take back trying to kill myself or that I was poisonous—
A Sweet Poison—Love me and Get Sick from and with me—
I can't blame my lover for trying damage me back.
I can't stop damaging myself more—I want a cigarette instead of love.
Then I'm ashamed that I'm a smoking yoga teacher and smell like cigarettes instead of universal love.
Because shame is deeply ingrained into the root of me.

Can one, having once located the residence of trauma-based physical damage in the body really just eject it by breathing into the intensity and exhaling into the atmosphere?
Where does all that bad energy go?
Won't it damage the plants or something?
My efforts and outreach to connect with love are frozen at the shoulder.

I am just so smart and clever and can make my suffering an entertainment and divert you from helping by making you just want to compliment my style of expression, make you intimidated by my ability and pride in what I don't love about myself, that which you do love, that you become so confused by what, if anything, I need, you laugh with me and buy me cigarettes.
Or it used to be dope and alcohol.
I used to regularly walk into this convenience store owned by a complete and foreign Eritrean stranger and elegantly explain that I was a heroin addict
and I needed $50 to $100 to buy some dope or I'd be really sick soon
and *He'd give it to me*!!!
Would he have helped me more by calling the police and having my charm arrested on the spot?
This misuse of my influence—evidence of my powerful charisma,
even at the lowest activity, makes me smile, self-satisfied.
Imagine my self-satisfaction.
Don't imagine it. It was, in reality, a very un-funny daily attempt to kill myself before I die naturally.
The truth is I'M AFRAID OF DEATH!!!
And it's closer and closer, in natural occurrence than ever now.
I have Misused
And Misspent
Most
of my talent, my love, my body ... and my soul.

Robert Trammell

The Cave

At the forefront of Styrofoam
technology in 1965 they sprayed
everything but the floors. Just left them slimy.
Made big, grey stalactites hanging
all over. It became a bar bail bondsmen
like Jerry hung out in. He knew every bar hustle
ever invented but he never could dance.
One night at closing time he invited
all the bar patrons to his car in the parking lot.
He opened the trunk, shined a flashlight
onto a tub full of iceddown cold cans of Lone Star.
After everybody got one Jerry helped his girlfriend
climb on to the roof of his car. He shined
his flashlight on her, took out his little .38 pistol
and as he fired it into the Dallas night sky
she started taking her blouse off
to the rhythm of his gun.

Robert Trammell

Cockatoos in Iraq

I heard on the radio that after the war
Cockatoos in Baghdad escaped the zoo.
Escaped the pet shops.
Escaped cages all over the city
& came together in the bombed out library
in the center of town. As they glided
in thru broken windows they made
the sounds of bombs & rockets,
of missiles & bullets. As they left they made
the sounds of bombs & rockets, of missiles
& bullets. As they flew over the city they made
the sounds of smart bombs & cockatoos
dive-bombed the citizens.
I heard it on the radio but my wife said
That's not true. They are trying to fool you.
I asked *Who? The Birds?*

Jeremiah Kelley

Visitation

Near Lorena, south of Waco, the radio tuned five beats to the bar,
the pulse of the prairie rippling the pavement into an electronic wave,
the salvation of cool jazz laid on the highway miles with athletic grace anointing
my car's metal body, in this spot of highway that I always remember,
where microwave radio antennae, watched for miles now
suddenly loom and close at hand appear gigantic and impossibly fragile,
one, then another and another, a whole mechanical forest.

But even with Bluebonnets and Indian Paintbrush flooding the April median
it's still difficult, this monthly drive to the ex wife whose neck still hardens,
whose voice still freezes at the mention of the money, visitation
to the kids who remain always just the kids, an ever growing collection
of report cards and birthday snapshots now taken by the boyfriend,
the phony smile and polite chat, football, he's the only one I really get along with.

Towards evening the highway becomes an orange sun setting behind a roadside cloud,
in the shadows it is a hitchhiker suddenly frozen I will not stop to pick up, a thumb,
a beard, a look, a backpack, then suddenly it's an abandoned farm house
lost in a fallow field, gently fading into prairie like old white wash,
imaginary history, the single Live Oak, imagine myself stopping
to climb from my car in engulfing silence, to hunt among the weeds
for artifacts, a doll's head, a screwdriver, a busted lamp,
anything to confound my understanding. I know I will not stop.

In the trees behind the farmhouse, some large dead thing—deer? cow?
I remember the story of Friedrich Nietzsche sobbing his heart out
hopelessly embracing a wounded dying horse, his last indictable act
before his sister had him put away. It is not fear that drives me on,
beyond this hitchhiker standing alone, but hopelessness,
the small voice telling me these things, kids, dead horses,
philosophy, will always be just memories, untouchable, insubstantial as radio waves,
telling me this desperate urge to feel and comprehend is really neither hope
nor help for pain, but biological imperative, instinctive as an erection,
this whole sprawl of humanity a reflex, an evolutionary spasm.

Here, where stars hang silver under the azure sky among jet aircraft landing lights,
every star a world unto itself, am I englobed, a drop of blood rolling across the prairie

in the radio heart beat; the winking lights of the microwave antenna forest laughing parodies of our gods, forever transmitting along incomprehensible wavelengths, milestones from Texas traveling forever into space.

Opalina Salas

Shut The Hell UP and DIE!!!

i want to know your city, picturesque dirty and painted with your thick tongue
full of sex and fueled by Benzedrine madness and hours of poetry talk
laid out on dirty floors, naked and eyes filled with smoke and teardrops
slabs of starlight bleeding in thru broken window blinds
and music floating in like faraway lullabies

oh stars
oh indifferent stars!
so indifferent now that a million billion years you were
earnest and bright
and shined like a star should!
now you are so indifferent to me,
never have a shining thought of me and of my
insignificance
but star!
oh star,
thank you for shining just the same.

I am 38 years old and I am dying a million prosaic deaths
each word that is spoken falls like dead branches from trees
at night I lay in bed beside my reclining Buddha and say goodbye to the universe
as if it is the last time. I spend uncountable hours recalling your brilliance
in tears and sighs and twisted pillows
i have now died a million times at least
only to be unremarkable and alive each morning when i awaken

i'll tell you this.
bury me with a book of Jack Kerouac in my hand
and if there is indeed a heaven, i'll get him to sign it for you.
but only after i ask him
what it was like to be here so long before i joined him
father, lover, brother thief and friend
heaven should be a meeting place for poets
fouling up the clouds with nonsense and parties
of the mindful kind
Plato and the Brontes cutting up rugs
Allen on accordian
and Burroughs puffing on a pipe

oh death march everywhere around me
laughing in the corners
cutting up everything with your scarlet ribbons
and i'm not even safe in my own bed
im not even safe between his thighs
or with his arms around me
if I had a mind I'd tear off my covers
and go looking for you, myself
dance the wild lines of street divisions
drink bottles of liquor and drive at ungodly speeds
while throwing you the finger
or sticking out my tongue
see I desire these mad nights in search of you
I dig the wild ponies in dusty bars
And nightclubs
The promise of ominous alleyways
And evil strangers
They carry death like a business card
Promises
Maybe we can all make the choice somehow
Maybe somehow we do
In the extra bottles,
The snorted lines
Riding cars without seatbelts
Picking fights with death soldiers
Strung out and with nothing to lose.

What have I got on you, death?
And why are you fucking with me now?
I've got at least 20 or 30 good years left in me

You show up in frightening health deterioration
Wild frenzy media blitzes of car crashes and shots in the head
And my favorite,
Whisking us away all warm in our beds ...
Fuck you, I'm going to go out reading poetry
Drinking whiskey and praying on a copy of on the road
But not anytime soon ...
And at least not until I finish this poem.

Opalina Salas

Jack

because you were a writer,
you posed with a railroad brakesman's rule book
in pocket, couch pillows airing on the fire escape
overlooking clotheslines
three flights up
on a lower east side Manhattan pad,
holding a smoke between the fingers that
pecked away
to the mouth that verbed deep colours
of consonant cues ...

because your hand
into fist fits so casually
in Levi's pockets,
you look like a lover i never had,
a lover i long for in the sickly green fadeout
black and white blues,

you were 'indulgent and huge'
tall thick and manly,
American
full-blooded red white and blue,
exalting the railroads, Negros, migrant workers, junkies,
homosexuals,
handsome girls and pretty boys,
and The Fabulous Beats

i daydream we celebrate birthdays together
smoke Mexican grass from your leather pouch
drink wine, eat hash,
wail to Charlie Parker on the phonograph
and dance barefoot together on dirty wooden floors

i dream i feel my first new york rain
as we walk to the diner together,
like dirty diamonds on our eyelids and lips,
and in the diner we hold hands and

flirt with the waitresses for more cups of
coffee

i hear your voice, Jack
reading my poems aloud
casual, punctuated and musical,
taking drags off cigarettes and telling me,
'it's awlright, doll'
and taking my pen you mark out all the
corrections and read and reread again

because you were a writer,
i feel your days of solitude in my head
where you hung like that clothesline
up above Big Sur
and tried to fill the whole that was
inescapable ...
but i know ...
that the booze stays bitter
and the cigs never satisfy ...
and the grass cannot sail us away ...

i think ... and i think i want to hang with you in
Big Sur ...
i want to avoid the outcomes of us
i want to avoid your demise
and someday mine ...
and i hope that mine
will not be so alone
like yours, jack ...

because you were a writer
i forgot your birthday again this year
as i fucked my husband on the living room floor
in the Sunday morning blues and greens
with bebop jazz crooning us back to sleep

but somehow ...
i know you think
thats
'awlright'

Lilly Penhall

Be My Neal Cassady

I want you to be my Neal Cassady ... someone who will feel the wind in their hair, someone to chase chase chase the edge of the horizon, someone who has the perfect road soundtrack, someone who will talk to me and listen back, someone who will stop on the side of the road in the mountains and dance. I need a Neal Cassady—someone to drive a hundred and fifty miles an hour across the long curling pavement with your dog's head hangin out the back window droolin down the side of the door ... someone who can drink whiskey from the bottle and smoke a cigarette and sing with the radio and get fingerfucked behind the wheel and keep it straight on til dawn ... someone who will sleep half naked in the backseat, won't wake up when I turn up The Electro-Magnetics but instead incorporate into their fishnet road dream while I sunburn my left arm hanging out the window smoking a cigarette. Someone who wants sunglasses on their face at all times—someone who will stop at 4am in whatever time zone we're in beside a glowing open field dyed turquoise in the moonlight stare at the stars not outshined and make up constellations about our own mad mythology—That formation is called the Johnny O ...can't you see, he's blowing up an air mattress—and these two red stars I'll name Hilgers Eyes. We'll map out City Lights in our stratosphere and aim ourselves in tomorrow's direction. Someone to talk about what it all means, someone to pass fat joints back and forth blowing out volcano smoke from the earth. Someone not afraid to get out there and do it. Someone who will be my Neal Cassady and dream dream dream and fuck fuck fuck and live live live and lead me to a life worth talking about, someone who will take me on adventures that legends are made of. I want a partner in crime and I'm a great driver but an even better passenger. Baby I'll light your cigarettes and unwrap your cheeseburgers so you can keep that lead foot on the wheel and just ride on, til we find somewhere to get a few shots of whiskey and get into some trouble and get a free place to sleep for the night—you'll be wearin your cowgirl hat and blue jean miniskirt making friends with the locals and charming the pants off every blue eyed American boy that makes eye contact. Someone who will kick some honkey ass if they even think about fucking with us. Someone who can adapt to wherever we land and always scrape something together that's not too dangerous or uncomfortable, and then again, so what if it is? I need a Neal Cassady, someone who doesn't give a shit about where we'll get the money or I won't have health insurance or I'd rather have air conditioning or my mattress is the only place I can sleep ... I need someone who's adaptable and authoritative because I'm never the leader, I'm the supporter—I'm the best little girl if you just tell me what to do—I need someone who's not tied down and who will take advantage of that freedom to get away from the same concrete I've been looking at for too long ... I love this city but there's so much more to see and so much more to experience, so many more faces to examine and so many bathrooms to use and so many bookstores to peruse and so many streetlights to pass and so many hole in the wall local restaurants to eat at—and there are millions of leaves on seas of trees to drive past and count by the acres ... there are hours of songs to listen to, days of words to be volleyed back and forth inside the six glass panes surrounding us, there are oceans to float and beaches to burn one, there are fields to frolic and raindrops to feel ... there are mushrooms growing right now waiting for someone to pick them so they can someday be sold to us by some hippies in a Winnebago somewhere in the western half of America. I need Neal Cassady, I need my co-conspirator, my comrade, a friend who I can share a brand new life every day with, someone who aint afraid to break

191

the law all day every day—and not because there's anything wrong with the laws, but just because that's the life we're choosing to lead—we're exempt from following the rules of the common man, because we're not common men—we're extraordinary holy fantastical women, the leaders of a generation of people who want to sit in their comfortable lives with their comfortable people and never step outside the boundaries that they're afraid will bounce them back to their miserable existence or shatter their illusions of what life really is—because life isn't what's on TV or what's showing at the movie theater—and our suburban problems will be a thing of the past because we'll be starving and sleeping on uncomfortable sofas in dirty living rooms with other beatniks passed out on the floors all around us, we'll be dirty and camping on beaches and shitting in the woods … but we'll be free from the weight of the technology and the media and this sad sad society that is ready to be told what to believe by electronic signals. And we'll write write write spilling out our minds and dreams onto spiral bound pages, write down conversations and haiku about the people we meet and the trucks we pass and the sights and the lights and the darkness and the loneliness … it'll be blue blue blue cerulean American skies as far as our dilated eyes can see … we'll make love and make art and live and die in orgasms of winged flowerpetal bliss … Be my Neal Cassady, before it's too late and we're finding more grey hairs in our temples and our breasts sag any lower, Be my Neal Cassady, let's start today, let's get our things distributed to storage or charity and buy a car with a little money we can scrape together … Let's make it happen, let's do it, let's go—I'm ready and I know that Neal has been haunting your dreams like Jack has been haunting mine, they're waiting to take us over and infuse us with their voracious appetites for truly experiencing life … it's all waiting, it's all out there waiting for us, waiting for us to go go go, so let's ball that jack, let's go … let's go mama, let's go—

Jolee Davis

How to Avoid Hate Crimes

*Avoid Dark or Isolated Places
it was the hesitation
as you reached for the 2% milk
imagined, if not for the grocery store's lighting
the truth was fluorescent, illuminated on the dew gathered glass
at that moment of decision, you decided the fate of the world
how one day, soon, you would come home
and everything will have gone bad

*Know Your Surroundings
i have ruined my soul
walking the hours before dawn like deserted fields
blistered thoughts on the endless sidewalk between the bus stops of my hope and my history
collapsed in the heat of following, beside highways of regret

*Never Travel Alone
at sixteen, i bought a bus ticket to san francisco
with money stolen from my mother's purse
the cops came before the bus
i told them i wasn't running from, i was running to
something beautiful
i realize, now, there is no difference
i have become practiced in leaving, without taking a step
my son will spend his life running to me
i have become practiced in not being found

*Know Where You Are
you are the koi pond next door, the concrete marshland beside the road,
the fountained pond filled with leeches, nestled in the duck belly of two story brick homes
you have taught me to build what i lack, taught me how to sustain life, become a habitat

*Say No to Strangers
i have given so much away because i didn't want it taken

*Plan an Escape Route
i was told, most people live their entire lives within a 30 mile radius of where they were born.
it would take 83 days, 8 hrs a day, 20 min. a mile, to walk to new york from here.
i read in a first aid handbook, once the jugular was severed it would take 3 min. to bleed out.

my favorite part of a map is the key. first knuckle to fingertip = 1 inch.
i am five fingers away from the sistine chapel, from the fingertip of god.
di vinci understood scale.
1 inch = our arms stretching across all of creation with the hope that we will finally feel, touched; we will, at last, forget the mathematics of escape.

*Leave a Trail
i retreat like a russian
burn it all, then wait
from my mother, i have learned the skill of turning vodka into blankets
from you, that patience is the same as a bullet

Johnny Olson

Joe

Some folks say there's no voice today that is willing to reach the hearts and minds of the average Joe. You know him. He's the:

The 50+ hours a week with no OT Joe

The let's build our lives on shaky credit with a 21% APR Joe

The one pay check away from living in the car Joe

The American dream that's drifting away Joe

The let's kill the pain with spirits, herbs and chemicals Joe

The fear for our tomorrow's in a world chock full of sorrows Joe

The class I was born into is going extinct and there's no moving up but only going down Joe

The masses that passes the classes and still works the mailroom Joe

The man on the street with nothing to eat Joe

The barely legal boys with their lethal toys who play GI Joe Joe

The dying too young my song never sung Joe

The teenager dad who wasn't so bad but got dealt the bad hand Joe

The drug addicted fool who sits outside the schoolyard retracing his steps to find his way back home Joe

The lonely poet who has lost his voice by no choice of his own Joe

The can't find it behind them and can't find it in front of them 'cos tomorrow may not be there Joe

The living in fear of the 6 o'clock news afraid to hear another 3,000 are struck dead in the name of God Joe

The seeker who seeks and finds nothing worthwhile Joe

The fool who struck gold only to let it go up in smoke Joe

The I'm too tired to deal with this head, sometimes I think I'd rather be dead Joe

The coping and hoping for someone to hear their plea Joe

I hear you Joe. And this one's for us Joe.

Johnny Olson

Welcome Back

It's been awhile. It took a spell to feel well but now I'm back on track. Ol' Humpty Dumpty me fell off the wall carelessly and my broken pieces scattered thin and it took all the King's horses and forces to put me back together again. But, I am back ...

I'm finding my heart again. Seems all I needed was a kick in the seat and just a little traction for my wayward feet. Now ... I'm planted firmly (sorta) and my head's back on straight (kinda) and my mind ain't dwelling and cloudy and shouting at my sleeve bleeding heart which is finally starting to feel and thumping excitedly at all the possibilities awaiting me. The ticker was sick but not no more. What's opened up with all this reconstruction from its mass destruction is a bigger door! From my heart's shore to its other shore, from tip-top ceilings to down low floors! Now there's room for so much more. I am back my friends and ready to feel.

I'm finding my eyes again. I'm no longer staring at yesterday's whats, whys, whos and whens. I grew so tired seeing only yesterday's classes with half-filled glasses. Now I'm looking out and seeing what is presently. My eyes have longed to see the here and now ... soaking in this urban scene, quietly chaotic and loudly serene seeing hot assed summer breezes waving dreamily to the pock-holed pavement, Tejano music bloating and fading, floating and falling, accordion chords ricocheting off these technicolor walls on this X+ street seeing all kinds of beat and diggin' on how beautiful it feels to see again. I am back my friends and ready to see.

I'm finding my ears again. All I kept hearing was chatter and lies, soul shaking sighs, breaking good-byes. But they opened up and I'm ready to sit and listen, to really hear, to perk up and give you my undivided attention and to fully absorb all these pictures you've been saying and praying and hoping just to be heard. Speak to my years, sing to my tears, shout to my fears, whisper in my ears, I hear you. I truly do. I am back my friends and ready to hear.

I'm finding my voice again. It was cracked and weak, ignored and meek. But it's no longer keeping quiet. I got some words that have been waiting to speak, patiently sitting and bidding their time to bounce out in shouts out of my mouth and pair up and make them some rhymes! I've saved up a few stories or two too, believe you me. And my shout is back on, along with my whisper, too. They've just been waiting for the right time to play and say ... "The time is now!" because I am back my friends and ready to speak.

I'm finding that the finding finds me finding more doors. Discovering something everyday as I'm scratchin' at my surface. There's still a whole lot more of me left to explore in this quest of rediscovering all of me. But you know what I really feel? I feel back, my friends, and really feeling real.

Tammy Melody Gomez

Brother and Sister Together

brother and sister together across table, discussing the conditions of his confinement behind bars in a Texas penal institution. she is, by turns, apologetic, apoplectic, resentful, and resigned. she recounts the day that she finally decided to pack his belongings, empty his room. weeks after he'd been revoked. she needed a new housemate to help share the bills and had to finally accept that her brother would not be coming home soon. it was not the proper burial. there are no songs yet, no songs exist to mourn this packing.

humming: she is alone and stacking, one by one, the folded shirts and pairs of socks. he kept things so neat, all she had to do was swipe off the dust and find the right size storage box. how big is the box they keep you in, bro? who dusts you off when you need the care? i am touching things you probably have no use for, in there. rainjacket, golf club, a wooden monkey head. i'll save your pennies for you, no worry that your savings might be spent. you add up the days, on the calendar blocks, red ink for days finished, and your innocence is safe with me. your innocence is safe with me.

she considers the smell of the apartment, on 7th avenue, the place he lived when it was time to take him in, they knew he was gonna be gone, straight to the courthouse, all neat steps leading to the punishing bench, concrete steps to concrete blocks of his warehouse cell. to be warehoused in storage.

that morning, they didn't wait to see him off. they didn't look past the barricades to catch the glimpse of manacles on his ankles, they didn't see him climb onto the long green bus. nor did they wait for him to wave. it was the smell, that smell back in the apartment that she recognized, like the smell of rancid cheese mixed with aerosol spray, an aquanet limburger cheese experiment, and then in a second, she knew he'd been up all night, smoking the pipe, cracking some jokes, killing some time before going off to do some time.

his friends floated out as sharply as the smell and somehow dissipated anonymously, no hellos. the nameless remain nameless. she will forever know that smell and connect it with him separating from himself before separating for real in order to go and meet his metal. it was pungent, piercing and had no shame.

on his back, he wore a little knapsack that was almost as small as the fake half-grin she knew was a put-on for mama and maybe a put-on for himself as well. he was going to hell and they weren't having a quotable conversation. they rode sullenly with Christian tunes on the dial and mama taking every last curve like she's driving a pregnant lady to emergency. it was the final drive, an aria without words.

in minutes, they pulled up to the jail. she snapped a picture of him against the light pole, standing there, when he hopped fake cheerful out of the car as if they'd arrived at a carnival park. another snapshot for the photo album of despair. she was thankful for a reason to cover her face. holding the camera up over her eyes, she could better hide the lump in her throat, distancing him through a viewfinder. to connect before separating is a difficult thing, so all they did was hug and drive away, leaving him alone to check in and belly up to the bars.

it coulda been kinder, shoulda been kinder. but this was the only way. this was the only way.

Joey Darrell Cloudy

One Time in the Corner

Tonight there will be no lies
about how your breast looks like the moon.
Nothing from the night sky has fallen
into your eyes. The lie of the metaphor is no more
desirable than the lie of omission.
"I do not know which I prefer" the beautiful
lie or the ugly truth.
Everything is what it is.
The horses are not boxers.
The ring is not life. Still,
I've put a little English on
a poem, enough to give
the hustlers grief.

Shin Yu Pai

Poem
for Wolfgang Laib

a life
of collecting pollen
from hazelnut bushes
a life of gathering word-grains
to find all you have wanted
all you have waited to say

five
mountains
we cannot climb
hills we cannot touch
perhaps we are only here
to say house, bridge, or gate

a passage
to somewhere else
yellow molecules
spooned and sifted
from a jar filled with

sunlight
      pouring
           milk
    over
          stone
you are the energy
that breaks form
building wax houses
pressed from combs

a wax room
set upon a mountain
an offering of rice
nowhere everywhere
the songs of Shams

Shin Yu Pai

feedback
    after John Pomara

the   push   and   p   u   l   l
of paint   sliding across a surface
  rolling   tremolo   machine
paint flows off
the hard edge of aluminum
      Rorschach drips
read on the horizontal:

a   graph   body's
       of the   progress
stut-ter-ing
on the vertical—
a
screen-
play
glitches
on
8 mm
race
across
a
film
strip
shifting
     cut up
        xerox
magnified
    blow up

d   r   a   g   g   e   d across an electric eye
emanations of light from behind the screen
    the absence of painter
      presence of machine
the television a template
     for a sketch enacted
in childhood
    boxes full of light
reaching through the screen

the human hand
leaves its traces

Sherry Riley

[McKinney Avenue in mid-sixties Dallas was home to a dozen or more beatnik coffee houses and night-clubs, including The Rubaiyat, the 90th floor Jazz Room, The Poet, and The 8th Day. At The Interlude, Sherry Riley read her poetry on Sunday afternoons accompanied by Jimmy Clay on jazz flute.]

Yes I am Gone
Gone with your wind
Low in your sax
And high in your flute
A wailing wind
James Clay's band.

Jack Estes

Interview with Rob Johnson
May 2014, Lebanon, Tennessee

I was in Waco originally, but I was in school at the University of Texas studying to be an actor. And when the first coffee houses opened up across from the college I was there with a friend and I asked if could borrow a guitar and the people started saying sing louder so we can hear and the next thing I know they had hired me. I was singing folk. They are long gone coffee houses. One of the coffee houses I remember playing was Jester's Cabaret. I discovered girls liked musicians so my career path was set.

When I was at UT in the fifties all the most intelligent people I knew were leaving school to go out and learn something. They weren't teaching you to use your brain at UT, they were saying, "Memorize this." Everyone was disappointed in what they were being taught in college. I had a friend who stayed there just so he could use the library—he rarely went to class. And he educated himself in the library.

We'd rented a big old ten room house, and we'd rent it out to party, and I'd come home 3 o'clock in the morning from singing in the coffee houses and there'd be people doing the deed in my bed. People were always coming in there from off the road. I smoked my first joint there from someone who was coming up from Mexico—he was the Apostle of Pot. It was just getting started good. So many of the people were artists and musicians and writers, and people were constantly coming through who were interesting. I had a couple of cartoons in *The Ranger*, and a little short story. There was some cool people.

I saw our generation taking to the road. I wasn't far behind them. I mean, I ended up at the Cellar. We had just left college, me and a couple of fellas, we had put together a folk trio. Anyhow, we were headed towards the Metroplex and one of the guys said, "Hey there's a good coffee shop in Fort Worth," so we took the left turn just past Waco and headed to Ft. Worth. And we got to the Cellar and I mean this place was unlike anything we'd ever seen 'cause coffee houses at that time were places where people plucked nylon strings and sang ninety-eight verses of "Lord Randall My Son." And the Cellar, this was already, even though it was just struggling to get started, it was already THE place to go to—everybody in Ft. Worth went to the Cellar at one time or another even if they wouldn't admit it. We just fell into a situation. My friend, he decided he didn't want to be with the group and the other one went on his way and I was the only one that stayed.

People thought the Cellar was just a coffee house, but it was just a coffee house 'cause [Cellar owner] Pat Kirkwood didn't want the liquor control board to tell him what to do. This place was a free for all seven-days-a-week all-out party. I mean it was a big black basement with all the slogans on the wall and the waitresses would wear the skimpiest things they could 'cause that's where they got their tips, and you could practically see their kitty feathers. And we had cushions on the floor and some great music there and lots of rowdies who wanted to take on the Cellar crew to their chagrin. This was when it had been opened maybe three months, the original Cellar, and I became a Cellar Dweller. I lived there singing in the club. It wasn't the money that attracted me, it was that if you couldn't get laid at the Cellar you were really lame.

I did a little of everything, mainly folk. I didn't have any original stuff in those days, but there was a lot of really good folk music around, and my challenge was that I never wanted to fit into anybody's mold, so I sang a little bit of everything. I grew up on the same music Willie [Nelson] did; I grew up in

Waco same time he did. We grew up on the same culture and the same music and that's what I did, a little of everything. Like Willie, he's liable to take on anything but an opera. I listened to everything folk I could find. I really liked Bob Gibson, grew up on Sons of the Pioneers, Hank Sr., thought he was next thing to Jesus. I loved The Weavers, they were pioneers, they really helped bring about the folk boom. Pete Seeger and Woody Guthrie. I've always liked songs with passion and drama, I don't like a lot of baby baby yeah yeah. I like story songs. I'm a storyteller that works in music. I did a lot of bawdy songs. I did some songs that were pretty bad. Hey everywhere I went people were requesting them, they were very popular. [Sings]: "A nymphomaniacal Alice/ used a dynamite stick for a phallus./ They found her vagina/ in South Carolina/ and her rectum in Buckingham palace." I had a string of 'em, and every time I'd do one someone would come up to me and say, "I got one for you." So I just gradually got built up where I could go for six or eight minutes with these limericks.

Johnny Carroll [Cellar music director and former rockabilly sensation], he was a helluva performer. I went to his house a number of times. The Cellar crew was really tight in those days. Pat Kirkwood was on the premises most of the time, and he and Dubber [Cellar manager] pretty well ran the place. It was like a family. Anybody there would go to jail for Pat 'cause they knew Pat would be down there in an hour with a fistful of money to get you out. If you were a member of the Cellar, you were a member of the baddest gang around. If anyone wanted to do you in, you had an army on your side. However, I'll admit there was a time when I had to carry a gun, 'cause it got pretty rough. Fortunately I didn't shoot anybody, I didn't have an occasion to. Back in the kitchen we had a rack where we hung the knives and the clubs and the brass knuckles and the slapjacks and all that stuff for the crew. There were big brawls all the time. People were allowed to bring in their own bottle long as they didn't flash it around, and they bought set-ups, and some people would overindulge and get out of line and try to slip a bowling-ball grip on one of the waitresses and that didn't go over too well, and next thing they'd know they'd have six or eight people on 'em out the back door, and I've looked down gun barrels there. We took on everybody in driving distance, even gangs. I can remember one time when six of our bouncers, all of them just average size, one of them even a little small, took on four TCU linemen and two Green Bay Packers and whooped those football players all around the block.

There's a time you may have heard of where this dentist got drunk, he was always drunk and always there, and he was fueled up and one of the waitresses found a pipe on the floor. She didn't know it was anything but a pipe, and she went over to Doc and shook it in his face and she said, "I'm gonna hit you over the head with this Doc," and it went off—it was a zip gun, with a .410 shotgun shell, but it only had about a quarter-inch of barrel and it just scattered. Doc got several pieces in the face. He was drunk, all fueled up, and suddenly we heard this POW! and we all went running up and all he knew was he got shot in the face and there's all these people charging up on him, and he got a little panicked there and I ended up pretty much toe to toe with him and he pulls a gun. He bounces bullets off the floor between my legs while cross-examining me and if he didn't like my answers, well POW! there'd go another one, and, hell, I didn't know what to tell him, I just went up there to see what was going on. Then Dubber went running across behind me and caught a ricochet in the knee. And when Doc realized he'd hurt somebody then suddenly he was all doctor. I've seen 'em fight some mighty brawls. I've seen Kirkwood up to his ass in cowboys just grinning from ear to ear.

Pat Kirkwood was a survivor. Very clever, very smart in his understanding of people. He's the kind of guy you could drop stark naked in the Amazon jungle and in a week he'd own the place. People would do whatever Pat asked them to do. And he was one of the most terrifying guys to see, I mean he had dark eyes and they were deep set—he could grin at you and chill your blood. And he could back it up. He was an ex-racecar driver, he was a "villain." He totally enjoyed being a racecar villain. Nobody around there who knew Kirkwood was going to cross him in any way. I went out and partied with Pat while he was living at the Four Deuces [Kirkwood Sr.'s casino on "Thunder Road"], we had some great parties there. We partied there and we partied at the Western Hills Inn, and I mean it was a free for all. Well he told me that the reason he opened the Cellar was to get his friends out of his living room. First few months it was touch and go but it was such a united effort and everyone was determined it was going to make it, we'd do anything to keep the Cellar open, because we knew there was no other place like it. Fort Worth was a conservative little cowtown. But he passed it off as a "beatnik" place long enough for us to get it established. And within a month or two of my being there, we were hitting newspapers and magazines all over the place. Hell, we even hit a couple of newspapers in Europe. Charlie Whomper, he was one of the original Cellar people. He was our resident beatnik, and Big Mike. They were party people. CW he looked the part and he was willing to play the part of the beatnik.

Pat was a master of publicity. We had a time where he put the waitresses out in the street in their no-nothings and got pictures in the papers and everything, and he went to court for this thing, indecent exposure with his waitresses, and Kirkwood notified every media outlet what was going on and he brought those two waitresses in in long coats and he said "Your honor, is this obscene?" and he opened up their coats and the flashbulbs went popping and yeah, Pat paid a big fine, but he got a helluva lot of publicity. They tried their best to close down the Cellar for a long time, and Kirkwood, between him and his daddy, they whooped 'em.

I saw some weird things. One night a couple of the waitresses ganged up on another waitress and took her bra off and we were up on the stage playing, then she got a friend and took some more bras off and next thing I knew bras were flying. Then they went up to the regular customers and took off their bras. We had bras hanging off our guitars and everywhere else, and then the cops came in the door. They stood there for a minute, looked around, shook their heads, and walked out.

I met my wife there. That was a strange thing. She'd been married three times previously, and she'd just got loose from her third boyfriend and she and her girlfriends were waiting on the steps to get in the Cellar. And she was telling her friends, "No more men, let somebody else have their problems and their dirty underwear," and they were standing there, Friday or Saturday night, and I started singing, and she couldn't see me she could only hear me, and I hadn't gotten through the first verse and she said to her girlfriends, "If that's not taken that's my next husband." We had one date and went out and got an apartment. Been together fifty-six years. When it strikes you, you can feel it.

I was only there [at the Cellar] for about 8 or 9 months before I took off for New York and Greenwich Village. It was something else in '59, '60. It was crowded, the tourists were wall to wall. Solid people, cops had to ride horses. A mob scene. I was playing basket houses. Told crowds god would punish them if they didn't give me money [in the basket being passed around]. I'd sing five different coffee houses a night, and I'd make 200 dollars. Knew Phil Ochs, we'd shoot bottle rockets out the window of my apartment. Gram Parsons stayed with me and his whole band. We had some great sessions in my apartment. All the Greenwich Village musicians would come to my apartment after the clubs closed down. I was there to hear Simon and Garfunkel play their first album at a "hoot."

I was in New York the day Kennedy was assassinated in Dallas, and I was singing in a Greenwich Village coffee house, and I was singing a song called "Stuval," about a racehorse, and I suddenly realized that the next line of the song was, "It was a big day down in Dallas, don't you wish you were there," and I thought, "Oh shit, I'm gonna get lynched," and I cut it off, I didn't go no further, cause I could just imagine something like that in New York City where Kennedy was popular, on the night he was killed? Self-preservation stopped me. I could just see me dragged from the stage down the street.

Beat East Texas

According to one editor's reckoning, and the reckoning of Texas friends whose families go back further than the Civil War, East Texas begins in and around I-45 that runs roughly north and south from Dallas to Houston, and then stretches east to the Louisiana border. Some may be surprised with this rough guess at its western border, but that's just about where the piney woods begin. Like any region of Texas, East Texas varies. The east Texas town Edgewood, where one editor owned a home for twenty-five years, integrated its schools before the Supreme Court decision in 1954. Edgewood has had a black mayor and black police chief, yet ten miles down the road, in another small town, no African-Americans lived and race riots occurred. Even driving through the town could result in police harassment for African-Americans up into the 1980s. It is this side of East Texas that William Burroughs satirizes in the "County Clerk" section of *Naked Lunch*. Edgewood is a town of mostly poor people. The town down the road with the race problems was mostly middle class. East Texas was the first place one editor saw men hunkered down in front yards, carrying on conversations. Time slows down in the piney woods. Even when shopping in stores, one needs to hang awhile and chew the fat, inquire how people and families are doing. One can't form simple stereotypes of East Texas. One editor had his deepest conversation about abstract art with a man from Crockett he met in an antique store.

William S. Burroughs

[Editor's note: Arch Ellisor was a moonshiner and neighbor of William S. Burroughs when he lived on a 99-acre ranch in east Texas. This is the last complete story written by Burroughs, and it was composed in separate parts in the journals collected in *Last Words*. The editors have assembled it with the blessing of the Burroughs estate. The story was inspired by Burroughs' 50-year-old memory of a *Time* magazine article about a policeman described as "a buck-toothed gunman with insolent eyes" who was killed by moonshiners in Harlan County, Kentucky ("New Grave in Harlan County," *Time*, May 2, 1949).]

Old Arch

Two of them droved out to see old Arch Ellisor, out where the sheep dip used to be and Clem Higgins got drunker than usual, fell into the dip, got stucked and drowned. Some said his fourteen-year-old daughter he'd been screwing incestuous held him down by jumping on top of him, up and down like they was screwing—and some says it was his old lady dumped a bag of hog feed on him, you know them dips is constructed like what a bitch has between her gams.

So here they stand, in suit and tie and black shined shoes, like they sprung up outa some place real different.

And there is Old Arch sitting on his porch, a mason jar of white corn in his hand.

And they say it together:

"We work for that *crazy* American government,"

And Arch says:

"Howdy."

Then they split up. One comes on fake-folksy:

"Hey, Pilgrim, how about giving me a snort of your bug juice?"

Arch passes him the jar.

He takes a swig:

"Phew!"

Goes into an act of fanning his mouth.

The other Fed is waving the Witness Protecting Action in Arch's face:

"You don't have to live in a shack like this. Why, you can have a nice place in town, TV, flushing toilet *and* $50 a month clear, free and all yours. How's that hit you?"

And he leans forward, punches Arch—soft and playful—on his chin.

Then they both gets hands on their hips, and their eyebrows shoot up and wriggle:

"It's the offer you can't refuse."

"It's the chance extraordinary."

And they is back smiling—"we know you"—a knowing smile:

("He's hooked, we got him. He is ours.")

—as they smack their lips.

"We got a job to do, Arch."

"Same as you."

"Just what sorta work you do, Arch?"

"Well now, I sorta steer folks the way they wanta go. Like someone comes here wants some action, comes to Old Arch."

Suddenly they stop the smiles, and chew up the words and spit 'em out.

"You were there."

"You saw it."

"Ever hear about obstructing justice?"

"We can summon you to Federal Court, and when you lie it's a felony."

They prance around him, jabbing fingers at him.

"Want to go into the can, Arch? Old ones like you do hard time."

"Know what they done in Marion Pen?"

They thrust their snarling faces at him.

"They fucked a ninety-five-year-old paralyzed man up his ass."

"He had a rectal hemorrhage."

Arch says:

"I reckon."

"I wouldn't want to see that happen to *you*, Arch."

He shoves his face an inch [from] Arch's, leering, all his teeth out.

They are going manic. They grab the jar of corn and swig.

Suddenly, from nowhere, Arch manifests a fiddle. His face is shifting, animals peeking in and out—goats and cats and weasels. He is dancing, cats gather and yeowl.

"Well, some music for the road, feller say."

"Faster faster round and round
swing your partner offen the ground
Faster faster round and round."

The Feds is capering, leering.

"Take off your coat and throw it in a corner."

The Feds take off their coats, showing their shoulder holster guns (which they pat and rub suggestively), drop their coats over the porch rail.

"Stay all night and stay a little longer,
Don't see why you don't stay a little longer."

On the way back to town a "freak wind" blew the Fed car off the road. Both agents were "killed at the scene."

"It was a terrible tragedy," said Bill Rogers, spokesman for the FBI office in Pitsman, [Montana]. "They were brilliant young operatives, with a grasp on sensitive cases. It is a tragic loss to the department, and the nation."

When Old Arch used his pipe, it could be plain panic for fake folk, because you can't hear that sound and lie.

Is there a basic lie in being alive in a body?

Of course. But most folks don't know that.

Neal Cassady

[In the Fall of 1947, Allen Ginsberg and Neal Cassady visited William S. Burroughs, his common-law wife Joan, and their children Willie and Julie on their 99-acre "ranch" in east Texas, located on Winters Bayou near Coldspring, Texas. Ginsberg's hoped-for romantic tryst with Cassady failed to materialize on the ranch and also later in a room at the Brazos Hotel in Houston; spurned, he left for Galveston, where he shipped out on a merchant marine boat bound for Dakar. Herbert Huncke, the New York hipster who first introduced the term "beat" into Jack Kerouac's vocabulary, also lived a spell with the Burroughses in east Texas. His description of that adventure is included in *The Herbert Huncke Reader*. Unfortunately, the Huncke estate did not allow us to excerpt his work for this anthology. In the following letters, "Carolyn" is Carolyn Cassady; LuAnne is Cassady's first wife, "Mary Lou" in *On the Road*. Kerouac's plans to join them all on a road trip from east Texas back to New York fell through because Burroughs needed room in his jeep to transport the marijuana crop he had raised on the "ranch."]

To Jack Kerouac
Sept. 20, '47
New Waverly, Texas

I received your letter, great to hear from you again. Went to a Texas football game last night. What a stupid business. The "Sam Houston Bearkats" vs "Louisiana State Wildcats." It was a college game & played at Huntsville several miles north of here. The announcer (typical Texan) was completely prejudiced for the home team (the Bearkats). It was not only unfair (his broadcast) but commanded absolutely *no* knowledge of football.

The fans in the stands were worse (if possible) & so upset me "I'd a 'fit' at the drop of a hat."

Needless to say the Bearkats outweighed the Wildcats 20 lbs. to a man & won 14 to 0. Enuf—

Friday morning (again) I dashed off to Houston with Huncke. This time we had to get some paregoric for Bill since he's got a slight habit again. Of course, we always pick up Benzedrine for Joan & Huncke.

We arrived about 1 PM. & Huncke bought some Nembutals (we always use them) & he & I got high.

I dashed about town gunning women shopping & Huncke wandered down Skid Row.

We finally got together—since nothing exciting could happen in the afternoon—& came home, getting here about dark.

Honestly now I can't [remember what I said in my letters to you ...]. I'm happy to have you say you like them, however, I've improved on the cardboard box, I now use a barrel.

Your coat idea sounds good, as does your anticipation of NY again; however, due to my fluctuating & lack of true knowledge or crystallization of my plans this winter I can't say for sure I'll be in NY. There are various reasons why this is so. I'll, enumerate briefly: 1. Fear of getting busted if I stay with Bill too long. 2. Hardship of getting set up (since I lack the basic drive). 3. Carolyn insists I come to San Francisco to spend the winter with her—she'll make a Hollywood salary by January. 4. Allen's absence—I had counted on him to get the ball rolling academically (or its equivalent)—etc. etc.—more of this later, in more concise terms.

Here, tho, are my exact plans for the next month. Stay here 'till Oct. 1. drive Bill & Huncke to NY, arrive first week of Oct. stay with Bill at least 2 weeks. After that? who knows.

Please, Jack, don't feel I've lost *any* incentive. I'm just making sure this time. Understand? I'm just making sure that what I do from here on out is for the best.

Thanks.

Apropos of this—Allen. No, he's not fallen out with Bill. He shipped out partially for money. The other reason is me. Don't be bugged at him for kicking the girl out. It was all my fault. I'll explain without delving too far …

I understand him & he, I. Finally, it became obvious we must part. It never came up who would leave who or anything on that corny level. So—he shipped out.

Well now, that night when I brought the girl up to the hotel room in Houston. I had promised (since it was his last night) Allen a ball from midnight to 6 A.M .—when he was to leave. Naturally, when l failed to kick the girl out at 12 o'clock he was righteously indignant.

I might add at this point, the whole thing was completely unknown to me because I really passed out about 10 PM. Boy! was l knocked out! To cut it short, Allen got rid of the girl & then struggled with my inert & lifeless body all night.

Bill has not reached the tear stage yet, but he's genuinely sorry that circumstances prevent your Plan "B" from working. Here are the circumstances: The jeep is small, so small that there is even talk of making Huncke (this is serious) hitchhike to NY. You see, Bill needs me to drive (Huncke can't) or else I'd hitchhike. There will be all kinds of furniture piled in the back, no room for anyone. Rash as it sounds, one of us may either ride the fender or drag out the rear end. Bill would send Huncke by train (as he is Joan) but, there is just no money. Bill has spent all & we'll be lucky (no kiddin) to get there at all. I'm sorry as hell. I've racked my brain to find a way for you to join us, but I have found no way. Bill is so concerned that you understand, he would have added a PS. explaining to you, but I said I would explain for him. Thereupon he said—"Well, I'm going to write back anyhow. I should have sooner." So that's the story—no room. Damn it! I suspect I've read more Balzac than you think, but, his personal life is even more interesting to me. *Lovin*, yea man!

Your entire letter was very nice, but, I like the last of it best
(NY etc.)

Afternoon

Just received another letter from Carolyn. She's written me *20* times since I've been here (18 days). See what a persistent cat she is. There's only one thing wrong with her—too middle class—Ha! Bennington. Oh well. I got a letter from Allen,—he left Sept. 13 for Dakar, Africa—stating his intention of being in NY about Nov. l.

Julie will really be something when she grows up. She's already hip now to many, many things. I want to keep an eye on her & when she's about 8 or 9 see just how far she's gone. It will be quite interesting, I'm sure. Willie, the baby, is just another kid so far.

Talk about story telling, Huncke gabs in my car all day & night, he relishes bullshitting with me. We sure whip up a breeze, especially when we're high. Bill & Huncke & I get high every night on tea & lush. It's "out of this world"—to quote Huncke.

Bill & I spend hours fishing [in Winters Bayou] like veterans, although he won't admit it—even to himself—neither of us know a damn thing about it. I've written LuAnne, requesting a divorce again. She's a fine girl, but not for me. How sad.

Write soon, pal, I like your style. This letter is just like the others—no good. I guess I haven't got it in me.

Neal

Mack Thomas

[Mack Thomas was a young Texan who was an in-demand jazz saxophonist in Paris in the late 1950s when he met William S. Burroughs, one of the many bohemian residents at the "Beat Hotel." Burroughs liked to trade east Texas stories with Thomas, who was a daily visitor. Thomas greatly admired Burroughs but saw him as someone who existed separate from the rest of humanity. A line from Thomas Merton (as he told Burroughs biographer Ted Morgan) summed up his view of Burroughs: "The night is my diocese and silence is my ministry." Thomas went on to write two fine autobiographical novels published by Grove Press in the sixties, *Gumbo* and *The Total Beast*, the latter about his experiences in prison after being arrested on drug charges in Texas. He and Burroughs read together in the Bowery in April of 1964 at a party hosted by artist Wynn Chamberlain. The character of "Orby Dobbs" in the following story may have more than a passing resemblance to Thomas's view of Burroughs, and the long audio cut-up section in the text was almost certainly inspired by Burroughs's and Brion Gysin's artistic experiments in Paris in the late 1950s.]

The Fable of Orby Dobbs

Shortly after Orby Dobbs was born his parents discovered that he was blind. Quite naturally, they abandoned him in a stone quarry, where he was found and raised by an eccentric family of diamond-backed rattlesnakes that had been forced to flee conventional reptilian society for taking too casual an attitude toward its traditions.

On the day that Orby was abandoned, the weather as calculated by snakes, was bitter cold. Nineteen members of the snake family were sprawled upon a sun-drenched slab of red granite, playing a game called "Hully Gully, Hully Gully, How Many Rattles Have I Got." For some reason unknown to his parents, the twentieth and youngest member of the family—whose name, by the way, was Clyde—did not seem to have too great a passion for the game and, as usual, was off by himself, probing the mysteries of adolescence and doing who-knows-what. But the moment his nose made contact with Orby's chubby leg, Clyde snapped out of his doldrums and went slithering over the rocks to the granite slab where the family recreated. He informed them excitedly of the strange thing he had found and without wasting a moment the entire family set out across the rocks with Clyde in the lead.

When the family reached the curious, gurgling creature, the patriarch—a nine-rattler named Fang who had gained wide notoriety in his youth for his unorthodox beliefs—made the rest of the clan wait at a safe distance while he examined the mysterious newcomer. He crawled across Orby several times back and forth, up and down, as if finding it difficult to accept what his senses told him, but at last he summoned the rest of the family and gravely stated his findings. He explained that the creature was comprised of a rather short but immensely thick snake, with two shorter but scarcely less impressive snakes growing from each end of the main body, and one wee snake which, for its own incomprehensible reasons, had chosen to grow from a spot between one of the shorter pairs. He concluded that, there being no other explanations possible, the creature was a god.

Upon hearing this declaration, the mother of the clan—a fat, kindly, somewhat scatter-brained but practical snake named Sally who had been raised in the old school—immediately took charge of the situation by sending all the children off gathering johnson grass to heap upon the god and keep it warm. With motherly intuition she divined that the god must be terribly hungry. She sent her husband off on the track of a sleek field mouse she had noticed earlier in the day and marked for her own supper but now felt would make a splendid, nourishing sacrifice to the new god. She chose for herself the task of gathering snapdragons so the god might have an immediate snack.

From these first spontaneous reactions to the appearance of the new deity a happy routine developed in which the family adequately if somewhat uniquely provided for Orby's basic needs, and so the first five years of his life passed uneventfully. Before he was six, however, minor troubles began to brew. As children reached maturity they came to resent the father's authority and to look for ways to reveal that they had a mind and a will of their own. Orby was not quite ten when the conflict finally came to a head. The climax came in the form of a fierce philosophic argument about the gathering of snapdragons on Thursdays. The meat of the children's argument was that, since Orby had been discovered on a Thursday, the gathering of snapdragons on that day constituted an act of sacrilege. The father conceded that the argument would he valid under ordinary circumstances, but pointed out that since the god himself, with such obvious relish, consumed the snapdragons, no sacrilege was being committed and that such talk was merely an excuse for a laziness that surely must have come from the mother's side of the family.

At the peak of the argument, sensing that he was somehow responsible for the rift, Orby slipped quietly away and groped along a dirt service road to the nearest city, a place called Pennsylchusetts, where he immediately became so involved with the problems of surviving without eyes that every trace of his stone quarry life vanished from his mind and never once influenced or interfered with his thoughts, attitudes, or behavior. In fact, these unimportant details of Orby's early life have been mentioned only because plodding, tradition-bound writers have trained most readers to feel cheated and even ill at ease unless some meaningless background information is provided that will permit them to imagine a connection exists between the things that happened to a person on one day and those that might happen on another.

After his initial adjustment, which is much too tedious to go into here, Orby became quite skilled in the shaping of brooms and the weaving of rugs and the twisting and braiding of dreams. He learned that the grocer would deliver groceries and the milkman would deliver milk. He learned that the people who paid him for making brooms and rugs would deliver materials outside his door and take away the finished products.

One day a radio was left by mistake outside his door. He took it and kept it forever. After a year or two of putting two million and two million together, he discovered what it was for. He made it a rule to listen to *Stella Dallas* and war news and *Ma Perkins* and *Gangbusters*. One day the things he had learned during twenty years of dedicated radio listening fell into place like the pieces of a jig-saw puzzle and made a pattern in his mind. With considerable surprise, he realized that he was living in an enlightened age. A faint hope was born in the back of his mind and his interest switched to *Buck Rogers* and *Young Doctor Malone* and other programs that dealt with science.

By the time he reached the age of fifty Orby's hope was so large that the radio could no longer feed it. The days of his contented isolation came to an end. For four decades he had loved his room as a hermit loves his cave. In all the years since his arrival in the city he had left the room not more than twenty times, but now his ravenous hope became more powerful than his shyness. It tortured and goaded him when he was awake, and made a Grand Inquisitor of his sleep. At last it drove him trembling into the streets.

For the next few years he wandered each night through the fearsome world of the city, counting curbs and remembering turns in order to find his room after each excursion. A time came when there was not a tree, fire hydrant, mail box, parking meter, phone booth or pole that his hands had not examined with movements that had much in common with caresses. His hunger to know the shape and form of things he sensed and heard drove him to feel the tires and stroke the fenders and hoods of trucks and automobiles. Once, when he felt there was no one about, he spent three delirious hours in an alley, examining a dog.

At last his senses were gorged and he withdrew to his room again. For more than a year he organized all the bits of sensations and classified all the suggestions of texture, sweep, and function that had been harvested by his ears and nose and hands. But when the last experience was integrated and the last conclusion drawn, his dissatisfaction was even greater than before. His insatiable hope made him turn to the radio again. The voices spoke of Salk vaccine and rockets and nuclear bombs, kidney transplants and satellites, computers and robots and automation and plastic valves for the heart; but nothing was said of the break-through he had hoped for all his life, nothing of a technique that would give him his sight and unburden the bloodshot eyes of his imagination.

He began to talk to the voices; he pleaded with them at first. As the months went by without news for his hope, he began to attack them with bitter, accusing words. The voices droned on and on in the most maddening, unconcerned way, reporting miracles as science plucked by them willy-nilly from the grab-bag of impossibility. At last the shattering indifference of the voices enraged him so that he attacked them with his cane. At the first blow the radio uttered a threatening roar of static, but at the second blow the static changed to a steady, pleading screech. The screech punctured his rage and permitted the abrupt return of his senses. A terrible fear made him drop the cane and fall to his knees by the radio. Fright made his fingers clumsy but he found the dial knob at last. Apprehensively, he gave it an experimental twist. The bland voices filled the room again. Orby sighed with relief. When he felt certain the screech would not return he moved his fingers to the other knob and switched the voices to silence.

Afraid to trust himself with the voices, Orby avoided the radio and spent the next few days and nights in a chair pushed close to the sill of his opened window. He dozed and brooded and listened and napped and awoke to listen again and again to the noisy, taunting voice of the street below. The separate sounds were lost to him; he heard them as part of a chorus forever sustaining a syllable of some unfathomable word started too many ages ago for the beginning to be remembered, a word that could not be ended since no one knew what it was. A policeman's whistle, the whine of tires, and the ring of a church bell were part of it, as well as the sounds of a derelict rummaging garbage cans in the alley and the brush and slap of children's naked feet on the asphalt street. The chorus rose, and fell, and rose, but the syllable did not change.

At last in utter desperation, Orby went to the streets again. As he tapped along one evening, trying to imagine himself a less ambiguous imagination, a hand touched his arm and a voice said, "Hello," and startled him almost out of his wits. Frantic, he tried to break away, but the hand closed more tightly on his arm and the voice said, "Whoa, old man, take it easy! Here, let's sit on the curb and talk."

"Stop, let go! What are you? What are you?" Orby cried.

The voice misunderstood. "Why, I'm Argyle P. Jones, that's who!" it said. "A little drunk, but used to it, so, believe me, there's nothing to fear."

"Argyle Jones?" said Orby. "Drunk? 'P?' What does it mean?"

"Something about being chained to a rock, and a vulture eating your liver."

"Liver," asked Orby. "Liver?" he asked, interested in spite of his fear. "Liver? ... Ahhh! Cirrhosis!" he cried exultantly.

"No," said the voice, "But you've almost got it. It's 'P,' not 'C,' ... for Prometheus."

"Prometheus?" Orby repeated, confused. "Is it new? My radio ..."

"Have a drink," said the voice and Orby felt a bottle pressed to his chest.

"Chained to a rock," Orby mused, "Hmmmm ... and a vulture eating your liver ... the radio mentioned black eyes and leeches once, but vultures ... what does it cure?"

"Okay," said the voice, "Then I'll drink it myself. It may be cheap, but it's good."

"Well, it must be terrible painful," said Orby. "Terrible! ... But if it works ... Do you happen to know if it has to do with eyes?"

"I'll not stand while I can sit!" said the voice. "It's cost me many a bottle."

"I suppose there's an anesthetic, though," said Orby. "For the pain, I mean. What's that new one? ... sodium ... something."

"Sit!" said the voice. "Or no more talk! Craning and twisting pains my neck."

"What??" asked Orby. "Excuse me, Voice. I'm old, and a little deaf."

"Voice?" said the voice. "Listen, old man ... there's not enough for three! But wait ... if we all chip in a quarter ... I know a store down the street ..."

"Instead of Prometheus," mused Orby, "Could it have been 'Prosthetics' you meant to say?"

"Old man, you calling me a liar? Argyle *P.*, for Prometheus ... not for prosthetics, cirrhosis, or sodium whatever, but P! for Prometheus Jones. Now, go to the devil!"

"Oh no, please, please!" said Orby, "It's all a horrible misunderstanding! Nothing but brooms the first twenty years ... and rugs! You wouldn't believe how many! Except for the radio, I'd know nothing about any of it! Absolutely nothing! Can you imagine what it ... 'Mr. District Attorney! Champion of the People! Defender of Truth! Guardian of our fundamental rights to life, liberty, AND THE PURSUIT OF HAPPINESS!' ... but of course, that wasn't nearly so thrilling as the time I ... 'Doctor Brent, Call Surgery! Doctor Brent, Call Surgery!' ... Yes, yes! That's what I ... don't you see how I owe it all, all! to Doctor Brent, and Doctor ... what was the other one? ... Doctor ... Doctor ... Oh, what was his name? ... Doctor ... something ... and his Secret Journal ... oh, there's no way I could have known all that about cirrhosis without Doctor Brent and the other one and the March of Time ... No, no! It's Dimes that I mean! Dimes! Dimes! And Doctor Brent! And the American ... 'America, America, God shed his grace with ...' no, no, it's 'on,' of course ... 'on theeee! And crown thy good with brotherhood from sea to' ... 'Oh, say can you see, by the dawn's early light, what so proudly ...' A citizen, sir! A citizen, I tell you! But all the same, you still have no idea how deeply grateful I am to the American, American, you hear! Cancer Society! ... even if ... Oh! I almost ... *One Man's Family*, brought to you by the makers of Lipton's Tenderleaf ...' ... but not that I wasn't ... and still, still, I tell you ... grateful for 'Mr. District Attorney, Champion of' ... of ... 'Buck Rogers! In the Twenty-Fifth Century!' ... and, and Gabriel Heater! ... and when Stella Dallas and Lolly were in that plane crash and for weeks and weeks the program was ... I'll never forget it! ... all about Plastic Surgery! and then Ma Perkins had that hysterectomy and Daddy Warbucks, bless him, bless him! performed a Tracheotomy on Little Annie with his penknife! and Walter Winchell went to press and sank all the ships at sea! and ... No, no! ... What is it? ...What is happening to my mind? ... To think that Walter had anything to do with the vultures feeding on your liver! ... but don't you see what I've been through these past forty-five years since the radio ... hoping ... someday an operation ... able to see? Oh, please Mr. P., P. for whatever you like, it's taken me sixty-five years to have this talk with another human being and you are the very first that I ... For Prometheus, by all means! Do you hear? I say '*P. for Prometheus!*' and a curse on any man, woman, or child who dares to question it! Or refuses to listen as I march this very street forever, in fact, all the streets, if you like, chanting, 'P. for Prometheus! P. for Prometheus!' for all to hear so there can be no confusion about it! ... if only you will tell me ... Oh! You must, for I don't believe I can stand it much longer ... you must! ... For the sake of my sanity! And my ... isn't there one drop? or not even that, but if there is only a drop of a drop of the milk of human kindness left uncurdled on your lips, you *must tell me what it is like!!*"

"Have a drink, old man," replied the voice.

"Tell me I say!" Orby demanded. He clutched the voice by the arms and began to shake it with all his strength as shouted, *"Tell me what it is like!"*

At the threat of violence the voice sobered immediately and, in a trembling, appeasing tone, asked, "But what, old man? What are you talking about? Only tell me what you mean and I will tell you, I will tell you gladly!"

"The World!" Orby screamed. *"Tell me about the world!"*

"Only the world? Why, of course, old man!" the voice replied with returning confidence. "Here, rest yourself and I will explain it fully. You see, the world is like ... well ... like ... like nothing that can be imagined! It's ... the world is ... it's unbelievable! In fact, it's indescribable! It's ... you have to see it for yourself to understand what I ... But believe me, old man, the world is something to behold!"

"Aaaarrrgghhhh!" Orby screamed in anguish. He stumbled down the street, bellowing, colliding with lamp posts and jostling trees as he fled once more to his room.

In spite of his maddening experience with Argyle Prometheus Jones, on the following day Orby went in the streets again. But he was not the Orby of the day before. He went without fear of the streets or the people; frustration had burned his terror away as a blow-torch burns paint from iron. In rapid order, he passed from shyness to boldness to utter recklessness. Only a short time before he had strained his senses to avoid brushing so much as a coat tail, but now, employing the same sharpened senses, he tried to collide with as many as he could. Day after day, he stalked the streets, and when he managed to bump someone squarely, he clutched their arms before they could move on, and demanded, "Tell me, what is it like?"

During the first few years of this he tried to restrict himself to collision with other men, but as he grew older and more feeble he switched his attention to women. Finally he became so weak that he had to content himself with stopping children.

The people he stopped reacted in may ways. Men, for the most part, brushed his hands aside, ignored him and walked away. They cursed him from time to time and, occasionally, one struck him and knocked him down. He came to expect it, and learned to accept it stoically.

The women were hardly kinder. Some giggled coyly and squealed such things as, "Stop it, you *dirty* old man!" Some screamed, "Rape!" and kicked his shins. Most, in their haughtiest manner, said, "I beg your pardon!" and moved on. Every so often one slammed his head with a heavily loaded purse. On rainy days those of this type thrashed him soundly with their umbrellas.

As for the children, when he caught them alone, most were cowed and kind, but when there were several on hand they called him, "Ol' Whazzitlike!" in their sing-song way and tormented him with tricks and pranks. They seemed especially fond of wiring tin cans to his feet and slipping beetles and lizards and pieces of ice and tacks inside his shirt. And yet there were times when some man, woman, or child would take his hands or touch his arm and do their best to explain. Some would conclude, "It's hard to say," and some, "It's just like always." Once a man said, "It's like a test," but Orby remembered and thought about most the time a woman with a gentle voice and soft hands raised his fingers to her lips and said, "It's like ... it's like a place where you wait to be born while your heart learns how to beat." Finally, when he was seventy-five and his mind dozed most of the time, there were many he stopped, placed his hands on their shoulders, and stood before in silence, unable to think the words and speak his question. At such times the person he stopped often stood quite still for a moment, then said, "Good luck to you, Grandpa," and slipped a quarter in his hand before walking away.

Late one morning he raised himself feebly and wearily from his bed, dressed, drank his coffee, ate his oatmeal, felt his way to the door, placed his hand upon the knob, and realized that it was over. He retraced his steps, sank into his chair and quietly cried himself to sleep.

He slept all that day and into the night, but when he awoke his mind was reasonably clear. Ignoring the protests of his bones, he hauled himself from the chair. After an hour of searching through piles of cartons, empty wrappers, grocery bags, clothes and rags, he managed to find the radio, silent for so many years. Doubtfully, he turned the switch. After what seemed an eternity the radio began to hum and crackle, then, suddenly, poured music into the room.

"Well, old friend," said Orby, "I guess you'll have to do."

He returned to his chair, and would have fallen asleep if the program of music had not come to an end to make way for the news. As the announcer began to talk, Orby's face formed the faintest of smiles. Remembering some of the things he once had said to the voices, he silently chided himself. "The voice sounds the same," he thought, "But it's a different man, of course. Well as for that, so am I ..."

Something the announcer was saying started tugging at his senses. Grudgingly, he pried his attention from the tone of the voice and listened to the words. Before the announcer had finished, Orby's hands gripped the arms of the chair. When the newscast ended he stood with a jerk and stumbled to the door. After several hours of asking directions and hobbling through the streets he arrived at the medical center. He went inside, stopped the first person he encountered, and asked about the doctor with the new operation for eyes.

The nurse he had stopped said, "Oh, you must mean Doctor A. P. Jones. Yes. He's on the eleventh floor."

"Jones?" asked Orby. "Doctor Jones? Argyle Prometheus Jones?"

"Why, yes," said the nurse, "Doctor A. P. Jones. Tell me, is something wrong?"

"No, no!" said Orby. "It's ... nurse? ... are you there? Would you point me toward the elevator?"

"Certainly sir," the nurse replied. "It's here, four steps to the right."

On the eleventh floor, immediately as he stepped from the elevator, Orby started shouting, "P., for Prometheus! P., I say! P., for Prometheus Jones!"

"What is it?" said a woman's voice. "Stop that shouting!"

"Quiet!" said another. "Don't you realize where you are?"

"P., for Prometheus!" Orby continued. "P., for Prometheus Jones!"

A nurse took his arm and said sternly, "We will be quiet and control yourself, or we will be asked to leave this hospital!"

"Take me to Doctor P.—for Prometheus! He'll see me! He'll see me, I tell you!"

"Here! What's all this commotion about?" asked a vigorous, masculine voice.

"Oh, Doctor Jones!" the stern voice exclaimed, "I'm terribly, terribly sorry, but this old gentleman rushed in here shouting your name at the top of his voice and insisting that you would see him! I'm really terribly ..."

"Never mind, nurse," said the doctor. "Now, old man ... Do I know you? I'm busy. Quickly, what do you want?"

"You're Argyle Jones?" Orby asked uncertainly, "Argyle Prometheus Jones?"

"Doctor Argyle Prometheus Jones, Junior. Yes," said the Doctor. "That is correct."

"Junior?" asked Orby, completely perplexed, "Junior? What does it mean?"

"It simply means that my father was named Argyle Prometheus Jones and that it struck his fancy to name me the very same thing. But, really, I don't think ..."

"Your father! Yes, your father!" said Orby. "He was the first one I ... yes! I remember all of it now, all of it!"

"I'm afraid you must excuse me" said the doctor. "I'll not stand here an ..."

"I'll not stand!" Orby shouted, "I'll not stand while I can sit! It's cost me many a bottle!"

"Er ... uh ..." stammered the doctor, "Perhaps I can spare a minute. But only a minute, mind you! Come, we'll go to my office." He took Orby roughly by the hand and led him down the corridor.

In the office the doctor seated Orby, then said, "Now, would you please tell me ... Oh, I've no doubt you were acquainted with my unfortunate father, but I do hope you don't expect ..."

"Your father?" puzzled Orby. "Oh yes! Your father ... I remember it clearly, now! It was the night ... you see, he was the first human being I ... but no, no! Forget about him! I've come for the operation. You must fix my eyes!"

"Oh, come now!" replied the doctor. "You can't be serious! You must realize that I am the only person familiar with the technique, which means there are thousands, literally thousands, mind you, of otherwise perfectly healthy, important people who are much more deserving of my skill than yourself. There are a great many things to consider in the selection of my patients, and I must ..."

"Deserving?" shouted Orby. "Consider? But I've waited all my life!"

"I can appreciate all that, but surely you understand that there are limits to my time, so I must choose those who might be of some benefit to the world, those with long lives ahead in which ..."

"Benefit? But I've waited all my life!"

"No," said the doctor, "I'm sorry. You see, it's completely out of the question."

The doctor rang for the security guard, and Orby was taken away.

Day after day, Orby returned to the medical center, making his appeal from dawn to dusk to any who would listen. His strength began to fail rapidly. Finally, even the security guards were moved to pity by the sight of his bent, gaunt, shuffling figure and the brittle, desperate sound of his voice.

The interns and nurses took up his cause. At every turn Doctor Argyle Prometheus Jones, Junior, was hounded and badgered with reminders of Orby Dobbs. Even his fellow physicians began to whisper in his presence about his lack of compassion for Orby Dobbs. In the end, he relented. He felt that he had no choice. Orby was admitted to the charity ward and tentative arrangements were made for his operation. He became a great favorite with all the nurses, and the entire staff coddled him as if he were their own delicate, admirable conscience.

At last the day came when Doctor Jones announced that, should the operating room be available between the hours of one and two, his schedule permitted him to grant Orby a half hour of his time. A quick check by the chief of staff disclosed that, at approximately 1:30, between a Caesarean and a hemorrhoid-ectomy, the operating room would be free for a period of eighteen and one-half minutes. The news spread like wildfire and the entire staff rejoiced. Orby was prepared.

Late that evening the anesthetic began to wear off and Orby regained a measure of consciousness, but the operation had taxed his pitiful reserves to the limit. Four days passed before he was able to speak coherently or comprehend the remarks made by his anxious new friends. His first words were "When will they come off," and his mottled hands rose to the bandages.

It happened that Doctor Jones was present, having stopped in for a moment on his way to surgery. "So," he said banteringly, "You've decided to acknowledge us, have you?"

"Please," said Orby weakly, "When do the bandages come off?"

"Oh," said the doctor casually, "In five or six months, I should think. The tissue must be allowed to heal, you know."

"Six months?" said Orby in despair, "Six months?" His chin began to tremble.

"Oh, come now!" said the doctor cheerfully, "Six months should seem like no time to a man who has waited seventy-five years!"

Orby was quiet for a very long time. Finally, he whispered, "You're young ... six months is nothing to you, but to me ... it's more than I've left ... I'll die, and never see what it's like."

"Oh, come now!" said the doctor, "We are experts, you know. We'll keep you alive."

Orby passed the next six months in varying stages of coma and senile stupor. Even the modern facilities of the medical center were strained to keep him alive. There was great concern among the staff that his mind would be too feeble for him to be aware of the great event, but he awoke miraculously lucid on the day the bandages were removed. The room was crowded with excited members of the staff. As Doctor Jones began to remove the bandages an expectant hush settled over the room. Doctor Jones spoke softly as he worked: "It may be a bit of a shock at first, but you must try your best to remain calm. That last heart attack five weeks ago, you know ... you're in no condition for excitement. There's no doubt about the success of the operation; so, when you open your eyes, you must understand that you'll be seeing the world as the rest of us see it is in actuality. Remember all I have said to you, Orby, and above all, don't permit yourself to become excited. One final turn and ... there ... now ... open your eyes, Orby. The bandages are removed."

Slowly, fearfully, Orby raised his lids and looked around. He blinked his eyes in shocked disbelief and began to roll them wildly. His cadaverous frame grew rigid and he uttered a terrible scream. Doctor Jones said, "Hypo, nurse!" Later, a priest was called.

At last, with the aid of adrenalin, oxygen, and many, many drugs, they managed to save him. When he opened his eyes he was silent for a considerable time as he looked around. Then, in a defeated tone, he asked. "Why did you lie to me?"

"But we didn't!" came from several throats, "We didn't lie at all!"

"Yes" said Orby, "Yes ... you promised ... you said it would be a success ..."

"But it was!" Doctor Jones said sincerely.

"Absolutely!" seconded a nurse.

The priest that had been summoned at the height of the crisis stepped to Orby's bedside and took his hand. "They are telling the truth, my son," he said. "As God is my witness, your eyes are now as ours."

"It's the same," said Orby, "The same as it was ..."

"Why, yes," said the priest, "Just the same."

"No, no!" said Orby. "You don't understand! As it was when I had no eyes!"

"Oh, come now!" said Doctor Jones.

"But there's no light!" said Orby. "What became of it? Where did it go? It's just a word! Don't you understand??? ... It's dark! It's dark!"

"Why, bless my soul!" admired the priest. "I do believe he's found the perfect word for it!"

There was a general murmur of excited agreement.

Andy Sanchez

I Love You, Van Helsing

We used to climb mountains.

I'm only your
wake-up alarm clock anymore,
your merciless ringtone
won't quit
seven in the morning.
Half hour later,
I'll check up on you.
You'll still be asleep.
And I'll still keep calling.

We used to
fight vampires,
paint cities,
pretend we could find God
together.
I remember when she left you,
the ten thousand conversations
we had.
But you haven't
mentioned her
in over a year.

We would
streak through the night,
teach each other
trumpet,
and write novels,

but I haven't seen you,
just glimpses
who you were
who we were.

Since the car accident
all the pot
all the bands that broke up
the poetry you never finished

—since last winter,
you've walked away.
Won't call at two a.m.
save my wacked out
voicemails
or pray.
We just
"chill,"
and Reminisce.
Like we used
to be young or something.

Jeff Callaway

Rode Hard and Put Up Wet

i've been rode hard
and put up wet a many a night
by dirty gin martinis
by fine moonshine
by the crucifix neon signs
of the bible belt of East Texas
where the liquor is always thicker
in one of those wet counties
and it always seems to find me quicker
over on the other side of the tracks
but back to what i was saying
i've been rode hard and put up wet
a many a night ...
i've seen the likes of mystics
madmen
six naked men on bikes
in downtown San Francisco
i've seen the likes of speedfreak succubus angels
creeping like snakes inside my beer bottles
listening to Radiohead, reggae
redneck romantics
who had also been rode hard and put up wet
i've written poems which i've put away
until now
and poems i put to you
today ...
i've seen the rain
from a train
from a Greyhound window
from a plane
i've seen the night inked in a blanket of fog
and i've sat and admired the moon from a hollow log
i've rolled my bones and joints
through cellar doors
through the Celis Brewery
through the celestial stars over California beaches
i love to eat the sweetest little peaches

i've read at Big Sur
i've loved English teachers
i love the sea
i love this poem that rages in me
i've combed the seashores
i've slept on floors
i've been locked behind bars and i've been free
i've been in a horrible mad raging sea
i've slept under the trees
i've watched evil TV's
and i've seen
the sunrise the sunset
and all of these wonderful people i've met
who have also been
rode hard and put up wet ...
i've been drunk and just went to bed
i've been underfed
i've had sex drenched in sweat and i've bled
i've thought for sure that i was dead
i've thought for sure the sun would not rise again
and i've made friends and i've made love
i've cried and prayed to the lord up above
i've felt and held in the beds of my lovers
endless nights of soft flesh
wrapped in covers
under Texas skies
beside cheerleaders' thighs
in smoky rooms
the scent of northern lights
and i've made love on through the night
and into the day
but what i really wanted to say
was i've been rode hard and put up wet
a many a night ...

Amber Foster

Unsent

Do you remember when we came here together? Five years ago, and we were raring to go, fresh out the gate and hungry. We ate and breathed the sea, diving all day until we started to see fish in the clouds, fish in sand-footsteps, fish in window grime. When we weren't diving we were talking about diving, because it was all about who had gone deeper, who had logged more hours. You wanted to beat my record because you didn't like it when girls beat you at anything.

I don't know why I came here again—I didn't know it was possible to be homesick for a place you don't belong to. Maybe I was remembering us in that little room on the edge of West End, the way we lay in bed, naked and sweating, listening to the *chik-chik-chik* of geckos on the ceiling. Maybe I was remembering the strange non-smell of the Caribbean Sea, and the waves that lap the shore in lake-sighs so unlike the roaring menace of the Pacific. Maybe I was remembering long nights sitting on the porch, drinking *Salva Vidas* and smoking home-grown weed, talking with Don Marcos about how *el presidente* just got thrown across the border into Nicaragua, practically in his boxers, and how in Honduras things always seemed to get worse and worse rather than better.

I came into town late, bleary and plane-wasted, my taxi bumping and rattling past crumbling walls and empty shop windows that stared out at the sand-pitted road like blind eyes. I went to our place first—call it nostalgia—but it was gone. A dusty For Sale sign tilted lazily on the beach, waiting for the next storm to wash it away. The buildings were still there, boarded up and fenced in, but somebody took the hammocks, leaving the tree branches naked and stripped of everything but memories.

José, my *taxista*, took me to Barefoot instead—you remember the place, a short walk up from the *baleada* shack where we used to watch Esmé turning and turning the balls of tortilla dough, stretching them out with her fingers and then slapping them back and forth between her palms until they were flat and round and perfect. Esmé is gone, back to her family in Ceiba, and there is an old black woman in her shack, a local, selling cheap jewelry and friendship bracelets to unwise tourists. But the hotel is the same, with its wobbly furniture made from compressed cardboard, its lumpy mattresses, and its windowsills coated in gecko shit.

I picked up some work at Sunshine—Hans is the manager now. That German bastard is in hog heaven, spending his days perched at the front desk, not having to put a single pinky toe in the water and collecting his check. He still waxes nostalgic at every turn about his love for "exotics," women with big asses and chocolate skin, women with dreadlocks and pendulous breasts jutting out from their chests like pirate ship mermaids. The local girl he was dating way back when is gone, replaced by a mainlander, a short, fat woman whose double chin and wide smile reminds me of Buddha.

We always did like talking about all the crazy characters on this island, this place of cruise-shippers and dreamers; *gringos* from Europe and Canada and the States looking for paradise; Honduran mainlanders looking for the same thing in the pockets of all the rich *gringos*; and black Garifuna folk, speaking their rhythmic island English and swaying down the street in their Sunday best, on their way to church to sing and praise *Jeeeesus*. I loved the sound of their hymns and their exuberant *Yes, Lawd!*s and *Amen!*s as it drifted in through the slanted glass slats of my bedroom window—it sang me to sleep as easily as a lullaby.

Yesterday, Hans had me take three young Dutch guys to Lighthouse Reef.

From the surface, the reef spread out below us like Martian topography, full of mysterious canyons and intersecting lines. We dropped down above the wall, my eyes drifting down to the sand bottom where it tilts off into the deep. I stayed above sixty, leading the boys on a winding path up above the dead coral, looking for morays and lobsters hiding in crevasses and waiting for night.

On the way up, we ran into a sleeping nurse shark cradled in a sand patch between two coral heads. I crept up close, and I could see she was watching me with her beady eye. I reached out two fingers and ran them gently down the sandpapery roughness of her skin, wondering if sharks ever wish they could stay in one place, or if they are fine to circulate the seas, going wherever the food goes without getting too stressed out about it. The Dutch guys came up and tried to touch her, but she got fed up with our bullshit and swam away, finding a quieter spot for her shark dreams.

I never told you this, but after you left with what's-her-name my mother died. Stroke. Didn't leave me anything, not that I expected her to. I missed the funeral—I got the email from my cousin a week after it was already over. You were the only guy I ever brought home, and she hated you. I became an instructor like you to spite her. She went to her grave thinking her daughter was a vagabond, as bad as the old bums in the 50s, riding the rails and drinking bottles of cheap wine from paper bags.

I don't know if I'm writing because I miss you, or because I miss the sense of direction that came with having another person there with me in the world.

I went diving alone last night. Hans gave me the keys to the shop, since he and his girl are off to the mainland today. I waited until two, when the bars were closed down for the night and the street deserted. I unlocked the gate to the dock and put my stuff on *Sueño*, using my dive light to navigate my way to the reef. The motor's kick and roar was so loud in my ears—a marching band amplified by a factor of ten—but nothing stirred, no angry voice shouted *¡Alto! ¡Ladrona!* at the little boat as it put-putted into the night. If anyone saw me, they probably thought I was a water *taxista*, taking some drunk tourist back to his resort.

I could navigate to Sea Quest in my sleep. Guide buoys, there, with red and green reflective strips warning boats to avoid the shallow reef on either side, then out into the deeper water, coasting along with the reef on the left, the light of the town insignificant compared to the dark mass of the island jungle behind. My hands shook as I tied the boat to the buoy and assembled my kit, my heart thudding like drums calling for blood sacrifice.

But splashing in was like coming home.

Looking up as I dropped down, I could see all the stars reflected back, a two-dimensional painting with the faint strip of Milky Way like a dirty brush stroke across the sky. I hit the sand at forty feet, my light illuminating a rolling undulation of sand unbroken except for a lone sea cucumber foraging for food. I lay out, spread-eagled and facing the surface, my fingertips resting in sand still warm from the day's sun. Then I turned off my light.

The feeling—how to describe it? At first there is nothing. No light, no sound except the steady bubbles of exhaled breath. Up and down are words without meaning in this darkness. Soon, though, your eyes catch flashes of light, little flecks of green and blue like strands of pearl floating in the water. Phosphorescent creatures coming together and falling apart. Mating, dying. The water tumescent with life, a living, breathing organism, beautiful and terrible at the same time.

I don't know how long I stayed down. I still had air left when I broke the starry surface. As far as I know, no one saw me return the boat or slip back out of the shop an hour or so before dawn.

Now I am lying in bed under the shroud-like recesses of the hotel mosquito net, trying to imagine where you are right now. I suppose you've gone on with things. Maybe you're married. Maybe you've got a kid or one on the way. Maybe you don't look up at the clouds and see fish any more. Maybe you don't even dive.

Somewhere between the Roatan of us and the Roatan without us, I got lost. But something in me is changing, I can feel it. The Roatan of now is a new place, a place without the ghost of you in it. Tomorrow, I will meet Don Marcos and we will drink beer and talk about how things only get worse and worse. Tomorrow, I will dive with Hans and see if the nurse shark has returned to nap in the refracted sunlight of Lighthouse Reef.

Tomorrow, I will throw this letter in the sea, watching it soften and disintegrate, merging with the water until it is gone, gone, gone.

Ryan Neighbors

Freight Train

You snore like a freight train, she tells me,
her eyes crusted and half-closed.
A freight train, I guess, that snores,
and sort of lies there, off-track,
not really freighting anything,
except maybe a tank car of gas—
yellow placard warns "toxic"—
that smells vaguely of our evening meal
but soured, fetid, under fluffed sheets,
or perhaps another filled
with flop sweat, ammonia-tinged,
from those damn dreams I have
recalling when, as a preteen,
I walked in on my mother
toweling from the shower,
pubic curls exposed
against pale, shining flesh.
But dream-mother only arches
an eyebrow and drops her towel, oops,
all while singing the theme song from *Aladdin*.
A whole new world, indeed.

My train-self thinks of Thomas the Tank Engine,
because I have a three-year-old
and he has poor taste in television.
Blue frame, red trim, leather interior ...
one assumes the last—
not a freight train, but close enough.
After a long day of dealing
with all of those bitchy passengers,
their immobile mouths painted on,
but still bitching,
"You're too fast, Thomas,"
or "Speed up, Thomas,"
or "Thomas, stop with the jostling,"
all narrated by Ringo Starr or Alec Baldwin,
an engine wants to relax,
recline his six wheels,
rest those radio-controlled eyeballs.
It's natural for him to squeak

to pass steam, or some other vapor,
to seep oil from well-worn joints, right?

I consider all of this,
sigh, and forget it.
And instead make a joke—
sexual, of course—
about something else I do like a freight train,
a freight train that does that other thing,
a freight train of looooove,
but she only tells me to stop snoring,
rolls her eyes, and then her body.

Janet McCann

Ginsberg

So he fell in love with a painting of Peter Orlovsky,
nude, red-haired, muscled, piercing-eyed—the paint still wet
and Peter was living there at the artist's house
and he walked out of the back room and Peter and Allen
spent the rest of their lives more or less together
despite Peter's mad behavior and penchant for women
and the artist painted others, and they too lived
right in the building, and other poets came by
and fell in love with them, and it was the fifties
and the blood of art was life and life was art
and ordinary singular people, itchy, grubby
blotchy and stoned, were brushed with liquid light

* * *

I'm skimming books for an icon to return to
gray day—sporadic light snow
and a mild chill-cataract of depression
eyes too dutiful in custody

a simple image, the self
vitalized and reified,
touch of otherness
as the library fills with sullen patrons

with hats and scarves—
maybe lights in a tunnel
getting smaller and smaller
I saw this often as a sickly child

in the folds of my bedcovers
perhaps a sound or a medal
of an unknown saint a train
hooing away in the distance

anything, sunflower, skull,
cityscape, horsehead, word
without meaning, chant, sitar,
something to hold in the heart in the dark

230

* * *

My friend and teacher said, I am afraid that you think getting old
has robbed you of some of the romance of life

His implication: but it is still there for you,
if (though only if) you trust in it

50 years ago he said, Good poem about the lake
but never would you say, "Beauty, beauty, beauty"

No, I wouldn't say that,
The words would stick in my pen, "Beau—"

* * *

the painter, smelling of turpentine,
the palette on a table with some rags
the model Peter, freckled, ordinary
there at the artist's house

trying not to move, his back sore
sweat running down his face (it's always hot
or freezing here) thinking would the sitting fee
cover a bottle of for once good wine

an abrupt knock on the door and
it swings wide open

Janet McCann

May 21

I am in a basement, where I see all my words I ever wrote in piled moldy heaps of old school notebooks and paper-clipped manuscripts and loose papers, parchment, onion skin, even carbons, and they all start coming apart, tearing, swirling around, disintegrating. The whole basement floor is now covered with torn, dirty papers and blurred words. Then they are a pile of illegible compost, a papier-mâché.

But now someone opens the floodgates of the Mississippi, and a huge wave sweeps through the basement, washing away the wall, and the ceiling collapses around me, just missing me, and sunlight blasts its way in. And everything swirls down a hole, dark mud with scraps of paper in it. There is a hoo-ing sound like wind on a prairie.

And now it's a flat meadow and something is gathering in the center, like an uprush of earth, and first a shoot, then a stalk grows there. It divides into whispery leaves, and finally a flower buds and opens–it is breathtakingly lovely. I try to find just a few words to describe it and I can't. I can't even name its color, which is nowhere on the visible spectrum.

In three months, in six, will anyone remember that today was the day the world did not end?

Chuck Taylor

Out by Munson Creek

"Give me my blowgun," Harry said.

Kyle handed him the blowgun from the floor on his side. It was dark and cool and we were on a county road sixty miles east of Dallas. The sky was autumn clear; a quarter moon hung low on the horizon.

"You can't drink beer, drive and shoot that blowgun," I said from the back seat.

"What are you going to shoot?" Kyle asked.

"I don't know. Maybe you," said Harry.

"Fuck," said Kyle.

"Fuck you," said Harry.

"You got poison?" I asked.

"Sure," Harry said. "Just hand me the box. It's under the seat."

"Shit," I said. "I'm too drunk." I found the plastic box. After a bit of a struggle I got the lid open and handed Harry a dart over his shoulder. Just at that moment we got to the bridge at Munson Creek and Harry handed me the blow gun.

"You load it," he said.

I took the blowgun and realized it was just PVC pipe. It had a rubber mouthpiece at one end. I put a dart in from the end, not sure what I was doing. "Where'd you get this?" I asked. "At Canton first Monday or a garage sale or something?"

"I ordered it out of the back of Soldier of Fortune," Harry said as we bumped over the open wooden bridge. "It's better than a gun. Zip and they're dead. No sound."

"Let's stop and shoot something," Kyle said.

Harry pulled off to the side a little beyond the bridge.

"You gonna shoot some fish?" I joked.

"Hell no!"

"You can't kill a turtle with that," I added.

"Turtle my eye," Harry said.

"We got to find something to kill," said Kyle.

"That's what we'll do," said Harry. "There's always something around to kill."

We all got out of the car. I could see a few old refrigerators stuck out of Munson Creek where people had shoved them out of their pickups off the bridge.

"All you'll find around here is cows," I said.

"Cows'll do," Kyle added.

"Zip a dee do dah," said Harry. "My oh my what a wonderful night."

"Save 'em the long ride to the slaughter house," said Kyle.

"Aren't they milk cows out this way?" I said.

"You country boys know about hunting?" Harry queried.

"No," I said. "We're small town boys. The only thing I know I got from listening to the good ol' boys drinking coffee down at the Dairy Queen on Highway 80."

"Cows should be hunted," Kyle quipped.

"Yeah. It's in their blood, and tonight we're tribesmen."

"Uga-booga," I said.

"There's a cow over there," Kyle said.

"Naw, you fuck, that's a log," said Harry.

"I bet you can't even hit that freaking log with that thing," said Kyle.

"What'll you bet me?" said Harry.

"I'll bet you the case I got in my trunk back at the house," I said.

"Naw, that's stupid," said Harry.

"It's dark as shit out here," said Kyle.

"You step in a cow pie?" I asked.

"What about shrooms?" Kyle said. "We could get us some shrooms right out of the cow pies."

"Naw," I said. "They put stuff in the feed. No shrooms anymore and no Kickapoo joy juice."

"Get over there," said Harry to me. "I'll shoot you in the leg. You won't hardly feel a thing—sorta like a flu shot."

"Do it," said Kyle.

"No way," I said. "You got poison on those darts."

"Did you bring the darts?" Harry asked.

"Kyle did," I said.

"Fuck that, man. You had them in the back seat."

"Fuck. I want to go to war," said Harry. "This is shit. Nothing to do but get drunk or do drugs. I want to go to war."

"I did Desert Storm, man," I said. "Let me tell you, you don't want any of that crap."

"Fuck yeah, man. That's why I joined the reserves," Kyle shot back. "I want to drink and defend my country. I'm ready to ship right now."

"My feet are covered with mud," I said. "The stars are cool out here, but let's go back."

"Just let me shoot something," said Harry. "Then we can go."

Beat Houston

must labor under an unfair prejudice because many know Texas' largest city only from its freeways and toll roads, and indeed, the daredevil spirit of this old wildcatter town shines in the unique style of driving its citizens employ. They know about living on the edge because they do it every time they get in their cars. Yet there is so much more to this city to inspire the independent Beat artist spirit. Public readings of literature go on all over the city on almost any night, mostly at bookstores and coffee houses. Dustin Pickering's Transcendent Zero Press celebrates in the pages of its magazine and books, and at readings, the outsider spirit. The Menil Collection, which focuses on the surrealist art that the beats loved, remains free to attend. Off of the freeways are beautiful neighborhoods full of character that inspire artists of all kinds. Many poets and writers, including Lorenzo Thomas, have produced fine work. Lorenzo pumped gas and taught university classes. Houstonites are an hour from the sea and the old port city of Galveston—a beat city in its own right. Houston sits at the edge of the piney woods of East Texas. Cultures mix in Houston and stimulate one another. KPFT, Houston's independent public radio station, was twice bombed off the air, and Arlo Guthrie came down in the 1970s for a benefit to assist the station to rebuild. What could be more beat than that?

Allen Ginsberg

Dear Neal

Claude [Lucien Carr] & I went to Mexico and returned to the U.S. A few days ago. Bill was in South America on some expedition. We took J. [Joan Vollmer] & kids riding all over to Guadalajara & Mazatlan—Mex Pacific Coast.

Car broke down near Houston—I spending week in Galveston on Beach. Claude flew to New York. He returns in 4 days by plane to pick up me & car & dog.

Note in newspaper I saw tonight says that Bill killed Joan in accident with gun last night. "An American Tourist trying to imitate Wm. Tell killed his wife while attempting to shoot a glass of champagne from her head with a pistol, Police said today.

"Police arrested: Wm Seward Burroughs, 37, of St. Louis, Mo., last nite after his wife Joan, 27 died in hospital of a bullet wound in her forehead received an hour earlier."

That's all I know.

I am sitting in a broken down shack across the street from the Gulf of Mexico. I have spoken to no one since I've been here, slept much, bathed a lot, walked around town, have an icebox.

Kells Elvins is in Mexico City. He is a great man, and on the scene so there is someone around to help bill & take care of kids.

Claude & J. played games of chance with drunken driving, egging each other on suicidally at times while we were there. I left with him from N.Y. at last moment after jack [Kerouac] dropped out to go hospital for leg and finish book.

Hope everything's ok by you. Write me 149 W 21 Street N.Y.C. care of Claude. I'm nowhere as usual, not doing anything though this summer I worked for a month as a book reviewer for Newsweek magazine.

My imagination of the scene & psyches in Mexico is too limited to comprehend the vast misery & absurdity and sense of dream that must exist in Bill's mind now—or whatever he feels.

All my love,
    Allen

P.S. Spent several days in Huston this trip—remembering 1947—but didn't visit Hotel Brazos—went to look at Shamrock Hotel, drunk

Derland Frost

New Novel for Young Bohemia
Houston Post 8 September 1957

ON THE ROAD *by Jack Kerouac, 310 pp. New York: Viking Press. $3.95*

Quite probably "On The Road" will be one of the most heatedly discussed novels of the year, though not among the cocktail set. This is a book for the dispossessed, for young Bohemia, for those whose lives so far have led nowhere, though not yet to the point of no return. It is not, however, a story of cynical attitudes or ennui toward a life that does not readily yield answers. It is a chronicle of restless, searching young men on a wild hunt for experience from one end of the country to the other, to whom this open road is life and the only possible response to everything is yes.

Sal Paradise is the voice of these "beat" characters, and says of them: "They rushed down the street together digging everything ... and I shambled after as I've been doing all my life after people who interest me, because the only people for me are the mad ones, the ones who are mad to live, mad to talk, mad to be saved, desirous of everything at the same time, the ones who never yawn or say a commonplace thing, but burn, burn, burn like fabulous yellow roman candles exploding like spiders across the stars and in the middle you see the blue center light pop and everybody goes "Awwww!"

"ON THE ROAD" is not ordinary writing. It roams without pattern as its characters roam, making no concessions to those who may like to see an unconventional subject presented conventionally. You will either be swept by its mood and footnotes go hang, or you will drop by the wayside, puzzled and probably a little uncomfortable for the exposure.

Few of us have ever encountered anyone like Dean Moriarty, the mad, holy, conman who is the acknowledged leader of this directionless but always moving group, some of whom get off at Chicago, are picked up in Denver, gather again for one or two wild nights in San Francisco's little Harlem. They scatter immediately, working the railroads, hitching rides, occasionally stealing cars for joyrides or arranging to drive them from one city to another, their destination a matter of whim and opportunity. Girls are absorbed into the group and ejected when they become too demanding, only to be readmitted during the course of another trip. There are no tragedies. Everything is a kick. Disaster in the ordinary sense is sadly lonely.

Occasionally one or another tries marriage: Dean himself maintains households on both coasts. In spite of his uncontrollable urge to go and keep going, he has a passion for roots. But his women cannot for long maintain the desire which Sal expresses for them all: "What is that feeling where you're driving away from people and they recede on the plain till you see their specks dispersing?—it's the too-huge world vaulting us, and it's good-by. But we lean forward to the next crazy venture beneath the skies."

Leaning forward, the wild adventures career from Chicago bop-joints to Mexican brothels, from California vineyards to New York pads, "rushing through the world without a chance to see it." There is no end, only a recurring wistfulness and yearning for someday solidarity and growing old together on a quiet street.

"On The Road" is not for everyone. Those who want to discover it, however, will find it a very special discovery.

Bongo Joe (George Coleman)

[A young folklore student named Pat Mullen recorded these improvised lyrics during a performance by Bongo Joe on the Seawall in Galveston, Summer 1967. While singing, Joe played two 55-gallon Superchief oil drums, tuned with a crowbar. Taped to his sticks were bandaid boxes filled with bb's. In the winter months, Joe was a mainstay during the early years of the infamous Cellar nightclub in Dallas, where JFK's secret service agents partied until 5 am the morning of the assassination. He also played his drums in Houston's Purple Onion club in The Montrose. Later, Joe was a fixture in front of the Alamo for more than two decades.]

What I Like About the Jungle

What I like about the jungle [drums]
—all them wild animals,
forests,
trees,
marshes,
Everglades,
woods [drums]
—well, jungles
—that covers all that,
—don't it?
Wild animals and beasts and things.
Get in the middle of the jungle,
and you don't have to worry about protection.
Texas Rangers won't mess with you out there [drums].
You don't have to worry about our present-day situation [drums].
Out there in the jungle you ain't got nothing but peace [drums].
You don't have to hang no sign on your door
talkin about "Please Don't Disturb" [pauses].
Might have to hang one on a tree [drums].
What I like about the jungle is,
all them barks,
and roots,
and herbs [pause],
and berries.
I could drink or eat as much as I want to.
Didn't have to worry about no federal control and
prescription and all that stuff.
They served their purpose for two,
ah, twenty thousand years.
Two hundred years did a good job of keeping one of them a secret,
til the Americans came over,

bombarded,
confiscated,
brought it over here,
slapped a label on on it,
called it LSD [loud drums].
What I really like about the jungle [pause]
is [pause]
I ain't there [laughs, drums].

Lupe Méndez

To Mi Tio, Joaquin
A response to *Yo Soy Joaquin*

Tio, let me show you.

I am protesting my own gente,
forgetting that I stood there,
near Harlingen feeder roads,
selling sandia with my broken spirit,
in Houston Worksource Centers, jobless,
while Azteca gods prayed
for me to succeed, and I did.

I moved to Austin, near SoCo.
I eat lime stone and sleep in pink granite.
I put three kids, —Nauatl, Ingles and Spanish,
in college, and bought a HUD home.
They graduted speaking todo mocho,
Fucking in a tormented Spanglish
And telling me—"Don't let any more of them in."

Help me remember
the stories you told me about
serenatas and rebellion like
hot red blood from Popocatepetl.
Angry because every mother and lover
knows temper for dealing with poverty,
abuse by man and our brown state.
I still hear you singing—

Hay mama, que yo no fui,
yo te lo juro que yo no fui,

NO,
That's the last song, Tio.
We have to leave Hallabaloo's.
Take your fingers out of her dress,
you don't live like that anymore.
I gotta go to work tomorrow.
I work like a burro with an ethic.
I should wear a red, white, and blue flag

with the words, "Don't Tread—Ya Chingaste"
underneath.

I owe no debt.
Paid in full, with you, Don Corky and Chavez.
Paid in the withering arms of a *Brazero*,
you signed your contract and never could send a dime home,
to feed me or my mother, who cursed you, who drowned me,
who searches for me in rivers. She searches hopelessly,
like pragmatic programs that leave every child behind.

Don't fret Tio, I got a plan.
I will live as you did in your youth.
I will reach out and repopulate the *frontera*
where everyone will be the
brilliant color of a rich Rio Bravo.

While you were fighting,
Tlazolteotl and Ehecatl cried for you.
They resurrected you; wrapped you in gold
and shot you at the sun.
You are better than Icarus ...

Entraste a la boca del sol, y
saliste cubierto en llamas que quemo
tu tocayo, tu maguey, tu maize,
tu Bexar, tu Goliad, tu El Paso,
tu peregrinacion, tu milagro.
—protect me Tio Lindo, protejame mi jaguar
for I am Mexico, y Soy Tejano,
hijo de Seguin y el Infierno de Espana
and
I SHALL ALWAYS ENDURE.

Carolyn Thorman

The Cut of the Cloth

Rags are the filets of fabrics once worn.
To make one, take off all buttons,
Adjectives, cuffs, collars and seams,
Excuses and stains
That show where you've been.

A rag is a failure of stamina, fit,
A material record of character flaws
The mistake in the plan, the fray in the seam.

Hard rags, say, linen
Never shed threads, inhibitions, or lint.
While soft ones, your flannels and old terry robes
Suck up the spills, slips of the tongue.

Give me the shreds
Of your time, let me see
The sag of your hem,
The holes in your past.

Give me your failures,
Lies and defeats.
Give me your stories.
Your reasons, your rags,
And I will give you
The shirt off my back.

Richard Peake

Ego Wheels

Cruising down the avenue
rolling slow
showing off your swangers,

envious eyes are watching
silver spokes
flouting rim-related murder

Would you put your Mama in this car,
or your baby?
"You gotta do what you gotta do."

Bro, would you strut this car
one deep at night?
"No, man, three deep and strapped,

you hate all the violence and death
provoked by these pokes,
but still you want 'em, you know."

Cruising down dark avenues
rolling slow
showing off your swangers.

Kay Cox

Ranch Ants

I love this place
I don't even mind shitting in the outhouse
in the middle of the night.
I leave the door open
and there, against the mountains,
are the sparkling lights of Santa Fe
grinning at me in the distance.
But it is snowing out there tonight, cold,
and I really need to pee.
Where is that empty water jug I cut the top off yesterday?
This won't be an easy task for a squatter.
Geezus, there's a damn line of ants in my room
and I trying to pee.
They're headed to my stash of chocolate.
Move the chocolate, pee, go back to bed.

Morning.
I'm thinking
these ranch folks are so ecologically bent
there's no way they'll go for bug spray.
Time for plan B.
Dum-ta-dum-dum
The ants go marching one by one.
Hurrah, hurrah.
I am tracking you critters out of here
to your holy front door in the sandy dirt.
I'm gonna drown you.
Yeah,
I'm gonna drown you in yellow piss.
Lookout, little red warriors, down the hatch
and if you dare cross my threshold again,
I'm gonna squash you and hide the evidence.
But right now, while no one is looking,
I am enjoying watching my pee roll down your hole.

So there!

Chris Wise

There's A Cloud Now

He sat
afternoon to sundown,
cross-legged on a five-gallon bucket.
His sign:
>   *"Hopeless drunk*
>   *Need food and beer."*
He had a dog for a time—
a thin, rough collie,
and a friendship with a bag maiden
who frequented him for talk.
People were always stopping by to talk.

I haven't seen him for a while now.
I'm not sure if the cops finally ran him off
or if one of the terrible things
that often happen to street people
                                   got him.
His spot is empty.

I never had anything to spare,
except the nods we shared when I passed,
but they were genuine.
I recognized him
as a man
neither vermin, nor waste,
who—for his own reasons—
has declared himself *hopeless*.

I'm not sure what he thought of me,
but maybe he saw the same dullness in my eye,
and that's why
he nodded back.

John Gorman

The Malted Milk Ball

like the world
is round, layered   gradually
over a core
    unlike the world
    is easily manageable
    (no sweat)
like the world
is being devoured
    unlike the world
    is sweet
—not that the world isn't sweet.
Death eats the world
      over time
    when I
              eat the malted milk ball
      it's sweet, sweet
I eat it quickly
        I'm having fun
me & death
    I'm better.

Dustin Pickering

Crossing Fertility

When the be-bop
dives
through the barrier of sound

the grilling of jazz
on the plate
like an egg fresh cooked

my mother comes close
to my ear
in the dreaming silence

i whisper my stony fright
to the ghosts
of her dead

mirror

Melissa Studdard

Subterranean

I'm not talking about the underside of a kitten's
belly, or the layers of dress on a modest woman's

corpse. I don't mean that beneath the skin there's
a world of vein, meat and bone. No, I'm talking about

mantle and core—the viscous, shifting substrata
beneath the camel's hoof, beneath the sand,

beneath the crust beneath the sand. I think there are
birds in there, flying around inside the earth's body,

birds flying over oceans, streams and lakes, children
laughing beside rivers, mothers calling them home

to supper by beating wooden spoons on the sides
of aluminum pots. It doesn't matter that we can't see

them, or even that my theory has been disproven.
I go where the laughter is, pure and simple, and I say

this ball of clay is really an onion, a snake coiled
around a bouncing ball, a swirl of petals exploding

from bud. It's simple, really: love is the pack on a
hitchhiker's back, everything he owns, everywhere

he goes, the only article that can't be left behind.
And we've all got our thumbs out, pointed towards

that other realm, the one beneath the skin, beneath
the bone and marrow and veiny streams of blood, where gods

await us like lovers, like dense smoke, like cracked
and forgotten mirrors, reflecting the singular route home.

Dru Watkins

All Night Chinese Diner

I want Kung Pao by the kilo
a pail of hot and sour.

I eat my cookie
with the fortune still inside.

Mr. Han handles the business.

He has a sports car that runs
on credit cards.

It's crowded all the time.

Cops make eyes at
girls through sodomy shades.

MSG and sautéed onions
are smoke signals
for salt and sex.

Translucent transsexuals flaunt
see-through genitalia
beneath the gaudy wall art.

Sophistication is a pair of
damp panties and an order
of skunk-fried rice.

Ken Jones

One Last Shot

To heal the Earth we must first heal ourselves
Of impurities we surely imbibed
At the shot bar of More Progress and Wealth.

We clean the bottles off the dusty shelves
To make way for the New Age we've described.
To heal the Earth we must first heal ourselves

And then never again dirty our wells:
Those storehouses needed for all the tribes
At the shot bar of More Progress and Wealth.

Unavoidable poisons, with shrewd stealth
Have stolen in with suicidal bribes.
To heal the Earth we must first heal ourselves

And learn the subtle cycle of her health.
She's not the whore our self-hate did proscribe
At the shot bar of More Progress and Wealth.

She is our source, our fountain whose vibe
Gives us the life on which we now inscribe:
To heal the Earth we must first heal ourselves
At the shot bar of More Progress and Wealth.

Ken Jones

Slices of Middle America

Doll cottages dot the dark tar boulevards
Glowing "home" for some animate animal
A temple of temperate comfort
And fixed feed time
In a frenzy of pituitary culinary
With his chosen monogamous mate
Who faithfully holds down the homestead
As he battles the elements for survival
They are not strangers.
Their ancestors conquered the virgin land
Fled famine for freedom, tamed
The Plains buffalo, hid
The misnomered natives
Who ferried across the Bering Strait
As slope nose Oriental anthropoids
The original Amerasians.
"Much deeper and you'll hit China!"
The grizzled prospector yells
At the spike driving coolie
Not thinking a gold Caddie
Awaits his descendants down the track
When they open a dining car
On stationary Chinatown plot
And net two million per annum
Feeding pink-skinned tourists
Who claim it as their special spot
"Our home away from home"

Stephen Gros

The Grand Adventure

I miss it.
The dripping yellow blood rushing down the expanse
Of my unknown black veins
Under the thinnest blue membrane of skin.

The chalky aluminum taste of disuse
in my dry mouth.
The warbling of strange radio
against my country tired ears
After 36 hours of driving.

I want to get back to that rest stop
where I was a hero for stealing some Fritos.
To the first time I saw the desert open up
like a huge book, its pages yellowed with age.
I want to return,
to the shimmering net of stars
floating in an endless black sea.
Me, bathing in silver
laughing as big as the moon
filthy and exhausted,
my breath a heaving labor,
my body floundering in the cracked earth,
the dry wind whispering soft truths to me,
the scorpions lying with clicking tongues.

I want to return,
to the simple nutrition of a piece of cheese
every 20 or 30 minutes.
Until it's gone.
The complexity of aimlessness.
Dirty love in the back seat.
Waiting at the bathroom door like a stone guardian.
Salt stiff clothes.
Booming thunder.
Trickling sap.
A coyote running across my eyelids.

I want to make a pass again

at the grand adventure,
of nowhere in particular.
I want to steal the breath from the passing wind,
and make it mine.

Stephen Gros

Acadian Blues

I'm a Cajun, a coon-ass, a bug-eating Bayou Wildman
and I have a great storied history
buried deep under
the filthy oil slick surface
of my swampy home.

I want to paint you a glorious portrait
of a forgotten culture
But my Acadian Blood
Runs hot and red with anger
It burns a channel deep and venomous
All the long way down the miserable Mississippi
And flows out in the red silt at its mouth

I can't tell my story in gentle tones
For my people were not treated gently
14,000 strong
Burned from their homes in 1755

      Have Mercy!

Le Grand Dérangement
The Great Expulsion
because they refused to take up arms against their French countrymen
Only 3,000 made it to Louisiana
That why this mud is so sacred to me
My family names are LaPoint and LeBlanc
2 of only 60 surnames to survive the ethnic cleansing
But we made it

      Have Mercy!

We thrived in an impossible wilderness
Found peace and nourishment below sea level

          Who is your mother?
          Are you a Catholic?
          Can you make a roux?
          Community

       Faith
       And Culture

     Have Mercy!

I'm a Cajun, a coon-ass, a bug-eating Bayou Wildman
I'm also an Acadian
Forever displaced from his home in the cold north
Forever attached to the wet black mud of Louisiana
Above all, of this, I'm proud

     Have Mercy!

Viens ici! I hear my momma calling
The gumbo's ready and the water's rising in the cobbled streets
The air smells raw, sticky and warm
It smells like suffering and injustice
Like untold stories
And forgotten ancestry
Hidden under Mardi Gras Masks
It smells like home, hope and family

     Have Mercy!

Robert Clarke

Buddha Came into a Hindu Culture

Buddha came into a Hindu culture,
With the over-riding concept of the Wheel of Life:
       Every time you die,
       You're born again,
       Into a new body
           Blip, blip, blip.
       And there's no escape from the Wheel.
So he took a good look at that old belief
That bound his people, and he said
       Yes, all that bullshit's true,
       But you can rest at the hub of the Wheel
       And be one with the one thing that everything is,
       And he called it Nirvana.

Jesus came into a Jewish culture,
With the over-riding concept of Good and Evil,
       And rules—so many rules you could never obey them all.
And he took a good look at that old belief
That bound his people, and he said
       Yes, all that bullshit's true,
       But there's forgiveness, reconciliation,
       And he called it Grace.

Now, you, take a long look at your culture,
And what it is that ties men down,
       For what once served as a frame of reference,
       If ever closed, becomes a cage,
And find a way to say
       Yes, all that bullshit's true,
       But …

Lorenzo Thomas

Ailerons & Elevators

Autumnal Equinox 2002

The backward see
The wise don't say a word

Three dreams, one foolish
And two meaningless
Are haunting me, disturbing me

One says
A golden road was plotted out for you
In dreams, of course

But that's not where you are
When you awaken

The danger is seeing the world
as two extremes
The afternoons of rushing home to see her
Balanced against
turning the corner
Hoping that her car will not be there

Daydreams are better

Nice—
watching the planes come in
On the last day of summer
Airport peaceful

Passengers are few
On flights answering demand
more than desire
Their stress has been at home
Or will come later
They deplane calmly

When the Wright boys
and their friend Paul Laurence Dunbar
Finished high school in 1890

Their neighbors knew
That they'd go high up in this world

Paul as an elevator boy in downtown Dayton
Orville and Wilbur
Going swimming in thin air

Unfortunately,
They'd never heard of Richard Gallup
David or Romare Bearden, either

Such are the baffling deficits that time imposes

They never dreamed
Someone would use an airplane
To drop bombs made of oilfield dynamite
and set Greenwood aflame
Andrew Smitherman fleeing in 1921
from Tulsa to New York
To the edge of America

What is this shadow
Cast across the coming season?

In the still watches of the Negro night,
Fear rising like mist off a bayou,
The danger in the world
Is seeing it as two extremes

Is this full moon so indiscriminate
That even liars prosper
if they have launched
Their web with the new moon?

This autumn equinox
A harvest of deceit
Leaves the ground rugged.
The harvest done, the fields outside the city
flat and sere
A single egret stands in the parking lot at the Post Office
Poised and confused

The world automatically recoils
Into itself

Are you ready for football?
For serious business
Are you ready for war?

People throughout all history
Have lived in ashen cities
or died in them
Marcel Duchamp was joking
Wasn't he, as always when he said
Dust-covered glass
Might offer auguries
Of our predicament

O mirror, mirror

How have my people been distracted so
They don't care any longer who they are?

How so misled that they believe
Punishment does not apply
To crimes committed in their name?

Must war morph from Nintendo game to spectacle
To get attention?

If all are suspect
Could my own duplicities
Be causing this—
The way we're all responsible
For air pollution
(if you keep breathing)

If you believe in magic, yes

And that same magic, yes
Could stop the rush to madness, too

There are still
scraps of summer laughter
On the street
There's still some music from two backyards away
The Funkadelics and Jay-Z resist denial

But here's
The truth:

You have the right to keep your mouth shut

Trust me,

Across the room
A person looking like a crazy version
Of somebody you once knew
Might be our Savior
One who can draw fire
Out of ashes
At least a lover, maybe
The one to take you up a little higher
Or let you down easy.

But don't look this way,

It isn't me

[In his "Stroller" columns for the *Houston Press* in the 1940s and 1950s, Sig Byrd uniquely captured subterranean Houston. As his friend Leon Hale says, "He was able to do this Damon Runyon stuff about the underworld. Nobody else has been able to do it," he says. "He wasn't afraid to go to 75th Street at 11 p.m. and sit and drink in a sleazy bar and get those stories." We feature two excerpts from *Sig Byrd's Houston* (1955), one set on Congress Avenue and another in "Catfish Reef."]

Sig Byrd

From *Sig Byrd's Houston*

Congress Avenue

He was a man you'd never notice unless you happen to know who he was, and the chances are you wouldn't know. He was walking up Congress Avenue, in his khaki trousers, pale yellow sports shirt, and the gray felt hat—the same gray felt hat he always wore, uncreased, as always, so that it resembled a derby.

His hair was black—at least the part that showed. Few have seen him with his hat off, and those who have paid dearly for the privilege.

His face was the same color as his trousers. His nose was slightly aquiline, and his eyes were very bright and watchful. I neglected to say that he was of medium build, except that if he had another twenty pounds on him you'd call him chunky. The only distinguishing feature about him was an old knife scar reaching from the right-hand corner of his mouth almost to the angle of his jaw. And the hat, of course. His age? Well, he looked anywhere between thirty-five and forty-five, but something about his eyes suggested he might be even older.

As he approached the first honkytonk he observed two persons standing in the doorway. A man in dirty slacks and a woman in dungarees were watching him and apparently waiting for him. But he observed them without looking directly at them. His black, shining eyes were on a black Ford parked across the street in the next block. There was nobody in the car, but he knew who drove it.

And as he drew near the honkytonk, he took a large, clean, white handkerchief from his hip pocket, folded it neatly, and began mopping his face and bare forearms.

Curiously, he was not sweating. It was one of those days when the temperatures were ten degrees below normal.

The man in the honkytonk door spoke to the woman.

"Hot," he said.

The woman looked as if she wanted to scream. With stricken eyes, she watched the man in the uncreased gray felt hat draw abreast of the joint, and then she spoke quietly. "The carpet," she said. "Please!"

But the man walking up the avenue ignored her. He kept on mopping. "It's real hot," the man in the doorway said. It was quiet along the avenue. The cars and trucks bumped along in one direction, the people in two, the cars stopping for red signals, the people for beer or for a pair of fifteen-cent socks.

Everybody was moving—slowly, yet they kept in motion. Even the characters kept drifting. The avenue was quiet, but restless. It was tense. The avenue needed a sedative.

The man in the uncreased hat passed on, mopping his face and arms from time to time. Many people saw him do this, and those whom it concerned understood. At last he reached the Azteca Theater, and here he quit mopping. He walked to the end of the next block, then turned down a side street.

A burly, neatly dressed man came out of a store farther down the avenue, got into the black Ford, and drove away quickly toward the courthouse. He turned right at the courthouse corner, and he turned against a red light, but the traffic policeman on that corner only threw him a soft salute. The car disappeared.

For half an hour nothing happened on the avenue. Then the man with the scar across his right jaw returned. He walked down the avenue now, on the other side of the street.

Every half-block or so he would pause, take the neatly folded white handkerchief from his hip pocket, and fan his face with it. As he moved on downtown, the avenue seemed to relax. He was like the cool hand of a nurse applied to the fevered brow of a sick person. He was a cool front moving into the parched city. He was a physician arriving in an emergency, a platoon of Marines come to prevent a riot; his briskly waving handkerchief was like a cry of "All's well!" in the dark streets of a besieged town.

The characters stopped drifting and sank wearily to the curbs and doorsills.

One went to the liquor store and purchased a fifth of synthetic muscatel, came out and sat on the stairway with two others, and they began passing the bottle.

In the doorway of the honkytonk, the man in soiled slacks said to the woman, "He's cool now."

The woman's jaundiced faced relaxed. She said, "I hope he remembers I've switched to blue eagles." Then she looked at the man through gummy eyelashes. "What are you on?"

"Bennies," the man said. "They're the best."

There was a walk-up hotel on the other side of the avenue. At the doorway, the man who was cool now turned in and looked up the empty stairwell. It was empty.

Nobody saw him take his hat off. Nobody saw the thin packages he slipped under the edges of the threadbare carpet. He didn't really like to do business this way. He preferred cash in hand. But he hadn't been cool very long. And anyway, if they didn't even leave the right amount he'd cut them off so tight they'd be screaming inside of twenty-four hours.

He came out of the doorway and walked quickly down the avenue, no longer pausing, but fanning his face with the handkerchief once more.

From the honkytonk, from the other joints, the ones who knew began drifting toward the hotel. They went in one at a time. The woman in dungarees couldn't even wait for a Coke or a beer. She was cramming the capsules into her flaky roughed mouth like popcorn as she came out.

Nobody was disappointed. There were redbirds where redbirds were supposed to be, yellowjackets for those on the yellows, and Dexedrine for those on dex. And they all left the right amount of money; so there was no trouble on the avenue that day.

Catfish Reef

Clyde and James Green, brothers, young men with eight beats to the measure of every breath they draw, were seated at the piano in Martin Nelson's recording studio in Catfish Reef. Clyde made his ten brown fingers flutter over the keyboard like butterflies in hobnail boots; his feet moved like the feet of voodoo dancer, slapping the pedals down, forte, forte, forte, never piano.

James on his right, embraced the base of the microphone amorously, spoke to it now tenderly, now menacingly, but always forte. The melody was intricate, the key a minor. The song was bluer than indigo, hotter than an atomic pile. It made your hackles stand; you wanted to say, "Yeah, man!" and take off your shoes and dance.

James Green smokes while he sings. Cigarettes. He wears a yellow sports shirt and has thin black mustache, invisible in the studio light that filters down through an inverted Japanese umbrella. He was singing:

"Houston is all around me; still I have nowhere to go.
Since my baby lef' me this mawnin', goodness knows I feel so low ..."

A red light flashed. Martin Nelson, wearing a sweatshirt and seersuckers, had to hold Clyde's arms to make him stop playing.

"What's the happenings?" asked James.

"It's the end of the groove, man," said Mr. Nelson.

"Well, all right," said James, still bouncing in four-four time in the piano bench. "Let's listen to ourselfs."

Mr. Nelson played the plate back. It was a good cutting.

"Talk to me," James said.

"Well, boys, it's like this," said Mr. Nelson. "You're good. You got talent. I don't know if you're ready for Hollywood yet, but you got the beat. You got it in you."

"He got it," Clyde said. "James got it. My brother-in-law got it on the electric guitar. But me, I don't know." Clyde works in a gas station at Sixth and Yale. He wears a yellow sports shirt too, but no mustache.

James snapped his brown fingers. Boogie still possessed him. "Lots of times," he said, "I go out to ankle a joint and spread my blouse. Because my feet is beat without shoes."

"Where do you get those songs?" asked Mr. Nelson. "You memorize 'em?"

"Just sing 'em," James said. "You name a thing, and I'll drop a light spiel into sound-catcher and overflow your knowledge-box. That is, if it ain't loaded."

"It's loaded," Mr. Nelson said. "I never encourage a man unless I believe he's got talent. You have got talent."

"I ain't," Clyde said sadly.

"Your bass was a little affirmative," James said, "but you had the beat. Lots of cats ankle to my plea. I drop the deuce of business when I drop my right to spiel."

"You got another side," said Mr. Nelson. "You want to cut the other side?"

The brothers said they did. They turned back to the piano. On the wall besides the piano was a large oil painting of a naked savage with ivory rings in his ears. Clyde began massaging the keys tentatively, like a surgeon feeling for an abdominal tumor.

A bell tinkled in the front of the shop, indicating that someone had come in, and Mr. Nelson hurried to see who it was. It was Raquel. Until she closed the door, the traffic noises of the Reef came into the studio like a kind of counterpoint in bebop, emphasizing the music of the Green boys in the back room.

"Hello, Raquel," said Mr. Nelson.

Raquel came in every payday to have her picture made in the fifty-cent size, and she never took less than three copies. Raquel is a very pretty girl. She smiled at Mr. Nelson, then sat in a brightly lighted booth and smiled at the shutter of a camera.

Almost before she got the smile off her face, Mr. Nelson handed her the three direct-positive prints. "I don't like 'em," she said. She always said that.

When he had her money, Mr. Nelson sad, "Tom and Harry was in, asking about your sister."

"I didn't know they was out of jail yet," said Raquel. "Was they on the weed?"

"Weed, or drunk," Mr. Nelson said. "I told 'em I'd tell you."

Raquel just smiled and went out. Mr. Nelson went back to where the boys were finishing up on the other side. James was dropping a wise spiel into the microphone:

"Goin' back to Houston, baby; get me a job on that Southern line;
Try to make myself some money and send for that little gal of mine.
I want all the people listen to what I got to say:
I'm crazy about that little gal they call Flora May ..."

"All right," said Mr. Nelson.

"How you like that one?" Clyde asked.

"I like that one better," Mr. Nelson said, lifting the cutting arm. "You boys need a backer. Need a get somebody to cut you some masters, get you some records on the jukeboxes."

"I can't even pick up on me no slave," James said. "Clyde, he slave on the grease-rack. I can't pick up."

"All right, boys," said Mr. Nelson, "now we come to the most important phase of this transaction. That'll be a rag and a half, please."

Clyde paid, and they ankled. The place was quiet now.

Beat West Texas

begins with the Balcones fault on the west side of Austin at the start of the hill country. Up in the northern part of the state, Fort Worth might be considered the Eastern most boundary. West Texas reaches up far north to Amarillo in the panhandle (which gets snow!), far west to El Paso, which sits on the border of Mexico and New Mexico, then deep down south to the Big Bend area. West Texas is giant, widely various and mostly dry. The folks tend toward the friendly, and an expression used when saying goodbye is "Y'all come see us." A new center for the arts in West Texas is the small desert town of Marfa, close to the famous apparitions of the Marfa lights. Marfa has a great bookstore, homes for visiting writers on grants where Robert Creeley worked right up to his passing, as well as a number of art galleries. Literary readings are common in major cities like Odessa, Midland, Abilene, Lubbock, and San Angelo. The small town of Lamesa, south of Lubbock about an hour, features a wonderful yearly poetry and music festival with an environmentalist slant, called Forrest Fest, run by poet and memoirist Connie Williams, who studied at the Beat writing school in Boulder with the unlikely name of the Jack Kerouac School of Disembodied Poetics. Connie Williams appears and offers commentary in a well-known documentary on the Beats.

Joe Ely

One Fuse of a Summer

I awaken to Lubbock crumbling
Hatch said roadie quit, gone to El Paso
Mark sick, mother in the hospital, all looks bleak
The night coiled in tension, attacked by fame

I went to Gregg's then to Robert's, no relief
Sharon said leave my house, she was serious
I wandered delirious at 7 - 11 and vacant lot
The weeds are breathing, the stars whisper *fool, idiot*

Felt bad Saturday and the dust was blowing
The air electrical and shocking negative static
The dust settled at rusty dusk and the band played
The music hot and the night went on until daylight

Slept late Sunday and went to the hospital again
Mother was doing better so I took in a movie, Black Stallion
Visual romantic sentimental tears of relief
Went to Stubbs to jam and TV's late night

Shot pool 4 A.M., accidentally insulted a black hustler
He hit me in the jaw and then reconciled
I studied this dangerous creature as we moved
To more dangerous joints in darkest Lubbock

Saw Eddie Beethoven at Broadway Drug
He showed me totem poles and woodworking tools
His mind is galactic but born in the wrong century
He wants to build monuments out of 2 X 4s

I dreamed for 3 days I needed the rest.
I went to Spain and rented a rubber Citroen
Tires inscribed with Each Man Becomes the Road He Takes
I was trying to avoid secret lovers of presidents

Sharon's wild, she cries day and night
"You're irresponsible," she screams
"Yes," I say, "I've misplaced everything."
"And don't really give a damn if I find it."

I returned to the hospital my mother worse
Ice packs and antibiotics and endless lists
She asks me to cancel Amarillo, doctors are torturing her
I feel so helpless, I pray for a miracle

I have inherited her distrust for doctors
She is the perfect mother for the life of a seeker
Passionate, suffering, visionary and weak
Life stacks the deck in certain games of solitude

Morning with Smokey, I leave to the land of my birth
Quick stop in Plainview for used store shirts and tux
On to Amarillo in a vicious wind in a vw
45 mph top speed wall of north dust, sandpaper air

Scene: Amarillo honky tonk red and black
I drink a beer as the band tunes for 30 min.
First beer in 5 days, tastes good, no sound check
The club feels ominous, wish I were down the road

We open with Hopes Up High full tilt
This bull has its head down. Take no prisoners.
I notice a disturbance on Jesse's side of the stage
His amp was crackling; he'd just gotten shocked

He's ok, the show misses not a beat
Next song the stage sparks and quakes
Jesse's eyes wide, mouth foaming,
Falling into Lloyd's steel, hands frozen on electric guitar

Slow motion spastic muscles
Dissonant chords flying chrome
Lloyd knocks Jesse's guitar away from electric snake
The dance floor stops and stares

The song self-destructs, we turn to Jesse
"Shit! You ok", "Man, what was that?"
"Try it again?" "Hell, I guess ..."
"One, Two, Three, Four ..."

We begin again, and then 10 minutes later I get a jolt.
Vision exploding, eyes spewing sparks
Arm twitching with voltage nerve terror
We announce we are taking a break. We hit the back door.

I woke up to the beat, Amarillo, Saturday
To hot rod, Bar-B-Q, Charlie's bar and hamburger mansion
Played wild to 2-steppers and ranch hands until retreat
To untamed outskirts of Route 66 and hoarse windy dreams

Sunday I rose in the afternoon and drove around memories
Recollections of childhood powerful and mystic
With clarity magic and reflective like glass
Like following subconscious sense of direction

Streets and alleys come alive again
In parts of town, dilapidated with decay
When certain veins of the memory are tapped
Springs of clear water erupt to the surface

Lubbock appeals to the sinuses of the mind
And to the allergies of the spirit
The eye sees horizons when none are near
The breath gropes for air in the sparkling dust

Feet feel for wheel when none are there
Receipts are a dime a dozen but business is bad
The fraternities chatter and the bar glasses clatter
But the rule of the cruel is dizziness

Got a cold in my nose and turned in my taxes
Ate a submarine thinkin' bout twin saxes
That played in my brain while I ate the guacamole
My boots got no shine but Lord, are they Holy

Lubbock Rox afternoon set-up
Night brings blown fuse and smoking amp
I am reminded of Lubbock's apathy, want to return to
          London ...
Some Vickie follows me around all night

Friday, I took my semiannual state of affairs tour
On a bicycle cruising Lubbock suburbs
I saw no other people on sidewalks, in yards, nowhere
To unconsciously circumvent the vastness of the prairie

Perhaps loneliness prefers to be inside with itself
I rode 20 miles before I was satisfied

I love to bicycle in Lubbock, there's no uphill
The wind is the biggest cliff there

I went to see Jerry Jeff and jammed till late
And talked in his wonderful nonsensical tone
I rode bicycle again the next day to Buddy Holly Park
Looking for a site for Tornado Jam

To TV's, again, I went after midnight
Always attracted to nightlife and danger
And my friends, Black Charlie, Shallowater Slim, Joe Murphy
Incandescent lights on green felt, neon on red Naugahyde

The clack of the balls, 8 in the side, the gleam in an eye
The cheap bright clothes, imitation snake and shark,
Shiny hair, patent leather and rhinestone gleams on Joe
Murphy
Cooking pork chop sandwiches on white bread wired
hotsauce ...

Sunday I sat in a nylon-webbed lawn chair with friends
And basked in the aroma of outside cooking
The day was clear and windy
And the sunlight was like New Mexico, sharp and revealing

Cadillac Mountain on the coast of Maine
Is the first point that the sun touches America each morn
And that's about the time I get home each night.
Sharon said leave; my guitar life-style does not suit her

Came the next day and got my stuff
I'm scatter'd to many winds. Mobile home gone to rust
My country house empty, covered in dust, belongings in boxes
Haven't unpacked from England, now packing again for
        Austin.

I talked to the parks department, silly details about future jam
They say the city's upset
Thinking we want to conjure up a cyclone. C'mon boys,
This ain't no fountain, it's the sea herself.

I rented a car and got the hell out, picked up Sharon first,
She had cooled down and drove that lonesome road to Austin.
We cooked out with the help of headlights
And on to Austin motel in a driving hurricane, 3:30 A.M.

I woke up to a ringing phone in a red room
Motellivin' is the life I lead. They say sound check off.
Chinese restaurant next door to Antone's loud music policy.
Jammed with angelic Angela, white queen of blues.

      Another play day, walk on glass
      Play late night to the shakin' ass
      Take this party to the lawyer's house
      And press our luck on what the law allows.

Sharon leaves mad feigning hurtness
I dont know why I hang around, or why she does
She needs more security and routine than I can give.
Singing, "All you need that I ain't got, is a little routine"

Back on the road, whew, finally, after a day off
Riding with Jesse talking dissatisfaction with band crew
Nothing works, amps, guitars. The band is slow onstage,
Sloppy dressed, thinking of itself as an endless bar band.

I dreamed I was walking between buildings on campus
I notice gun-turrets on tops of buildings
A biplane dives and the students spray it with white powder
I realize it's all a joke.

The pilot barely misses the tall bell tower
And stalls after a hard turn and clunks down to the ground
A couple of girls fall out giggling. One takes me by the arm
We walked, she talked, I was deep in thought.

I dreamed Chinese sex and delicate weave of carpets
Jesse sat in one room grinning with peroxide hair
One girl took me in a room running her fingers through my hair
And said, "I'll show you how it's done."

I rode a bicycle around Lubbock shopping for binoculars
We played with the Planets at the Cotton Club
Saw Gene Glasscock fresh out of Houston drunk charge jail.
He slipping back into pre-prison pattern

Saw fire 3 A.M. in small wooden alley 2-story
Silhouettes of firemen spraying orange water

Against blue violet sky. The full moon argues
With flashing lights and people crying

Another Cotton Club night berserk and Jesse said he quit
And I said I quit then did an encore
When the stage beckons, I cannot refuse
I didn't blame Sharon when she kicked me out at dawn

I met with the Mayor of Lubbock to talk Tornado Jam
He was cordial and serious, owns a TV station and is divorced
I felt like a seagull on ice, I was not the right person
To represent myself in these concrete matters

We arrange for a stage, P.A., lights, etc.
And figure how to pay for it or else skip town
That night we go to TV's. Sharon finds me like a bloodhound.
Silence like ice. I'm always in jail.

Johnny Green arrives from England with wife Lindy
Like a breath of fresh air straight from Clash tour
At dinner we discuss news from both sides of Atlantic
Hell fire, let's go, I'm bustin loose

Johnny finds the Coldwater cowboys amusing
As well as void of familiar personality.
Will his sense of adventure justify his culture shock?
Tune in later for more ...

Coldwater again. Johnny asks why we play here
There is no excitement, he says
Everyone sitting on their fucking asses
I agree, by cracky! Wake up! Start your engines!

The big day of the Tornado Jam and I feel like shit
My eye and throat are infected and swollen shut.
A pain rips like a power saw from my jaw to my temple
The crowd seems unreal, aquarium like.

I recoup for a few days, my eyes very bad.
Friday we go to Palo Duro Canyon with Johnny and Lindy.
This landscape must look like the moon to them.
Farm road 400 plowed and barren

Johnny admires the TV dinner packages at gro store in Plainview
Lindy looks for English tea and finds Lipton's

We arrive in the canyon at sundown,
Build a fire, and then watch TV like true gypsies.

We woke to the river and climbed a red mesa
Me and Johnny walk to the store and buy a Winston radio
Back at camp, we battle another camper's loud radio
With xtra loud rockabilly and reggae

A storm approaches over the canyon wall
The rains wail and our van rocks violently
We sleep rocking like crazy
And pray for low water not holding our breath

Sunday we go to the drags, outskirts Amarillo
Hot rods and Modifieds lined up for miles
Super stocks roar down the quarter-mile mouths open
Dragsters explode in terrifying smoke and decibel scream

The asphalt melts leaving the smell of nitro and burning rubber
Six seconds later the crowd gasps as the monster smashes 240 mph
I feel empathy as the drivers tear down.
We drive to the Cadillac graveyard and shoot it full of holes.

I dream Mario Andretti tells me performers have a need for speed
Some find it in women, some in danger.
I'm talking long distance to a parachutist whose chute won't open
"I hope you ain't calling collect," he says, "Reverse the charges."

Goddamn Dust! I was born in It, swam in It,
Swept in It, mowed and moved in It.
I've cried in It and woke with mud stains on my pillow.
I've resisted the draft, scattered wild seeds, and attended
        funerals
        in It

I've run with It and against It,
Swallowed acres of It, fought It and flowed with It.
My wise conclusion is only; Let It blow! Let It blow!
Blow you goddamn dust, blow!

Terry Allen

[From an interview with singer/songwriter/playwrite/multimedia artist Terry Allen: "It's funny, you think about those little permissions that you run into. When I was a sophomore in high school, the beatnik thing hit Lubbock, with coffee shops and people in leotards and berets and sunglasses and beatnik poetry. And I loved all that, whatever you could get your hands on, Kerouac and all that. I had an English teacher, and we were doing Shakespeare, and I remember writing a beatnik poem when we were supposed to be following her reading. She stopped the class and said, 'All right. Stand up and read that.' So I stood up and read this horrendous gibberish, fully expecting her to throw me out, and she just looked at me and said, 'You keep doing that.' I was stunned. And she was dead serious. 'You keep doing that.' That's the first— maybe the only—thing I can remember getting out of high school. It means so much to have somebody cross that line with you and give that to you."—Interviewer, Robert Faires, *Austin Chronicle*.]

Amarillo Highway

Well
I'm a high straight in Plainview
Side bet in Idalou
An a fresh deck in New Deal
Yeah
Some call me high hand
An some call me low hand
But I'm holdin what I am ... The Wheel
'Cause
I'm panhandlin
Man handlin
Post holin
High rollin
Dust Bowlin ... Daddy
An I ain't got no blood veins
I just got them four lanes
Of hard ... Amarillo Highway
Yeah
I don't wear no Stetson
But I'm willin to bet son
That I'm a big a Texan as you are
'Cause
There's a girl in her barefeet
'Sleep on the back seat
An that trunk is full of Pearl ... and Lone Star
(chorus)
So
Gonna hop outta bed

Pop a pill in my head
Yeah, bust the Hub for the Golden Spread
Under blue skies
Gonna stuff my hide
Behind some power glide
An get some southern fried ... back in my eyes
(chorus)
As close I'll ever get to heaven
Is makin' speed up ol' 87
Of that hard-ass ... Amarillo Highway

Bobbie Louise Hawkins

Beauty Contest: Ms. More Usual Person

A Beauty Contest I might have a hope of winning would include as values: chewed-up fingernails; hair with split-ends, matte finish, unlikely color, tired roots, and exhausted curl.

A pretty girl is like a melody ...

(Well, sort of like a melody ... A not so great melody ... A melody that never quite resolves its beginnings into a negotiable middle and then on into a usable finale.)

That haunts you night and day ...

(Haunts is a good one ... a real pale face that doesn't invite a vigorous tan, as in a vampire that can't stand to be touched by sunlight ... I mean, any light, any light at all can drastically interfere with the delicate patina of my personal charm.)

That haunts you night and day ... Just like the strain of a haunting refrain ... She'll start upon a marathon and run around your brain ...

(Yeah, that's the gist. When I really get my grip in it's like that, like I really look good when I start upon a marathon and run around your brain ... with my chewed-up fingernails and my pale but interesting face, and my really drab hair.)

She'll start upon a marathon and run around your brain ... You can't escape ... She's in your memory ... Morning, night and noon ... (We're starting to get close to it now, to what I really require if I have a hope in hell, me and my hairballs and my frazzled-out wash-the-color-in-it's-good-for-six-weeks—that's six times you wash it and you're back to nondescript and it's time to start over again—me and my hair going through our six weeks up and down, running through your brain, you can't escape ... I can see where you might want to, I mean I'd like a little relief myself, six weeks in, six weeks out; you think beauty is easy?

Why isn't it like school, where the teacher graded you according to what you started with and how much you made out of it. Where the kids who were brilliant had to do even better and the ones who didn't have a hope in hell were given a little encouragement. Misleading, sure. Not the way to toughen up the young for the streets of the world. More like a brief breather, with the implication that Authority operated on the lost-sheep ethic where the lost lamb gets desperately looked for and there goes God getting enthused about here comes back that one lost sheep. And the teacher looks past the class geniuses writing genius papers and checks me out, dyslexic, can't read, can't write, live in a trailer with my mama and daddy here from the old countries can't even understand each other's language; the only thing I have to read is joke toilet paper we bought on sale because of the typos. My book, I call it.)

Just like the strain of a haunting refrain ...

(Oh my god, the strain, the strain, of a haunting refrain ... I'll start upon a marathon and run around your brain if that's what it takes.)

She will leave you and then, come back again ...

(Tenacity. That's what us beauties know all about, tenacity. Beauty is not easy to come by and it is not simple to maintain. Starting at the ground like a beautiful little plant, let's go up and up: Toes, Ankles, Calves, Knees, Thighs, etc. You know, and I know, that there's more than that to beauty. It isn't enough to have the parts in place. Beauty is when the parts work in wondrous harmony with the current social desires running a hardline counterpoint. So let's get into stuff like *rhythm and cute* and Hedy Lamarr and Greta Garbo, Marlene Dietrich ... There she is, Ms. Amerika ...

Aw hell, I don't know. It's all so overwhelming.

You have to start small.

You have to start somewhere.

I've been working on my hair for four weeks this time.

I'm just ready to go from Rich Dark Brown to Heaven's Own Purple, what the hell.

I'm ready to get down to business here.)

She'll leave you and then, come back again,

and come back again,

and come back again ...

Bobbie Louise Hawkins

Things

The thought of unpacking my "things" and sitting in the middle of them curdles my soul. Apparently I'm making other choices. If only choices were solutions ... Over-the-falls is my style, a choice that precludes most others. Over-the-falls feels like hope to me. I am waiting for a miracle. A miracle is whatever might happen to resolve all this. I've cleared the slate. I'm ready.

Connie Williams

To Lawrence Ferlinghetti
who stole my maidenhead with a poem

You were my first poet
The first one to hover near my nakedness, telling me
That birds would go mad when I gave myself
Stretched eagerly upon the dirt brown earth
A hot summer upon me

You were the first to lift me spinning into the world of words
My virgin intellect bursting into existence with each plunge
of earthy freedom, freed at last to live it, to write it all down

Years later when I saw you for the first time
Sitting at that table in Naropa
My heart could not be still
My body could not move
My breath strangling me
My silent mind frozen, framed around your profile
Like that photograph of you on the back of *Coney Island of the Mind*

But real, fulfilling all my fantasies
Your flesh and blood
Close enough to touch
Close enough to smell
Yet still unavailable
Untouchable
Unknowable
Forever pure

Connie Williams

I Might Have Cried
for Chuck Taylor

I might have cried pulling into a strange city
had someone else been driving, but always
It has been me behind the wheel. Tears came later.
When the complications of living became how to
pay the bills, or where the next meal was coming from
or where my child would go to school and how I could
Take care of myself without compromising my familial
Responsibilities. Always watching each new companion's
Eyes for pedophilia or abusive lies. Being a single mom
is a double role. Being a hermaphrodite might work,
then father and mother could come rolled into one.
Strange cities have an allure drawn from the imagination
near fantasy, the good job, the things to do, the culture
Like California beaches or New Orleans jazz. Always
we have expectations that may or not come true, and only
If we have the flexibility and mind to start anew.
Perhaps it takes years before we discover what we learned
From each new town and life we tried on for size
Sometimes it never quite makes it to the conscious mind
Remains a mystery for years to come and curious how we
Take it out to ponder why from time to time.

Joseph Stamey

The Day Allen Ginsberg Died

We will summon Gautama to do
A command performance of the flower sutra
And the angel Gabriel to recite
Dozens of Hail Marys
And let Jesus repeat Beatitudes
And have Kid Ory play the blues
And each of us add a koan
Or sutra, then we will place
Pennies dimes and nickels
On his eyes who welcomed us all
Decades ago to paradise
Where hipsters hopped
Boxcars, could forget angry
Fixes, and glory hallelujah
All night long until in the icy
Dawn we were one with plants
With animals with the third rail
Of any line we chose
Like Whitman before we were burning
To merge with ever loving ocean
To be swallowed like every Jonah
And lost on shore alive.

Catfish McDaris

Washing Machine Blues

In the laundromat my
voluptuous neighbor & I
watched our dirty clothes
make soapy love

"Some people are beautiful
until they open their mouths"
she yawned "Some are only
fantastic when expressing
their personal vision"

"People without vision are
not only blind but they are
less than strutting peacocks"

Her head tilted to one side
like a Picasso looking in
thought into my eyes

She discovered the Amazon,
the Sahara, Rachmaninoff, &
Coltrane in the gray rain.

Catfish McDaris

Fat Cats

A campaign? who are you
at war with, politician?
your own people?

Using children as cannon fodder,
keeping fat cats, FAT

"Ask not what your country
can do to you, just be assured,
it will do it" lawyers, CEO's,
rich selfish gluttonous pigs

Dancing on avoidance, hollow
words, forked tongues, broken
promises, treaties, & bribes

Together we stand, divided we
fall, LOOK around, then put
on your parachute

If politicians don't keep their
WORD, let's put their asses
in jail, like ordinary citizens

I've heard Alcatraz is vacant,
let them bugger each other
instead of us for a change.

Roxy Gordon

Junked Cars

I spent my mysterious childhood
hunting human sign
over miles and miles
of empty
Texas West.

I hunted rusted tin cups and
broken bottles where adobe houses
melted and where dryland farmers'
deserted shacks moaned low in
summers' winds.

I spent my lonesome childhood
hunting rusted human sign
over miles and miles
of the empty West.

I treasured rusted old tin cans
and purpled broken bottles
where dugouts had collapsed
in drywash creekbeds
and where empty limestone
ranch houses stared out
blind from broken windows.
Junked cars were beautiful to me then
because they once had lived themselves
of human living beings.

Roxy Gordon

Living Life as a Living Target

The idea came from prairie dogs.
Prairie dog towns used to stretch
all over the West. Prairie dogs
are funny little animals that stand
on the dirt mounds by their burrows
and bark like the devil when
something threatens.

Prairie dogs have no real defense but to
head underground
(just like human beings)
and even then, they are likely to
be followed, dug out and
eaten (just like human beings).

–PAUSE–

Prairie dogs seem
born mainly to furnish
nourishment.
Living life as a living target,
living life waiting for
the ferret
living life waiting for
the fox
living life waiting for
the coyote
living life waiting for
the hawk
living life waiting for
the white man–
running always, offering
a moving target,
fighting like the devil
to stay alive,
but keeping others alive
by dying.

–PAUSE–

Prairie dogs are an endangered
species now, except up on the
northern plains and
the ranchers up there would
like to see them that way.

But we expect they'll survive—
in name and in fact. Because
the world still needs those who
die
for the survival
of the races

—PAUSE—

And then on the other hand,
there are those moving targets
that move so fast
they just never get caught.

Roxy Gordon

An Open Letter to Illegal Aliens

It wasn't that those old Indians
had such bad immigration laws,
It's just that you
European wetbacks came
in such vast numbers,
the Sioux and Comanche border patrol
couldn't keep up.

And even after you've overrun them
and taken their jobs and stolen everything
you could steal,
Still, they'll let you stay.
It ain't you, you see, illegal aliens
that the American continents don't want.
It's that baggage you slipped through customs—
Send it back; you can stay.
Send back your capitalism.
Capitalism kills and steals.
Ask virtually every imperialized human being
in the whole suffering world about that.
And send back your communism.
Communism kills and steals.
Ask the Kirghis of Afghanistan.
Ask the Miskito Indians of Nicaragua.
Send back all your green-frog-skin materialism.
Money kills and steals.
Your green dollars have worked the working class
to death for generations and stolen from them
the possibility of life lived like human beings
are supposed to live.

Ask the water and the air what
grief your green dollars have wrought.
Ask the cut, bleeding, poisoned earth.

Send back your Christianity.
Christianity kills and steals.
Ask every Indian whoever
ran into a Spanish priest.

Ask the uncounted dead of your own
holy wars.
And send back your Judaism
Judaism kills and steals.
Ask the Palestinians;
Ask the Lebanese.
Why did you smuggle all that stuff
in, anyway?
Things had been going along pretty well
here for thirty- or forty-thousand years.
Why didn't you try to learn American ways and
American realities?
If you liked your European -isms and -anitys so much
why didn't you stay in Europe with them?
You want to be an American,
Then be an American.
Love it or leave it.
Any gringo born in America
is as native American
as Crazy Horse.
Why in the hell don't
you act like it?

Johnny Hughes

All Those Things That Don't Change, Come What May

Jake inherited the Magic House when his drinking Uncle tried to empty a rabbit out of a long irrigation pipe and the pipe hit a high-line wire. The 1940s furniture clashed with Jake's beatnik, coffee-house conversational monologues sanctioned only by the weekend wannabe artists, singers, writers, and actors from the college [Texas Tech] that came to his regular parties, called Jake Parties.

Stilt Momma took me to one of Jake's scratchy-jazz-records-spilled-red-wine-bullfight-poster-smoky rent parties. Pseudo intellectual was the pose du jour.

Over one hundred optimistic souls, mildly costumed, loved each other there every weekend of 1964 and 1965. Faded blue work-shirt was already the uniform of the day for this flock of alleged nonconformists. Magic House and the parties were Jake's life and livelihood.

Jake would meander regally to small groups of impressionable college kids, pontificating and pretending to speak knowingly. His weapon of choice was the caustic, shocking insult, a brief cryptic challenge. It was Jake's gig. He was the only legend in town that year. I thought he was a con, and sometimes cruel to his drunken guests/suckers.

It was cheaper to go to the strip for your own booze and hide it somewhere in the spacious Magic House than to be badgered by Jake to chip in for his profitable trips to the strip or later to buy beer outright from him. My first night there, two gorgeous, ironed-blond haired bookends were glued to Jake reading aloud from Kerouac's *On the Road*.

For them, being hustled by, buying wine from, and ultimately being Jake's temporary girlfriend would be the adventure story to take back to Dallas.

"I have a right to tall women," he gloated. Jake was five-eight, not good looking, with this bramble patch of thick, black curly hair which he conditioned and fussed over to get the exact, unkempt look. His flashing, chocolate eyes stayed hidden by his signature shades day and night until he needed to remove them dramatically for effect. His wispy and uncooperative goatee betrayed him.

The Magic House was Jake's rice bowl. Revenue trickled in from love offerings, a volunteer cover charge, bootlegging, and the sale of you-cook-your-own hamburgers and pork chop sandwiches. At two bucks, I'd buy one right now. The place always smelled of the variegated stale of red wine, tobacco, and pork chops. Usually, Jake had compelling reasons not to actually cook or clean or hold a job over three weeks or a fiancée over a semester.

Some of Jake's stories originated with trips to Selma, Denver, Mexico City, North Beach, and Venice. He did the Beatnik grand tour before he was self-incarcerated in the never ending party of Magic House. For some, graduation was delayed. For others, the dream of graduating was partied away. I feared I'd miss some folk singers or some heartbroken Freshman girl rejected by rush or some radical politico with news of the outside world. Magic House was my flame. I was the moth, returning, returning.

Karen began to pretend to love me during the third verse of a group sing-a-long of "Four Strong Winds" and I really believed her. Under the year 'round Christmas tree lights and the spell of the song, "twelve voices glued us together," Karen later said. I cooked her a pork chop sandwich. The black leotards, oversized men's dress shirt, dishwater ponytail, and copy of Kahlil Gibran made Karen seem ordinary that year. She was a skilled romantic with little notes, poems, morning toothpaste kisses, worn pink wool pajamas, and small shoplifted gifts. We'd have romantic dinners at fancy restaurants, dressed to the nines, and walk the check. She'd pout and cry and leave and I'd go after her and keep going. Her elitist belief in Ayn Rand's objectivist philosophy somehow justified her life of petty crime.

Her notes, presents, day and night phone calls, and obsessive, controlling jealousy convinced me of the ocean floor depths of our love. Stalking wasn't known then. Karen climbed a winter-brittle elm tree to the second floor window of my alley pad to leave a lime on my pillow. Jake's unvarnished warnings all slid past me. She secretly tape recorded my drunken benedictions.

Three months into it, Karen quit me in a Furr's supermarket produce section. We were shopping for French bread, noodles, garlic, and tomatoes.

"I don't like you or Jake or your so-called friends," she said.

A history major with a long slide rule on his belt observed all this and drove me back to Magic House. He baked the garlic bread, drank half a gallon of red wine, and left a new, tan corduroy coat with leather elbow patches. Jake claimed it, as he often did with lost articles.

When the mean blood-alcohol level of the Magic House was precisely right, Jake led a group sing-a-long to the Beatles' first album and everyone knew every word. He was shaking his own mop top and dancing on the couch. I had thought Karen and I were engaged. No one saw me cry.

Sororities warned penitents about Jake and Magic House and his well-intentioned but ephemeral engagements to a parade of young women, dissimilar in appearance and background but remarkably alike in their intense need to prove their intellectual worth and unbridled devotion to the dawning of the counterculture. Jake's future bride of the semester always had a car to loan, but Magic House was hard on monogamy.

My last semester, I was so broke that I had to move into Magic House. My clothes always smelled of cigs and pork chops. After a few weeks, Jake wanted me to go with him in Karen's car to steal food from deep freezers in richie neighborhoods. Sometimes, he stole beer or whiskey which was amply stored in a dry town. I wouldn't go but knew Jake and Karen were an item. I baked one of the stolen, frozen cherry pies the next morning and moved out before Jake woke up.

A couple of years later, on my way home from Viet Nam, I ran into a guy from the debate team in the Los Angeles Airport. He said the Magic House, and the parties, and Jake were still the same. On the airplane, a reed-thin, textbook salesman, who smelled of Old Spice, provided his opinion of the manhunt for James Earl. "He'd been to New Orleans just like Jack Ruby and Oswald. Probably been to Cuba too," he said.

The flat, flat land of home and the checkerboard fields glided by outside the window. While filling out the papers for a rental car at the Lubbock Airport, I began to have jagged, second thoughts about a reunion with Jake. The kitchen door of Magic House was open when I arrived. The walls had the same tired, printed slogans I had seen in magazines, "Hell no, we won't go." The college-bar smell welcomed me. From the next room, I could hear Jake reading aloud from Kerouac's *On the Road*. A youngish female voice said, "Wow." I retreated, silently.

Beat El Paso

blazes at the far Western edge of Texas, bordering both what is called there Old Mexico and New Mexico. The drive from Beaumont to El Paso is farther than the drive from El Paso to Los Angeles. Native John Rechy wrote his great beat-inspired novel *City of Night* there. El Paso county is 82% Mexican-American, and Mexican-American writers all over the city, like John Rechy and Dagoberto Gilb, were in part inspired by the Beats because Beat writing is full of authentic *corazón* sincerity, and does not come out of comfortable backgrounds. Artists of all ethnicities in El Paso are mostly homegrown and fiercely loyal to their city and region. As with others who consider their work part of the continuing Beat movement, El Paso writers and artists often have a political edge to their work. They are inspired by the remote desert, by the half naked mountains, by the relatively low rents, by the strong sense of community, by hard time suffering, and by the exciting borderland mix of cultures. A major literary press, Cinco Puntos, operates there, as do other presses and the independent literary project, Tumblewords, run by Beat inspired poet Donna Snyder, also a lawyer and activist. One editor of this anthology, when he returns to this city where he once lived, will go on a bar tour with friends and bump into folks he has not seen for many years. Together they may cross the penny bridge over the Rio Grande to hit bars in Juarez. These El Pasoans are always welcoming.

Jack Kerouac

from *The Book of Dreams*

El Paso

SO I'M GOING THROUGH EL PASO, a clear dream and vision, it's all wild and merceds and shacks jumbled like Thieves' Market and just like it with green shacks, fruit littered dirty mud walks, Arabic filth behind, squatting brown ragged figures, blocks and blocks of it under the clean blue sky of Indian City morning, smoke rising from a thousand noxious pots, strange hidden robes, wild, orange peels, bananas, the end—I'm driving through with somebody and cry out "Look at this wild Es Paso! –the cat told me it was the wildest place in America if you live downtown!—this is sure downtown!"—and blocks to the fore began the skyscrapers of a spectral city but it wasn't Mexico City it was on a plain in Texas and not only that the Texas of raw snow and moons and mountains for suddenly I saw Apache Navajo Indians with their shaggy ponies at a dismal rack, in front of almost buffalo tents in the general rueful wreckage of the market shacks and they wore floppy rider hats stained and rolled by snows of the Texas plains, and brilliant big blankets which also were thrown over their mournful little paints—the Texas, the St. Joe and the Independence of the Old Real America, dismal, cold, vapors rising from their brown mouths, feeble thin smoke from fires not warm enough, the cold blue keen February morning sky—El Paso of the frontier border, of the Navajos and Indians, of the market shacks and dung heaps and ponies, of the sad Indians and dumps of poverty—downtown wild huge Merced El Paso—I was stoned! I wanted to get off the car and live there, work on the railroad, dig it, like I'd planned—Get high! ——

LONG BEFORE I WORKED ON THE RAILROAD, in earlier dreams of traveling down the ribneck Mexican continent, it was always rails—railroads—sad mountains—the railroad, the yellow ground—long sad trips—Now I'm in Mexico City, I go to live in the suspicious apartments of Bull and June, June is still alive after all—They have rich town furnishings, but somehow they got hungup to live with a paternal older couple and awful bores, an Okie 40-year-old painter or carpenter, goodnatured but suspicious, mock gay, and a funny type middleaged thin whacky woman with (like Vera Buferd) a husky voice, Tallulah like, sexy—I go into the bedroom with an understanding with June that we're gonna do some fucking, we get in bed together, June rambles and talks, but suddenly the woman jumps in bed too and that brings the Okie and it appears he's not pleased about that or something's wrong and dammit I'll have to leave the comfort of this house—so I never get to bang poor sad June—and Bull is somewhere in the house, silent, isn't interested in those El Paso Navajo ponies of mine—(like when I lay in bed beside June one time in the dark at 118th street on benny and Bull came in and sat talking to us, I guess)—The wacky woman doesn't really want to screw but to create an issue that will get me out of the house, as I long suspected of E. So I'm out in the Indian cold again, and return to El Paso, and walk in the dirty snows with angels in my soul, whoopee! That Es Paso! !

John Rechy

City of Night

LATER I WOULD THINK OF AMERICA as one vast City of Night stretching gaudily from Times Square to Hollywood Boulevard—jukebox-winking, rock-n-roll-moaning: America at night fusing its darcities into the unmistakable shape of loneliness.

Remember Pershing Square and the apathetic palmtrees. Central Park and the frantic shadows. Movie theaters in the angry morning-hours. And wounded Chicago streets ... Horrormovie courtyards in the French Quarter—tawdry Mardi Gras floats with clowns tossing out glass beads, passing dumbly like life itself ... Remember rock-n-roll sexmusic blasting from jukeboxes leering obscenely blinking manycolored along the streets of America strung like a cheap necklace from 42nd Street to Market Street, San Francisco ...

One-night sex and cigarette smoke and rooms squashed in by loneliness ...

And I would remember lives lived out darkly in that vast City of Night, from all-night movies to Beverly Hills mansions.

But it should begin in EI Paso, that journey through the cities of night. Should begin in EI Paso, in Texas. And it begins in the Wind ... In a Southwest windstorm with the gray clouds like steel doors locking you in the world from Heaven.

I can't remember now how long that windstorm lasted—it might have been days—but perhaps it was only hours—because it was in that timeless time of my boyhood, ages six through eight.

My dog Winnie was dying. I would bring her water and food and place them near her, stand watching intently—but she doesn't move. The saliva kept coming from the edges of her mouth. She had always been fat, and she had a crazy crooked grin—but she was usually sick: Once her eyes turned over, so that they were almost completely white—and she couldn't see—just lay down, and didn't try to get up for a day. Then she was well, briefly, smiling again, wobbling lopsidedly. Now she was lying out there dying.

At first the day was beautiful, with the sky blue as it gets only in memories of Texas childhood. Nowhere else in the world, I will think later, is there a sky as clear, as blue, as Deep as that. I will remember other skies: like inverted cups, this shade of blue or gray or black, with limits, like painted rooms. But in the Southwest, the sky was millions and millions of miles deep of blue—clear, magic, electric blue. (I would stare at it sometimes, inexplicably racked with excitement, thinking: If I get a stick miles long and stand on a mountain, I'll puncture Heaven—which I thought of then as an island somewhere in the vast sky—and then Heaven will come tumbling down to earth ...) Then, that day, standing watching Winnie, I see the gray clouds massing and rolling in the horizon, sweeping suddenly terrifyingly across the sky as if to battle, giant mushrooms exploding, blending into that steely blanket. Now you're locked down here so Lonesome suddenly you're cold. The wind sweeps up the dust, tumbleweeds claw their way across the dirt ...

I moved Winnie against the wall of the house, to shelter her from the needlepointed dust. The clouds have shut out the sky completely, the wind is howling violently, and it is awesomely dark. My mother keeps calling me to come in ... From the porch, I look back at my dog. The water in the bowl beside her has turned into mud ... Inside now, I rushed to the window. And the wind is shrieking into the house—the curtains thrashing at the furniture like giant lost birds, flapping against the walls, and my two brothers and two sisters are running about the beat-up house closing the windows, removing the sticks we propped them open with. I hear my father banging on the frames with a hammer, patching the broken panes with cardboard.

Inside, the house was suddenly serene, safe from the wind; but staring out the window in cold terror, I see boxes and weeds crashing against the walls outside, almost tumbling over my sick dog. I long for something miraculous to draw across the sky to stop the wind ... I squeezed against the pane as close as I could get to Winnie: If I keep looking at her, she can't possibly die! A tumbleweed rolled over her.

I ran out. I stood over Winnie, shielding my eyes from the slashing wind, knelt over her to see if her stomach was still moving, breathing. And her eyes open looking at me. I listen to her heart (as I used to listen to my mother's heart when she was sick so often and I would think she had died, leaving me alone—because my father for me then existed only as someone who was around somehow; taking furious shape later, fiercely).

Winnie is dead.

It seemed the windstorm lasted for days, weeks. But it must have been over, as usual, the next day, when I'm standing next to my mother in the kitchen. (Strangely, I loved to sit and look at her as she fixed the food—or did the laundry: She washed our clothes outside in an aluminum tub, and I would watch her hanging up the clean sheets flapping in the wind. Later I would empty the water for her, and I stared intrigued as it made unpredictable patterns on the dirt ...) I said: "If Winnie dies–" (She had of course already died, but I didn't want to say it; her body was still outside, and I kept going to see if miraculously she is breathing again.) "—if she dies, I wont be sad because she'll go to Heaven and I'll see her there." My mother said: "Dogs don't go to Heaven, they haven't got souls." She didn't say that brutally. There is nothing brutal about my mother: only a crushing tenderness, as powerful as the hatred I would discover later in my father. "What will happen to Winnie," then I asked. "Shes dead, that's all," my mother answers, "the body just disappears, becomes dirt."

I stand by the window, thinking: It isn't fair ...

Then my brother, the younger of the two—I am the youngest in the family—had to bury Winnie.

I was very religious then. I went to Mass regularly, to Confession. I prayed nightly. And I prayed now for my dead dog: God would make an exception. He would let her into Heaven.

I stand watching my brother dig that hole in the backyard. He put the dead dog in and covered it. I made a cross and brought flowers. Knelt. Made the sign of the cross: "Let her into Heaven ..."

In the days that followed—I don't know exactly how much later we could smell the body rotting ... The day was a ferocious Texas summerday with the threat of rain: thunder—but no rain. The sky lit up through the cracked clouds, and lightning snapped at the world like a whip. My older brother said we hadn't buried Winnie deep enough.

So he dug up the body, and I stand by him as he shovels the dirt in our backyard (littered with papers and bottles covering the weeds which occasionally we pulled, trying several times to grow grass—but it never grew). Finally the body appeared. I turned away quickly. I had seen the decaying face of death. My mother was right. Soon Winnie will blend into the dirt. There was no soul, the body would rot, and there would be Nothing left of Winnie.

That is the incident of my early childhood that I remember most often. And that is why I say it begins in the wind. Because somewhere in that plain of childhood time must have been planted the seeds of the restlessness.

Before the death of Winnie, there are other memories of loss.

We were going to plant flowers in the front yard of the house we lived in before we moved to the house where Winnie died. I was digging a ledge along the sidewalk, and my mother was at the store getting the seeds. A man came and asked for my father, but my father isnt home. "You're going to have to move very soon," he tells me. I had heard the house was being sold, and we couldn't buy it, but it hadn't meant much to me. I continue shoveling the dirt. After my mother came and spoke to the man, she told me to stop making the holes. Almost snatching the seeds from her—and understanding now—I began burying them frantically as if that way we will have to stay to see them grow.

And so we moved. We moved from that clean house with the white walls and into the house where Winnie will die.

I stand looking at the house in child panic. It was the other half of a duplex, the wooden porch decayed, almost on the verge of toppling down; it slanted like a slide. A dried-up vine, dead from lack of water, still clung to the base of the porch like a skeleton, and the bricks were disintegrating in places into thin streaks of orangy powder. The sun was brazenly bright; it elongates each splinter on the wood, each broken twig on the skeleton vine ... I rushed inside. Huge brown cockroaches scurried into the crevices. One fell from the wall, spreading its wings—almost two inches wide—as if to lunge at me—and it splashes like a miniature plane on the floor—splut! The paper was peeling off the walls over at least four more layers, all different graycolors. (We would put up the sixth, or begin to—and then stop, leaving the house even more patched as that layer peeled too: an unfinished jigsaw puzzle which would fascinate me at night: its ragged patterns making angryfaces, angry animalshapes—but I could quickly alter them into less angry figures by ripping off the jagged edges ...) Where the ceiling had leaked, there are spidery brown outlines.

I flick the cockroaches off the walls, stamping angrily on them.

The house smells of Rot. I went to the bathroom. The tub was full of dirty water, and it had stagnated. It was brown, bubbly. In wild dreadful panic, I thrust my hand into the rancid water, found the stopper, pulled it out holding my breath, and looked at my arm, which is covered with the filthy brown crud.

Winters in EI Paso for me later would never again seem as bitter cold as they were then. Then I thought of El Paso as the coldest place in the world. We had an old iron stove with a round belly which heated up the whole house; and when we opened the small door to feed it more coal or wood, the glowing pieces inside created a miniature of Hell: the cinders crushed against the edges, smoking ... The metal flues that carried the smoke from the stove to the chimney collapsed occasionally and filled the house with soot. This happened especially during the windy days, and the wind would whoosh grimespecked down the chimney. At night my mother piled coats on us to keep us warm.

Later, I would be sent out to ask one of our neighbors for a dime—"until my father comes home from work." Being the youngest and most soulful looking in the family, then, I was the one who went ...

Around that time my father plunged into my life with a vengeance.

To expiate some guilt now for what I'll tell you about him later, I'll say that that strange, moody, angry man—my father—had once experienced a flashy grandeur in music. At the age of eight he had played a piano concert before the President of Mexico. Years later, still a young man, he directed a symphony orchestra. Unaccountably, since I never really knew that man, he sank quickly lower and lower, and when I came along, when he was almost 50 years old, he found himself Trapped in the memories of that grandeur and in the reality of a series of jobs teaching music to sadly untalented children; selling pianos, sheet music—and soon even that bastard relationship to the world of music he loved was gone, and he became a caretaker for public parks. Then he worked in a hospital cleaning out trash. (I remember him, already a defeated old man, getting up before dawn to face the unmusical reality of soiled bloody dressings.) He would cling to stacks and stacks of symphonic music which he had played, orchestrated—still working on them at night, drumming his fingers on the table feverishly: stacks of music now piled in the narrow hallway in that house, completely unwanted by anyone but himself, gathering dust which annoyed us, so that we wanted to put them outside in the leaky aluminum garage: but he clung to those precious dust-piling manuscripts—and to newspaper clippings of his once-glory—clung to them like a dream, now a nightmare ... And somehow I became the reluctant inheritor of his hatred for the world that had coldly knocked him down without even glancing back.

Once, yes, there had been a warmth toward that strange red-faced man—and there were still the sudden flashes of tenderness which I will tell you about later: that man who alternately claimed French, English, Scottish descent—depending on his imaginative moods—that strange man who had traveled from Mexico to California spreading his seed—that turbulent man, married and divorced, who then married my Mother, a beautiful Mexican woman who loves me fiercely and never once understood about the terror between me and my father.

Even now in my mother's living room there is a glasscase which has been with us as long as I can remember. It is full of glass objects: figurines of angels, Virgins of Guadalupe, dolls; tissue thin imitation flowers, swans; and a small glass, reverently covered with a rotting piece of silk, tied tightly with a faded pink ribbon, containing some mysterious memento of one of my father's dead children ... When I think of that glasscase, I think of my Mother ... a ghost image that will haunt me—Always.

When I was about eight years old, my father taught me this: He would say to me: "Give me a thousand," and I knew this meant I should hop on his lap and then he would fondle me—intimately—and he'd give me a penny, sometimes a nickel. At times when his friends—old gray men—came to our house, they would ask for "a thousand." And I would jump on their laps too. And I would get nickel after nickel, going around the table.

And later, a gift from my father would become a token of a truce from the soon-to-blaze hatred between us.

I loathed Christmas.

Each year, my father put up a Nacimiento—an elaborate Christmas scene, with houses, the wisemen on their way to the manger, angels on angelhair clouds. (On Christmas Eve, after my mother said a rosary while we knelt before the Nacimiento, we placed the Christchild in the crib.) Weeks before Christmas my father began constructing it, and each day, when I came home from school, he would have me stand by him while he worked building the boxlike structure, the miniature houses, the artificial lake; hanging the angels from the elaborate simulated sky, replete with moon, clouds, stars. Sometimes hours passed before he would ask me to help him, but I had to remain there, not talking. Sometimes my mother would have to stand there too, sometimes my younger sister. When anything went wrong—if anything fell—he was in a rage, hurling hammers, cursing.

My father's violence erupted unpredictably over anything. In an instant he overturns the table—food and plates thrust to the floor. He would smash bottles, menacing us with the sharp fanged edges. He had an old sword which he kept hidden threateningly about the house.

And even so there were those moments of tenderness—even more brutal because they didnt last: times in which, when he got paid, he would fill the house with presents—flowers for my mother (incongruous in that patched-up house, until they withered and blended with the drabness), toys for us. Even during the poorest Christmas we went through when we were kids—and after the fearful times of putting up the Nacimiento—he would make sure we all had presents—not clothes, which we needed but didn't want, but toys, which we wanted but didn't need. And Sundays he would take us to Juarez to dinner, leaving an exorbitant tip for the suddenly attentive waiter ... But in the ocean of his hatred, those times of kindness were mere islands. He burned with an anger at life, which had chewed him up callously: an anger which blazed more fiercely as he sank further beneath the surface of his once almost realized dream of musical glory.

One of the last touches on the Nacimiento was two pieces of craggy wood, which looked very heavy, like rocks (very much like the piece of petrified wood which my father kept on his desk, to warn us that once it had been the hand of a child who had struck his father, and God had turned the child's hand into stone). The pieces of rocklike wood were located on either side of the manger, like hills. On top of one, my father placed a small statue of a red-tailed, horned Devil, drinking out of a bottle.

Around that time I had a dream which still recurs (and later, in New Orleans, I will experience it awake). We would get colds often in that drafty house, and fever, and during such times I dreamt this: Those pieces of rocklike wood on the sides of the manger are descending on me, to crush me: When I brace for the smashing terrible impact, they become soft, and instead of crushing me they envelop me like melted wax.

Sometimes I will dream they're draped with something like cheesecloth, a tenebrous, thin tissue touching my face like spiderwebs, gluing itself to me although I struggle to tear it away...

When my brothers and sisters all got married and left home—to Escape, I would think—I remained, and my father's anger was aimed even more savagely at me.

He sat playing solitaire for hours. He calls me over, begins to talk in a very low, deceptively friendly tone. When my mother and I fell asleep, he told me, he would set fire to the house and we would burn inside while he looked on. Then he would change that story: Instead of setting fire to the house, he will kill my mother in bed, and in the morning, when I go wake her, she'll be dead, and I'll be left alone with him.

Some nights I would change beds with my mother after he went to sleep—they didn't sleep in the same room—and I surrounded the bed with sticks, chairs. The slightest noise, and I would reach for a stick to beat him away. In the early morning, before he woke, my mother would change beds with me again.

Once—without him, because he was working on his music—we were going to take a trip to Carlsbad Caverns, in New Mexico: my mother, my sister and her husband, my older brother and his wife, and I. My mother prepared food that night.

In the morning, before dawn, I woke my mother and went to my sister's house to wake her. When I returned, I saw my mother in our backyard (under the paradoxically serene starsplashed sky). "Dont go in!" she yells at me. I ran inside, and my father is standing menacingly over the table where the food we were taking is. Swiftly I reached for the food, and he lunges at me with a knife, slicing past me only inches short of my stomach. By then, my sister's husband was there holding him back ...

There was a wine-red ring my father wore. As a tie-pin, before being set into the gold ring-frame, it had belonged to his father, and before that to his father's father—and it was a ruby, my father told me—a ruby so precious that it was his most treasured possession, which he clung to. As he sat moodily staring at his music one particularly poor day, he called me over. Quickly, he gave me the ring. The red stone in the gold frame glowed for me more brilliantly than anything has ever since. A few days later he took it back.

During one of those rare, rare times when there was a kind of determined truce between us—an unspoken, smoldering hatred—I was crossing the street with him. He was quite old then, and he carried a cane. As we crossed, he stumbled on the cane, fell to the street. Without waiting an instant, I run to the opposite side, and I stand hoping for some miraculous avenging car to plunge over him.

But it didn't come.

I went back to him, helped him up, and we walked the rest of the way in thundering silence.

And then, when I was older, possibly 13 or 14, I was sitting one afternoon on the porch loathing him. My hatred for him by then had become a thing which overwhelmed me, which obsessed me the length of the day. He stood behind me, and he put his hand on me, softly, and said—gently: "You're my son, and I love you." But those longed-for words, delayed until the waves of my hatred for him had smothered their meaning, made me pull away from him: "I hate you!—you're a failure—as a man, as a father!" And later those words would ring painfully in my mind when I remembered him as a slouched old man getting up before dawn to face the hospital trash ...

Soon, I stopped going to Mass. I stopped praying. The God that would allow this vast unhappiness was a God I would rebel against. The seeds of that rebellion—planted that ugly afternoon when I saw my dog's body beginning to decay, the soul shut out by Heaven—were beginning to germinate.

When my brother was a kid and I wasn't even born (but I'll hear the story often), he would stand moodily looking out the window; and when, once, my grandmother asked him, "Little boy, what are you doing by the window staring at so hard?"—he answered, "I am occupied with life." I'm convinced that if my brother hadn't said that—or if I hadn't been told about it—I would have said it.

I liked to sit inside the house and look out the hall-window—beyond the cactus garden in the vacant lot next door. I would sit by that window looking at the people that passed. I felt miraculously separated from the world outside: separated by the pane, the screen, through which, nevertheless—uninvolved—I could see that world.

I read many books, I saw many, many movies.

I watched other lives, only through a window.

Sundays during summer especially I would hike outside the city, along the usually waterless strait of sand called the Rio Grande, up the mountain of Cristo Rey, dominated at the top by the coarse, weed-surrounded statue of a primitive-faced Christ. I would lie on the dirt of that mountain staring at the breathtaking Texas sky.

I was usually alone. I had only one friend: a wild-eyed girl who sometimes would climb the mountain with me. We were both 17, and I felt in her the same wordless unhappiness I felt within myself. We would walk and climb for hours without speaking. For a brief time I liked her intensely—without ever telling her. Yet I was beginning to feel, too, a remoteness toward people—more and more a craving for attention which I could not reciprocate: one-sided, as if the need in me was so hungry that it couldn't share or give back in kind. Perhaps sensing this—one afternoon in a boarded-up cabin at the base of the mountain she maneuvered, successfully, to make me. But the discovery of sex with her, releasing as it had been, merely turned me strangely further within myself.

Mutually, we withdrew from each other.

And it was somewhere about that time that the narcissistic pattern of my life began.

From my father's inexplicable hatred of me and my mother's blind carnivorous love, I fled to the Mirror. I would stand before it, thinking: I have only Me ... I became obsessed with age. At 17, I dreaded growing old. Old age is something that must never happen to me. The image of myself in the mirror must never fade into someone I can't look at.

And even after a series of after-school jobs, my feeling of isolation from others only increased. Then the army came, and for months I hadn't spoken to my father. (We would sit at the table eating silently, ignoring each other.) And when I left, that terrible morning, I kissed my mother. And briefly I looked at my father. His eyes were watering. Mutely he held out the ruby-ring which once, long ago, he had given me and then taken back. And I took it wordlessly. And in that instant I wanted to hold him—because he was crying, because he did feel something for me, because, I was sure, he was overwhelmed at that moment by the Loss I felt too. I wanted to hold him then as I had wanted to so many, many times as a child, and if I could have spoken, I know I would have said at last: "I love you." But that sense of loss choked me—and I walked out without speaking to him ... Only a few weeks later, in Camp Breckenridge, Kentucky, I received a telegram that he was very sick.

And I came back to EI Paso.

I felt certain that this time it would be different.

I reached our house, in the government projects we had moved into from that house with the winged cockroaches, and I got in with the key I had kept. There is no one home. I called my brother. My father was dead.

I hang up the telephone and I know that now forever I will have no father, that he had been unfound, that as long as he had been alive there was a chance, and that we would be, Always now, strangers, and that is when I knew what Death really is—not in the physical discovery of the Nothingness which the death of my dog Winnie had brought me (in the decayed body which would turn into dirt, rejected by Heaven) but in the knowledge that my Father was gone, for me—that there was no way to reach him now—that his Death would exist only for me, who am living.

And throughout the days that followed—and will follow forever—I will discover him in my memories, and hopelessly through the infinite miles that separate life from death—try to understand his torture: in searching out the shape of my own.

The army passed like something unreal, and I returned to my Mother and her hungry love. And left her, standing that morning by the kitchen door crying, as she always would be in my mind, and I was on my way now to Chicago, briefly from where I would go to freedom: New York!—embarking on that journey through nightcities and nightlives—looking for I don't know what—perhaps some substitute for salvation.

Ricardo Sanchez

Ain't Nuttin' for a Stepper

Ain't nuttin' for a stepper,
old timer,
for this chuquío paseño
is now going about to step
and strut his way
to the cantón.
i am a-steppin, long timer,
'cause i am now
chicano short timer
and time no longer hurts,
it just haunts,
but i've gotlessthanamonth
NETA-less THAN A MONTH-to go
and kiss them bricks
and swallow
El Paso dust
and hear mariachis
in Juaritos
and jive and galavant
and see those groovy rucas
and make out all night long;
look, esos,
i will catch a groovy broad
and scam and shuck and jive.
me voy para el cantón,
yes, i'm going home again
to eat my mamma's cooking
and feel alive again
and just relax and bask
beneath el paso's sun
and don't you give me no jive, ese,
about my coming back.
            like hell i will,
not that i've learned my lesson,
it's just that it's a drag
to feel despondently,
to know this emptiness.

Ricardo Sanchez

I Know You by Your Smile-Filled Songs, Chinto

I

Jacinto-Temilotzín,
you arrived
within our lives
when clouds
kept the sun from view.

your first cry
broke
up darkening patterns,
a song wafted
over our landscapes ...

II

in Salt Lake City, Chinto,
you would pull me by the hand,
down Truman Avenue
'til we could cross State;
inside that monument
to hectic Amerika,

you would smile at the Denny's waitresses,
ask in song-filled voice
for fries and a coke,
never knowing
that such places
are usually anathema
to my quests for beauty ...

III

i recall those little books
you would make,
cutting papers
into tiny one inch pages,
gluing them together,
and then writing

miniature verses
and childhood caricatures;
joyously did i read you
as i saw images dance
through your smile-filled
serenades to life ...

IV

i know you, Chinto,
through your human delicacy,
as your inquisitive senses
peruse all notions of the universe,
I know your anxious voice
wafting
through bookstores and galleries,
your smile floats
about books and paintings,
your voice demanding
of countless poets
to proclaim
a beauty beyond the ken
of societal keepers of the keys;
I know you through a lovefilled family,
you running about
sweaty and juvenile
caring only about enjoyment,
asking serious questions
about death and heart attacks,
digging into familial lore
with a pungent seriousness
caught somewhere between
a daring laughter
and a joyous hope for understanding ...

V

more than just know you, Chinto,
I sense you everywhere
as you explore Paperbacks ... ¡y más!,
nine year old wizard,
you take customers by the hand
and then convince some

to buy the things
you feel are valuable ...

VI

there probably is no need
to tell you or your sister
that you are loved, nor
need we remind Rikárd
that he, too, is loved,
you three know
the power of embraces
as well as the beauty
of familial kisses—we
only say it
because it is our greatest truth,
the only truth worth knowing
is the one bespeaking love ...
still, Chinto, I must again admit
that i love
that you which
swims in smile-filled songs ...

Dagoberto Gilb

The Death Mask of Pancho Villa

It's late, very late. I've been in bed since eleven o'clock, for almost four hours, trying to get some sleep. I haven't been going to bed this early, but it's Sunday night and there's nothing on television. Not that I really like to watch television late at night the rest of the days. I do it too much because I don't know what else to do with myself. Probably I could listen to music on the radio. That's not true, I almost forgot. There's nothing on the radio anymore, and around here, whether it's El Paso tejano or Juarez ranchera, pop from Mexico City, hard or soft American rock, it's all boring, and anyway there's commercial after commercial, just as irritating, maybe even more so, as the ones on late-night television. Okay, so maybe it's me.

Really it's not late, it's early, early morning, and one other reason I need to get some sleep is that I have to be somewhere in the morning. I've arranged, finally, to see about getting some work. I've been treating it pretty easy for a while, telling myself I was sick of doing physical labor and trying hard to blame my age for feeling that way. Unsuccessfully. So I've been sitting around, not doing as much as I probably should, getting soft. Doing too much television, I'll you the truth. I gotta admit, that isn't what I consider having a great time, but it can't be called suffering either. Our bills might be getting paid, my kids might be running around laughing and breaking things, my wife might finally keep a job for a while, but we're not getting rich. Not that I ever really lived my life trying to get rich. Which is why I've been feeling guilty about my working situation, my lack of it. It's gotten me jumpy and nervous, worried about something really bad happening to us while I'm doing nothing about a paycheck. Which might help explain why I think the worst when I hear the pounding at the door. I don't even realize what it is, and my wife's so asleep I have to shake her awake.

What I do is pick up my son's aluminum baseball bat. I even think of putting on my boots. I guess that's some deal I have, not wanting to get into late night violence barefooted. Why do I think it might be something violent? Good question. I guess it shows how I'm thinking, even if it doesn't make much sense because obviously violent criminals aren't going to be knocking on the door, ringing the bell to wake me up. I'm just asleep and not reasoning too clearly. Also there's been a lot of talk in the papers about thieves breaking in. Desperate young punks from the other side of the river disobeying all the rules of thief etiquette.

But when I finally get the door open it's just a friend and some other guy I don't know. One of my oldest, best friends in all the world, a guy I started hanging out with in high school, then after that worked a few construction jobs with. We shared a lot of girlfriends, a lot of bottles and cans, and traveled together often when we did ... well, outlaw business years ago. All to say that I've had some of the best times I've ever had with the guy. We're still friends, but time has passed. We both ended up married—him first!—and we both have kids, and our wives talked to each other more than we did. Which is how I heard he was having some home troubles. First he got suspended from his job at the railroad. Then he got caught, or accused, of being bad with another woman and Dora, his wife, threw him out of the house. In fact she did the whole routine—threw his clothes out onto the driveway with an empty suitcase and locked all the doors and windows.

"You whore," I tell him after I turn on the yellow outdoor light. Gabe's wearing a tight, too-small, white T-shirt and still looks in good shape, particularly for a man in his late-thirties. It makes me feel bad that there he is, like always, a beer in his hand, a glaze in his eyes, somehow being healthier than me, drunk and whatever else. The only thing not like him is that the T-shirt and jeans are a little dirty and wrinkled, and his hair, which when he worked steady he didn't keep so long, looks like it just got off a pillow, the same as mine. Stuff his wife, it would seem, has been taking care of for a long time.

I open the door and go onto the front porch with my socks on. "Everybody in the house is asleep," I say, an explanation for why I'm not offering them the indoor accommodations. We shake hands, then wrap arms around one another for a longtime-no-see abrazo. "I been wondering about you. Hear about you having too much fun."

"Gotta have fun sometimes. You know that." Gabe's grin is almost exuberant.

"I heard about the clothes on the driveway too."

"Which ones?" he asks, still smiling.

"Whadaya mean?"

"There were two sets of them."

I don't understand, and I don't say anything.

"A day or two after the old lady handed me a suitcase, that other bitch came over and threw a pile she had on the driveway too," he tells me, and we laugh pretty good. "You know what I said when Dora called me about that? 'She didn't hit the grease spot, did she?' When she hung up on me my fucking ear hurt."

We're both laughing while Gabe's friend keeps this steady smile throughout. "This is Ortiz," Gabe says, finally introducing us. "Roman Ortiz." I shake his friend's hand. Despite the mile, the man's gauntness, for me, translates into something else I can't quite put a name on, and my first impression is that his loose western style clothes don't seem to suit his character.

It gets too quiet for a moment. Not a dog, not even the shuffle of a breeze. It looks very dark beyond the yellow porch, though it isn't.

"You wanna beer?" Gabe asks me, plucking a can off from the vine of three he'd carried to the porch.

"No. It's kinda late for me. Or early."

Gabe looks at me disappointed and the other guy looks at Gabe, though still with that smile. Gabe breaks the tab from the can he'd offered me.

I feel bad, immediately, for saying no. Somehow I've done something to spoil the visit, I've brought things down a notch.

"So how you been really?" I ask.

"All right," he tells me, uneffusive. He takes a couple swallows of beer.

"What about that job?" I ask. "You gonna get back there?" Working at the railroad, you have to understand, is one of the best paying jobs in the city.

Gabe makes a sour face and leans against the porch railing.

"A bunch of suckass culeros. I'll find something better."

Very few people could. Very few people would want to leave that job. Gabe can do both. I know it as well as he does. I used to feel the same way about myself, though not anymore. I try to blame that on El Paso or the times or my age. But I'm only a year older than Gabe. It's another thing I admire about him and dislike about me.

Ortiz hasn't so much as moved except to sip on his beer. "You mind if I piss over there?" he asks, indicating beyond the porch.

"Of course not," I say. "I do it all the time." I don't do it all the time, but once in a while, just to keep in practice.

Gabe and I don't say anything until we hear Ortiz's stream hitting the hard dirt that is my front yard.

"So what's up?" I finally ask.

"This guy has something I thought you'd want to see," Gabe says. "Remember that time we were in Mexico and that old dude said he had pictures of him with Pancho Villa?"

I was into collecting Pancho Villa stuff years ago because he was my hero. More than that really. Anyway, I'd found letters he'd written, bought a holster and pistol that were supposed to be his, and in our front room I still have a framed document Villa'd signed for my great-uncle saying what an honor it'd been to fight together during the revolution. It has been a while since I'd thought about any of this though. I guess because I had children and got married. And worked a lot. And because I got older. I've got all kinds of excuses if I let myself think about it.

"So he has photographs?" I say, trying to sound interested. I'm not at all.

"A mask," says Gabe.

Ortiz is stepping back up onto the porch. "His death mask."

"I never heard of such a thing," I say.

"There were three of them made," Ortiz says. Same smile.

"A Hollywood producer has one and a senator has the other." Ortiz opens another can of beer. No change in the smile, but the face around it seems prouder now.

My first impression isn't improving. I'm pretty sure Gabe's just met the guy in a bar, and in my humble opinion ... well, I'd call it bar talk.

Gabe lights a joint. I'm wishing I were back in bed, the door locked. Which makes me feel bad again. What's happened to me? I don't think anything's wrong with marijuana, and I like smoking it the same as I always have. That's what I say anyway. The only thing is I don't smoke it very often anymore. I even have about two or three joints worth in a bag that was given to me almost a year ago. I guess I never want to smoke it by myself, and I'd be embarrassed now to use it with anyone else because it's so dried out. I should throw it away. I will throw it away.

I go ahead and smoke some because I don't know how to say no to this too, though the truth is that's what I feel like saying. I don't know why we're not talking. I think it has something to do with me, with me standing in my socks, not inviting them in, not saying let's go. Though maybe it's Gabe. He's too quiet, and it can't only be that he's unhappy because I don't feel like drinking beer. Maybe it's something between him and Ortiz. When we used to hang out together a lot, it was Gabe who usually met the guys like this in the first place. Gabe was the one who'd listen and believe, while I was the one who was skeptical. Gabe'd get all the information, I'd put it together, then we'd both come up with a conclusion, a decision—you know, we'd solve another little human-oddball mystery, and sometimes actually do something with the person. Either buy or sell. Was this guy trying to sell Gabe something? Or trade? Or was Gabe thinking of a sale to him? But why would he need me after all these years? And if he did, why doesn't he just say something to me straight out? Then maybe he thinks I'd just want to buy it. But why right now? It's about three a.m., or later, and I can't think.

"So are you selling this thing or what?" I ask Ortiz.

"Absolutely not."

He stares at me with that smile. I look for some kind of indication from Gabe, but there's none. We're finishing off the joint.

"Then what are you doing with it?"

"He's got it at his place," Gabe says. "Let's go see it."

"You haven't seen it?" I ask him.

"Sure. I want you to see it. All you gotta do is get some shoes." He drops the roach and grinds it out with the sole of his boot. Then he pops another can of beer. He stops leaning on the wrought-iron railing around the porch and stands like he's ready to get going.

Gabe's push isn't out of exuberance now, but it's along the lines of it, some excess of something, and I can't figure it out. I start thinking about the problems he's having. No job, being away from his kids. Except that's not Gabe at all. I know him too well. He'll get back together with Dora whether she thinks she never wants to see him again right now or not, he'll get his job back or a better one, and I know he believes that too, and even if it didn't turn out that way a few years from now, I know he wouldn't think it wouldn't. So it's not that, it's not like he needs me, needs a friend or some TV emotion like that. And somehow it doesn't seem like he really wants me to hang out either. He wants me to go with him, but it doesn't seem personal, it doesn't seem to me like he's asking. It's more like he's telling me to go with them. Like it's for my own good or something.

"I can't go tonight," I say, thinking it's not tonight but this morning.

"How come?" Gabe asks. He's disappointed again.

"I gotta do things. In a few hours, as a matter of fact. Normal shit."

All the sudden a cop car cruises by. Not slow and not fast, just on a routine pass through the neighborhood. Except from behind us, from the dirt alley where we wouldn't have expected that blue-and-white to come from, and a dog starts barking at him because a dispatcher talks over the police radio and the window on the driver's side is down.

"Normal shit?" says Gabe. "Since when did you worry about doing normal shit?"

That stings because he's right. Or used to be. "Why don't I just see it tomorrow? You taking it out of town or something?"

I'm feeling a little defensive now. "Somebody buying it?" I look at Gabe. He's not looking back at me.

"I'm giving it away," says Ortiz. "There are only three of them, and I'm sending mine to Moscow." His smile is the same but it's fading.

"Moscow?" I look at Gabe once more and feel stoned. He hits on his beer.

"In Russia," says Ortiz.

"I know where it is," I tell him. "Why there?"

"Because that's where John Reed is buried," Ortiz says. "John Reed wrote about the Mexican Revolution, then went to Russia and wrote about the Russian Revolution."

A smile starts to come on me because now the cop car is crusing by again, only this time in front of us, and it seems so ridiculous especially because we're about to talk about communism or something at three or so in the morning and I don't have shoes on. Then another cop car goes by. We know it has to be another one because it's coming from another street, toward us, too soon after the last one. It turns right, opposite the direction the first one did. And now more dogs are barking in the neighborhood.

"I better turn off the light," I say. I open the screen door, then the other, and reach inside to turn off the yellow porch light. A cop car passes a second later. "You guys better not leave for a while."

"I don't need a DWI," says Ortiz.

Ortiz's car, I notice for the first time, is faded green, or blue, I can't be positive in this dark, with a peeling vinyl roof.

"So how'd you get this mask?" I ask.

"I just did," Ortiz says, finishing his beer.

"How do you know it's Villa?"

"People have seen it. Warren Beatty saw it and wanted it."

Warren Beatty, the actor. Now I am smiling the most. Dogs are barking all over the neighborhood and another cop car passes us. I swear it's a third one. I'm sure we can't be seen without the porch light on though.

"Why not just keep it right here, right here in El Paso?" I suggest. "Probably a lot of people would like to see it. It'd be a great contribution. It seems to me anyway."

Ortiz turns his head away from me and my naiveté. "People here wouldn't respect it enough, and it's fragile. Over there they care about things more than they do here. All of Europe is like that too. They have museums to take care of important cultural things. In Germany there are probably thirty opera houses to every one here." The speech erases Ortiz's smile, and he steps over and reaches down to get the last can of beer.

"So you've been to Europe, to Germany?" I ask.

"No," Ortiz says, humorless.

It's that I've stolen his smile. I'm looking for cop cars and watching lights go on in the house across the street where a dog is barking the loudest and steadiest. "Moscow, huh?"

Ortiz gathers himself after a big swallow of the beer. "The Mexican Revolution was the first in the century, and the bolsheviks used it as an example of common people rising up. John Reed was there for both revolutions and was buried at the Kremlin as a hero. They'll put the mask near him as a memorial!"

I'm still smiling, but not because I'm unconvinced or skeptical. More that the cops have quit driving by and the dog across the street won't stop barking, which is probably why another dog still barks farther down the street. I'm smiling just thinking about how we're having this conversation about Russians and death masks in the dark and quiet right on my El Paso porch with the light out, all while I'm in my socks.

''I'd really like to see it some time," I say.

Neither of them say anything.

"I guess I should probably get a couple hours in," I say.

Gabe looks a little disappointed again. Or maybe apologetic. I don't want him to feel bad for coming by, for banging on my door. I haven't done anything for weeks but watch the stupid television.

"You guys better look around to see if the police are waiting for you to pull away," I say. I wish I knew how to say more.

Gabe just shrugs my worry off. He never did care about things like that, and, maybe because he didn't, never had to.

They both stop and piss before they get into Ortiz's car. It starts with a cheap gas and old motor sound, and finally rolls away without headlights for a few yards.

I lock the door and climb back in bed. I'm thinking that I probably can wait on seeing about this job, and I'm thinking how nice it feels being stoned and sleepy. My wife asks me who it was and I say it was Gabe and wait for her to ask me some more. She doesn't, but in my head I start asking questions for her and answering them. Or asking for myself: He wanted me to go out with him. To go see something this guy he knows had. No, I don't really know why I didn't go. No, I really don't know why he wanted me to. Maybe he thought because of Pancho Villa. Or maybe because he thought I'd have a good time. Which I haven't had in a long time. No, I don't know why I didn't go, I don't know why it didn't seem like I should. I used to not think about it, I used to just go. Gabe and I used to do things together. Things just like this.

I'm on my back in bed and my wife, after I've been lying there all this time, finally asks me what Gabe wanted. Nothing, I tell her, except he wanted me to go look at Pancho Villa's death mask. That makes me smile all over again. At what? she asks. Don't think about it, I say. But what time is it? she asks. What's the difference? I say.

Daniel Peña

Bang

It was to Cuauhtemoc's liking to pour scotch over the ice cream to start the meetings. A surly body guard slopping scoop after scoop into bowls no bigger than the size of your palm. He worked like the designated ugly girl at a brownies retreat. "Beer under the bridge," Cuauh would say and offer up heaping bowls to the big wigs of the competing cartels, bowls filled high above the fallout radius so that they'd have to catch it with their mouths before the shit dropped to the floor. And nobody, cabron, wanted to be from the messy cartel, especially El Gallito. There was pride to up keep, dick inches to be measured. And though it was a nice gesture on the glossy outside of things, I'm sure Cuauhtemoc (though he's never told anyone to this day) did it to humiliate them: "this is what it looks like when the ——— cartel sucks a cock." We could afford it for we controlled the whole trade route, cabron, from Bogota all the way to Branson, Missouri. You wouldn't believe the cocaine that trucked itself up that spine of those Sierra Madre (trucked itself, cabron, because a kilo would pay its fair share, all the huff n' snuff goons to kill Rasputin and a little extra for cositas), all of that cash moving along the carreteras and US Highway I-35 inside one of those eighteen-wheeled affairs disguised as an H-E-B truck. It carried our goods by the ton across the Texas-Mexico border through Matamoros. Left lane for multiple axles and there'd be an alphabet boy who'd handle the fake documents forged in Monterrey. "Business or pleasure," and we'd look at him just the way you would if you pulled up to the border crossing in a grocery truck. What kind of fucked up question is that? "Business," I'd say and we'd drive clear on through to San Antonio, Austin, Dallas and cops all around, oiled leather and aftershave in the breeze. "What you haulin'?" and the answer was always the same. "Cheese." Me in front because I spoke the best English, Cuauh in the back lying prostrate on the goods, palettes of coke wrapped three inches thick to avoid drug dogs. You could hear him unsticking his skin from the cellophane. When you get to sitting on those palettes so long it's a furnace, all of that body heat trapped beneath you. And could you believe we used to wrap people up in that stuff? Them sweating a thousand beads inside that cellophane jacket, faces looking as though they were about to pass out. And I'll tell you that it was my idea, to suspend them over a pristine white Chinese rug, three of them at a time, and swear on their mothers' graves, "a drop of sweat, a gallon of blood," and it would always happen that by the third hour, as right as religion, the first drop would fall to the fibers below. A hubbub about a ruined carpet and wouldn't it be a shame if the whole damn thing were ruined too. And you should have seen the shake of their eye, cabron, you would have been right proud—a thousand micro-movements a minute like the oscillations of a tuning fork smacked right across the table. That hum, that hum in the air (a glassy jaw yet to be broken), a throbbing inside the nose, that thousand-yard stare that replays like a B-movie murder in the back of your eyelids when you're making love, when you're yelping a corrido, when you're washing that skunky blood from your skin—translucent pink and a cloud of red. All of that cellophane on the spool put to good use even if it was just for rest.

A knife plunged deep into the belly of the brick and cocaine crumbled out all over the hotel coffee table. A dozen hands flesh forking right for the pile and Cuauh saying, "Take your leave, gents, there's enough for the whole class," but a junkie never knows how to handle himself when he's in the presence of free food. There's a running joke in Mexico how the wealthy indio can't handle abundancia. We all end up fat fucks with rotting livers and rotting eyes and failing kidneys. Take a look around you and tell me if I'm wrong. A hotel room full of coin jacking men dressed in their Sunday's finest—trajes made from elephant skin and black satin, guns on full rock and roll, gilded and gold (the ones shown in the narco museums of Mexico City), all of them hanging inside the waistband of those Dickies pants that slide so well over the boot, perfectly pressed, killing pants, vaquero pants. See the bodyguards, the assassins, the book keepers, the doctors, all of them travel weary and paunchy and sweaty and bored. Their boots clack-clacking against the white tile covered in dust and everyone who's not snorting coke, shooting the shit. Not one man giving two fucks about what the other has to say and everyone thinking the same things, gimme a room to myself, a shit, shower, and shave and a broad who can suck the chrome off a tailpipe, a broad who knows all of the cheers and I'll be pleasant, jefe. By God, I'll be pleasant and just like clockwork see the women pour into the room like a band of slags, the door left ajar, all of them dancing and snorting and lifting belly to the Mariachi perched atop the bed of a truck outside. A surprise! A gift from El Gallito, notes as loud and obnoxious as a yelping dog, a mariachi just a-wailing on those instruments like they were in it to win it. Doing it for the money. None of them able to remember the words to Cielito Lindo if you were to put a knife to their neck and yell, "Sing, goddamnit! Sing!"

And wouldn't you know that some of those Mariachi were low pro too; some of them not much better at guitarron than they were at gathering leads. One torso-tossing violinist getting john law angry because no one's biting her bait, gordibuena but ugly as the Lord makes them. We could tell by the way she moved that she was a paper pusher who took the mattress route. A rube if there ever was one, mariachi Barbie. You could smell her arrogance, vomit all over the fucking table. This was a job too messy to handle and she was going to be the one to clean it up, make a name for herself—guffaw-haw-haw—this shit wasn't Memphis Beat. You could tell it by the way she spoke the es-pan-yol, bitchface stolid. You ain't from around here, missy and she's oblivious to the fact that she's fooling no one. An agent from el otro lado chatting it up with El Gallito, fist bumping her chest to let him know they're tight the way the cholos do in Los Angeles. She doesn't know that here it means something completely different. Ignorant cops just like fags (fuckin' new guys): a dime a dozen, Mexicans the same wherever they are. She's really implying he's a maricon, a puto, a faggot right to his face—fist bump right to the heart, that double bounce and a lifeguard smile. And quicker than it takes to tell it, cabron, the gag is up, we bid our adieus and take our leave. And it's not until we're stone drunk that the deals are made. All of the tight laces cut and El Gallito and Cuauh acting just like brothers.

Nobody wants to hear about the wheel-horse loneliness. The kind of lonely that goes beyond guilt. The feeling when you were twelve years old, when you asked the priest about Santa Muerte in confession, that dark saint of the poor.

You had a dream of her speaking to you in a manly voice on a park bench. She was cutting something, silver strings with a machete from the banana groves, the rotten stink of fertilizer in the air with each swing. A language you didn't know but understood. And you asked her if you were going to die. "No," she said grazing your cheek with the back of a wet finger, "but you'll have a glorious death, boy. I can promise you that," which was just enough to get you right with religion.

So, you went to confession the next day. "Is it wrong to pray to her?" you asked. "What is she?" You've seen the altarcitos, the offerings from your family to a skeleton woman that's scared you since before you had a tooth in your head. Your mother told you to look the statue in the eye (no fear here) and you could have sworn that they were smoldering maroon, a dark, velvety maroon you could feel on your face when you spoke the Lord's name. "Ask her for her justice," your mother told you, "ask for food," and she placed your hands together. "Ask her for the return of your father, whatever it costs," and so you did.

"Yes!" said the priest, "Yes, you satanic, idol worshipping fool! You've prayed to evil's sister in the guise of a saint, you've forsaken the Holy Spirit and you've put a cloud over your family which you'll never abjure."

So, you said you were sorry, that you'd never do it again and then you said your penance.

"Wait there, young man," said the priest. "I want you to go home, I want you to prepare a dish, I want you to take it to field across the railroad tracks on Calle Ocotepec and I want you to come back in the morning and tell me what happened."

So, you did. You prepared the only thing you knew, chicken mole, and you were hungry with the fasting that comes with penance. It wasn't until you reached the edge of the lot that you smelled the tires burning inside of the cardboard houses, a dozen bodies walking toward you, dark, naked, and dirty. Dusk.

"And what happened," said the Father.

"They beat me," you said, "they beat me until my dish fell to the ground. They beat each other over the tender flesh and ripped it from the bones with their teeth like hounds. They licked the mole from the dirt. They beat me for my money."

"And did you give it to them?" the father asked.

"Yes," you said.

"What did they say to you?"

"We'll cut you a deal," said the tallest boy, "your money for your life."

"How did you feel?"

"All alone," you said.

"And *that*," said the Father, "is Santa Muerte."

You prayed with him the Act of Contrition. The Sign of the Cross.

"In the name of the Father, and the Son, and the Holy Spirit."

"Amen," said Cuauh. "Amen," said the rest of us. We bit into our tacos al pastor, tiny slivers of meat carved right from the rotisserie. Slivers so thin they were transparent. Nothing like the cube cut shit the night hawkers served thirty yards away in El Paso. Truth be told, cabron, I enjoyed those times when it was quiet and rainy and there were tacos, pockets on swole. It was a Sunday morning and we could still hear shooting in the streets of Ciudad Juarez, the kind of shooting that came from a gun that never stopped, tiger's wife angry, something hinky in the air. You could hear it from the rattle.

"Who you think that is?" I asked. Cuauh salted his pork.

"Felix," he said, "probably Felix. He don't know you don't work on the Lord's day."

"Or El Brujo."

"Or El Brujo," he said matter of factly.

"Or El Gallito," I said and laughed the kind of laugh you do to make yourself right again, my nervous laugh. Cuauh just stared back at me, his taco dripping grease mid-air. "Think he'll come back?" I asked.

"No," said Cuauh.

"Not even for us?"

"No," said Cuauh, "not even for the ice cream." We laughed, a dark humor of the gallows kind of laughter and we put the bills on the table, waved for the mesera to come over. "Aguita, por fa'!" It wasn't until she rounded the counter that you could smell it from the door. A car parked out front. Fertilizer in the air.

The heat pulled our faces taut and you could taste blood on your tongue before that ratfuck fire

315

poured into the taqueria like a screaming demon. Paint and crucifixes and hair and animal flesh and human flesh all fused together in midair; nails too for the car was filled bumper to brim with packages of barbed ring-shanks that splattered against the walls like coins hitting the ground, ricocheting into the flames, that metallic sound about the only goddamned thing you could hear over our screams.

We screamed, cabron, all the way till kingdom come. Right from the gut, a shit kick from your brother when you were nine, loud just like that, and the ripping of your flesh like the dictionary definition of pulled pork. *All* of that fucking flesh burned to ash on contact and all of that ash floating away right before your eyes, right before the rabbit blood heat boiled the marrow in your bones and you were a bag of splinters covered in nails.

And we were cooked, cabron, everyone inside of that goddamned place but Cuauh. Our ashes blown out the back window with the glass and flame, blown into the rain of the sky. And as much as I want to say that we floated in the air (out into the four winds), as beautiful as that image would have been, instead we were turned to mud in the streets of Juarez like dirt looking for a field to rest only more lonesome.

Louis Bardel

Plucking the Petals Off the Texas Rose

Lights on the squad car martial the El Paso night
I scoot by
American as long as I am free

Statue of Liberty
From sea to shining sea

I am sick of dour faces

Obama the torturer?

I gulp coffee and grip the wheel
I guess I'm a bean fiend
But hot java is a friend on the road, you dig

I stare straight

Charging up my phone in Ozona (Texas)
Washing my ass in the gas station john

250 miles to go ...

La Vista Motel
Followed by the sheriff when I drive in to the parking lot

They call this place Junction, Texas

2AM

"Can I have a room?"

"You got any warrants out for your arrest?"

It was that kinda place

317

Donna Snyder

Gone Man Gone

He's buried in a potter's field
Nothing but tumbleweeds
Stumblebums come to drink and cry
Birds sing that same old cheerless song
My best friend long gone
So gone
Long gone
So gone
So long

Gene Keller

For the Unknown Beat Mother of Poetry

Who was that sad angel?
La belle dame with mercy
in her slacks and sandals,
nursing their beat hangovers.

Who was that sad angel?
Goddess of the Golden Gate
in her benzedrine nightgown,
knitting blankets of spaghetti.

Who was that sad angel?
Muse of the disappearing moment
in her bra and panties,
holding their fevers in her lap.

Who was that sad angel
who blew the cool flute
they all turned to
to sing in rapturous chorus?

Who was that sad angel?
Beat Mother of Poetry,
maid to Saint Francis,
wiping pigeon shit off their heads.

Who was that sad angel?
Betrayer in the jazz hours,
pleading with the stoned poet
to get a job. Any job.

Who was that sad angel?
Hearth-keeper and layer-out
in cheap rooms on low-rent hills,
too busy to dream her own songs.

Who was that sad angel?
Companion to the bards,
waiting for Wandering Aengus
to return from Mexico.

Who was that sad angel?
Desperada of Miltown
and the Tokay alleys,
saving their existential tears.

Who was that sad angel?
Protector of makeshift libraries,
of napkin-scrawled epics
to the atomic wasteland.

Who was that sad angel?
Inventor of paper and ink,
swooned by the fumes
of their male fame.

Who was that sad angel?
Cunt of the virgin birth,
pregnant with 10,000 poets,
Mother of American Light.

Who was that sad angel?
Caroline? Judy? Margaret?
Daughter of the cross-country days
and bohemian nights.

America, who was that angel?
Who were those sad angels?
Who was that sad angel?

Gene Keller

Phlebotomy

Dazed by 10,000 ambiguities, the moon and nether lights,
electric with the energy of my time, I sit in the plasma
center with We the Beautiful Poor. I am reading Octavio
Paz on alchemy and communion, amazed by the poetry of being
and the form of the sacred. An aide asks, "Donor number?"
"792." It's a radical strangeness: that boy with Indian
cheekbones, that girl with swirling hair.

When I cast the I CHING, it tells me, "Gradually." Gradually
the needle enters. My blood is lowing. "Steadiness is profitable,"
says the oracle, as gradually, like a cow with tubes to tits,
I am being milked. Voznesensky says, "Poetry is blood." This
is phlebotomy: they take blood, extract the plasma, and
reinfuse the cells; after 48 hours of cellular regeneration,
the lost cells are gradually replaced.

I drift. I recall a Street of Two Prophets in Poland where the air
is prescient with sage. Is there a desert in Poland? Octavio
Paz mumbles, "The prestidigitator anticipates the feast
of immortality." I am distracted. My blood arrives, and
I have sold my first poem. $10. My hand is blue.

Lawrence Barrett

about jim

Jim laughed
in a poem he wrote.
He laughed
as he cried
as he died in
a smooth shot
of heaven;
a rush of needles
shimmering sunlight
as a hundred holy mothers
bow down
like the great
virgin mother
on an old funeral card ...
(she touches his pale skin
right on the flesh)
and yeah, jim felt
the breath of the mother,
the beauty of the water
(and its wetness)
as he slept on the sidewalk.
He laughed at you;
He laughed at me;
He laughed in the music
of jukebox rain
in the morning surf,
as his dreams fled out to sea,
like his prayers,
through holes in his jeans.
He was a good catholic boy,
but he laughed,
he laughed at it all,
caught in his traps,
busting head,
double rectified,
drinking double barrel
in the daylight.
He used to say
"nobody's clean,
but it's nice to believe."

Jonathon Penton

The Way Buckeyes and Beers Taste Just Like the Lone Star

So the ink-stained asphalt stretched before me across that dotted yellow line
sleeping like a leather domme who never looks inside

and all the stars came out to celebrate my reminiscing
in every place that is deserted and all the places that are brave

and   i remembered
                              a thousand points of light when all the cigarettes could burn in unison
so i sat down with a Raleigh in Montezuma's bed to dream the sweet hard heart of Roosevelt Island on
game night

i   have wrapped
                    my lips 'round Indians east and west who tried to teach me to love
                                        folks who weren't like me
but I sank my thumbs into Schenectadian mud and remembered i never loved no folks at all

                    i don't mean to get political

i just remember great-uncle Jack told us to travel like a child even after pappy shot that hole in
gramma's head

Joe Olvera

Jack Kerouac as a Mexican

Jack Kerouac's descriptions of Mexico—and of Mexicans—are breathtaking in their simple beauty and in their beautiful simplicity. Once he discovered that an ancient civilization waited just across the dry-river bed that is the Rio Grande/Rio Bravo, he didn't waste any time learning everything he could about the ancient Azteca Kingdom—-with its dark-skinned Indios looming over sunken prayer wheels. Sometimes Kerouac even fancied himself a Mexican.

In the "Mexican Girl" chapter of *On the Road*, Kerouac (aka Sal Paradise) says this about that:

There was talk that Terry's [the Mexican Girl's] husband was back in Sabinal and out for me; I was ready for him. One night the Okies went berserk in the roadhouse and tied a man to a tree and beat him with two-by-fours. I was asleep at the time and only heard about it. From then on I carried a big stick with me in the tent in case they got the idea we Mexicans were fouling up their trailer camp. They thought I was a Mexican, of course; and I am.

And from then on, Kerouac becomes a defender of things Indian—los Indios son de la noche, los Indios son de la tierra. In another part of that magical book, as he drove into Mexico proper, with Dean and Stan asleep in the back seat of Dean's decrepit jalopy, Kerouac marveled at Mexico's tortilla-carpeted streets and dawnish fragrances intermingling with the sweat from one million farm workers drying in the sun and adobe bricks baked with work-toughened hands.

... The boys were sleeping, and I was alone in my eternity at the wheel, and the road ran straight as an arrow. Not like driving across Carolina, or Texas, or Arizona, or Illinois; but like driving across the world and into the places where we would finally learn ourselves among the Fellaheen Indians of the world, the essential strain of the basic primitive, wailing humanity that stretches in a belt around the equatorial belly of the world from Malaya ... to Morocco to the selfsame deserts and jungles of Mexico. These people were unmistakably Indians and were not at all like the Pedros and Panchos of silly civilized American lore—they had high cheekbones, and slanted eyes, and soft ways, they were not fools, they were not clowns; they were great, grave Indians and they were the source of mankind and the fathers of it. The waves are Chinese, but the earth is an Indian thing. As essential as rocks in the desert are they in the desert of 'history.' And they knew this when we passed, ostensibly self-important moneybag Americans on a lark in their land; they knew who was the father and who was the son of antique life on earth, and made no comment.

But back to Terry, as Kerouac fell in love with Terry's blue timidities, and recognized that she was a damsel in distress. He forced himself to talk to her:

I had bought my ticket and was waiting for the L.A. bus when all of a sudden I saw the cutest little Mexican girl in slacks come cutting across my sight ... Her breasts stuck out straight; her little thighs looked delicious; her hair was long and lustrous black; and her eyes were great blue windows with timidities inside. I wished I was on her bus. A pain stabbed my heart, as it did every time I saw a girl I loved who was going the opposite direction in this too big world.

But Kerouac didn't give up on Terry—the blue-eyed Chicanita fell for Kerouac too. She thought he was a "nice college boy." Oh, I'm a college boy, Kerouac assured her. And so she fell in love, as her blue eyes reached out to him in that City of Night, with its lonely platform streets and its immensity swallowing them whole. With Terry, Kerouac experiences first-hand a little bit of the discrimination that Chicanos have faced since that time when they lost the right and the promise:

We stood under a roadlamp thumbing when suddenly cars full of young kids roared by with streamers flying ... Then they yoo-hooed us and got great glee out of seeing a guy and a girl on the road ... I hated every one of them. Who did they think they were yaahing at somebody on the road because they were little high school punks and their parents carved the roast beef on Sunday afternoons.

While Chicano mothers yawned in the early dawn, fixing the beans for that day's eating, and tortillas-calientitas filled the air with a soft yearning and good things to eat, but soft. Later, Kerouac and Terry see the self-same kids at a diner:

We had battered bags and all the world before us ... all that ground out there, that desert dirt and rat-tat-tat. We looked like a couple of sullen Indians in a Navajo Springs soda fountain, back bent, heads at a table. The school kids saw now that Terry was a Mexican, a Pachuco wildcat; and that her boy was worse than that. With her pretty nose in the air, she cut out of there and we wandered together in the dark up along the ditches of highways.

Pachuco wild-haired throngs of L.A., cutting across the world making their presence known. Talking the talk and walking the walk, as switchblade knives spent entire days cooped up inside pants pockets, safe and serene as a cool summer breeze. Terry and Kerouac are, of course, no Pachucos, but they could be if they wanted to, que no? But, they weren't, you see. But Chicanos in East L.A. or in L.A. proper, were always accused of being Pachucos, and of being bad, no matter if they were sensitive, prolonging a love affair with life and the common ground. No matter the soft tears and the tender hearts.

As Pachucos are misunderstood in L.A., so are they misunderstood in Sabinal, Terry's hometown. Terry is a blue-eyed Chicana, but very few people know that there's nothing novel or amazing about that. It's only people not knowing that mestizos are the blood and the fury that blanketed the Aztec night when the Spaniards came a-calling. The lust carried over when white European blood mixed with brown skin and la raza cosmica was born. Mestizo is as Mestizo does, but ignorance is the blot that falls and covers tremulous and shaky bones.

That blue-eyed bull must've jumped the heavenly fence, guffaws one ignoramus. Kerouac had been staying in farmer Heffelfinger's barn. They talk:

> "How you doing, young fella?"
> "Fine. I hope it's alright my staying here."
> "Sure. You going with that little Mexican floozie?"
> "She's a very nice girl."
> "Pretty too. S'got blue eyes. I think the bull jumped the fence there ..."

Yes, and so the Spanish nightmare—gachupin glory hounds lapping up Aztec Princesses, and impregnating them with the seeds of doom. Impregnating and leaving blue eyes behind so that the brown hordes were left dangling in their common misery—cold, blue eyes stringing together curses and love songs, but only to rape and to merge blue bloods with brown-skinned calzones.

And Kerouac understood mañana as he worked to understand Terry and her crazy brother, Freddy. Mañana with that golden-throated promise of tomorrow:

"Mañana," she said, "everything'll be alright tomorrow, don't you think so ... honey-man?"
"Sure, baby, mañana." It was always mañana. For the next week that was all I heard. Mañana, a lovely word and one that probably means heaven.

Right you are, my boy. Mañana! the mana from heaven. And it means everlasting hope—because la esperanza es lo ultimo que muere—que no? To Chicanos like Terry and Freddy—and even little Raymond (Terry's little boy)—mañana is what keeps them going. What has kept them going beyond the gates of heaven. What has kept them going beyond the misery, beyond lackluster days of trying to survive, beyond devilish flashes of pain–to Nirvana. Tripping along, high on life, with Freddy and Ponzo, Kerouac lets himself be carried by these California Chicanos. Hugging Terry like there's no tomorrow, making love to her under the yum-yum tree, with little Raymond wide-eyed at their heated exploits. Caring for Terry and little Raymond, Kerouac sees himself as a man of the land, with his little family waiting for him and dependent on his bringing home the bacon, or the pork and beans, whichever comes first. He thinks he's found his life's calling. But Terry knows better: "You see, you see, it's very hard picking cotton. If you can't boogie, I'll show you how." And, so no boogie, no mambo, no cumbias rocking the morning star. Kerouac works his fingers to the bone for his lovely little family–a man of the earth is he. "Pshaw! No such thing!" Kerouac says to Terry, wanting to prove his manliness. But he sees beauty in even the most humble things.

We bent down and began picking cotton. It was beautiful. Across the field were the tents, and beyond them the sere brown cottonfields that stretched out of sight, and over that brown arroyo foothills, and then as in a dream the snowcapped Sierras in the blue morning air ... But I knew nothing about cotton picking. I spent too much time disengaging the white ball from the crackly bed ... Moreover my fingers began to bleed ... My back began to ache. But it was beautiful kneeling and hiding in that earth; if I felt like resting I just lay down with my face on the pillow of brown moist earth.

Like everything that Kerouac wrote about Mexico, and Mexicans, the love and respect shows through. For he is much more than a mere writer, he sees beauty even when there's no beauty, but only the lustful, bloody carcasses of life. He knows. He sees. He understands that brown-stroked folks, those with hard and calloused hands–hands that go digging in that dark earth–must also be pampered and protected against that cold, wintry rain. He knows. He sees. Kerouac is a Mexican. Yes, he is. He said so himself. Orale!